A Mirror For Our Times

Also available from Continuum:

Religious Diversity in the UK, Paul Weller
Time for a Change, Paul Weller

A Mirror For Our Times

'The Rushdie Affair' and the Future of Multiculturalism

Paul Weller

continuum

Continuum
Continuum International Publishing Group

The Tower Building   80 Maiden Lane
11 York Road   Suite 704
London SE1 7NX   New York NY 10038

www.continuumbooks.com

British Library Cataloguing-in-Publication Data
A catalogue record for this book is available from the British Library.

ISBN: HB: 0–8264–3276–X
     978–0–8264–3276–6
     PB: 0–8264–5120–9
     978–0–8264–5120–0

Library of Congress Cataloging-in-Publication Data
Weller, Paul, 1956–
  A mirror for our times : 'the Rushdie affair' and the future of multiculturalism / Paul Weller.
   p. cm.
  Includes bibliographical references and index.
  ISBN 978–0–8264–3276–6—ISBN 978–0–8264–5120–0
  1. Rushdie, Salman. Satanic verses. 2. Islam and literature. 3. East and West in literature. 4. Freedom of the press—History—20th century. I. Title.

  PR6068.U757S273897 2009
  823'.914—dc22
        2008042406

Typeset by RefineCatch Limited, Bungay, Suffolk
Printed and bound in Great Britain by Antony Rowe Ltd, Chippenham, Wiltshire

This book is dedicated to Geoff Heath, a former colleague and Head of Counselling and Psychotherapy at the University of Derby, and a continuing friend. His critique of religion and its place in the life of believers and the wider society, as well as in relation to multiculturalism and human rights in the modern world, has always been honest and has often been challenging. It has also sometimes been rather too close to the bone for one who continues to affirm that within religious traditions there is a witness to the importance of the things that cannot be seen, touched, smelled or tasted or heard, for a more balanced perspective on things that can be experienced in these ways.

This book is also dedicated to the work of the Dialogue Society (http://www.dialoguesociety.org). Based in London, this is an initiative of second-generation British Muslims. It aims to promote intercultural dialogue and understanding. It sees Islam as its inspiration, and especially the exposition of Islam offered by the Turkish Muslim scholar, Fethullah Gülen. Gülen does not teach a "liberal" or "modernist" version of Islam. Rather, his teaching offers a robust renewal of Islam that is engaged with the contemporary world. It is rooted in a deep knowledge of authentically Islamic sources. It is committed to dialogue as an Islamic value, and it has been given expression in a range of civil society movements inspired by his teaching.

Contents

Acknowledgements

General Acknowledgements

The origins of this book go back to a time when I was employed as Resources Officer for the Inter Faith Network for the United Kingdom (1988 to 1989). It was then that the controversy around Salman Rushdie's (1988) book, *The Satanic Verses*, began to develop. As a by-product of my employment within an inter-faith organization, I became aware of the controversy's significance at an earlier point than the generality of other than Muslim people.

Because of my day-to-day work I became convinced that what, in due course, became widely known as 'the Rushdie Affair', was likely to continue for a long time. Acknowledgement should therefore be made of the opportunity provided to me by the Inter Faith Network for the UK to be concerned with these matters as a normal part of my work. At the same time, the Network should not, of course, be held responsible for any of my views and perspectives on the controversy or for the content of this book.

When I left the Inter Faith Network in 1990 to take up a post at the then Derbyshire College of Higher Education (which in 1993 became the University of Derby), I started six years of part-time doctoral research into the controversy and aspects of the issues arising from it, conducted at the University of Leeds. Acknowledgements are therefore also due to Professor Kim Knott of the University's Department of Theology and Religious Studies for her supervision of that research; to my employer for its financial support; and to the management of the (then) Faculty of Education, Humanities and Social Sciences for releasing me from most of my teaching commitments during the three final months of 1996 prior to the submission of the thesis. At the same time, again, none of the above are to be held responsible for any of the views and perspectives contained in this book.

Acknowledgements and Permissions

Both at the time of the origins of the controversy and in the years since, I have remained a close academic observer and engaged participant in these issues and debates arising from them. For at least a decade following the inception of the controversy, I collected relevant published and other materials that were available in the English language, and closely monitored the voluminous debates to which the controversy gave rise.

Around the beginning of my research, when the controversy was still at its height, I published some short works that related to aspects of the controversy, including a book chapter (Weller, 1990a) on 'The Rushdie controversy and inter-faith relations' in Dan Cohn-Sherbok's (1990) edited collection, *The Salman Rushdie Controversy in Inter-Religious Perspective*; an article (Weller, 1990b) on 'Literature update on the Rushdie affair' in the journal, *Discernment: A Christian Journal for Inter-Religious Encounter*; and a 'think-piece' (Weller, 1990c) on 'The Rushdie affair, plurality of values and the ideal of a multi-cultural society' in *The National Association for the Values of Education and Training Working Papers*.

The monitoring and collection of materials and the above publications eventually fed into the information and arguments that were included in the successful submission of my doctoral thesis (Weller, 1996) on 'The Salman Rushdie Controversy, Religious Plurality and Established Religion in England'. This was a thesis that documented, charted and reflected upon the key incidents in, and issues arising from, the controversy, and linked them with the primary focus of a thesis that argued for a new configuration of religion(s), state and society in the UK in time to supersede the current role of the establishment of the Church of England. The present book – and also one of my previous books, *Time for a Change: Reconfiguring Religion, State and Society* (Weller, 2005a), draws upon material that was originally developed in that thesis.

In the present book this is especially the case in chapters 1 and 2, which record the principal features of the controversy and some of the key actions and reactions that played a part within it. Chapter 3, which identifies some of the key issues arising from the controversy, also draws upon material from the thesis. In the sections on 'Christian Reactions', 'Other Religious Reactions' and 'Inter-Faith and Cross-Community Reactions', Chapter 2 draws on material from a paper on 'The Rushdie affair: an overview' that I gave at at the University of Kent, Canterbury, on 11 May 1990, at the public launch of Dan Cohn-Sherbok's (1990) edited collection on *The Salman Rushdie Affair in Interreligious Perspective.*

In the fifth section of Chapter 3, 'Law in Contention', and with the agreement of my own publishers, Continuum, materials are used from the chapter (Weller, 2008: 155–77) on 'Religious diversity, hatred, respect and freedom of expression' in my otherwise most recent book, *Religious Diversity in the UK: Contours and Issues.* With thanks to Leeds Metropolitan University Press to do so, three sections of Chapter 4 ('Bombings and "Hard" Wars', 'Culture and "Soft" Wars' and 'Religious Radicalism') draw on my conference paper (Weller, 2007b), 'Robustness and civility: themes from Fethullah Gülen as resource and challenge for Government, Muslims and civil society in the United Kingdom', in I. Yilmaz, ed., *The Muslim World in Transition: Contributions of the Gülen Movement* (conference proceedings of a conference of the same name, held at the House of Lords, the School of Oriental and African Studies and the London School of Economics, London, 25–27 October 2007), London: Leeds Metropolitan University Press, pp. 268–84; as well as my paper (Weller, 2007c) on 'Dialogical and transformative resources: perspectives from Fethullah Gülen on religion and public life', in I. Yilmaz, ed., *Peaceful Co-Existence: Fethullah Gülen's Initiatives in the Contemporary World* (conference proceedings of an international conference of the same name, held at Erasmus University, Rotterdam, 22–23 November 2007), London: Leeds Metropolitan University Press, pp. 242–65.

The section on 'Social Policy Challenges' in Chapter 4 quotes materials from a book chapter (Weller, 2007a) published as 'Conspiracy theories and the incitement of hatred: the dynamics of deception, plausibility and defamation', in M. Fineberg, S. Samuels, and M. Weitzman, eds., *Antisemitism: The Generic Hatred. Essays in Memory of Simon Wiesenthal,* London: Vallentine Mitchell, pp. 182–97. That chapter, in turn, was based upon a paper on 'The dynamics of hate literature: specificity, deception, plausibility and defamation' that was given at the expert seminar 'At the Centennial of the Protocols of the Elders of Zion: A Paradigm for Contemporary Hate Literature', organized by the Academic Response to Racism and Antisemitism in Europe (ARARE) in cooperation with the Italian Historical Studies Centre

Olokaustaos, under the Auspices of UNESCO, at the UNESCO Regional Bureau (ROSTE), Venice, on 7–8 December 2003. The first and fifth sections of Chapter 4, 'On the Other Side of Terror' and 'Religious Radicalism', draw upon an unpublished paper on 'Terror, religious radicalism, religious freedom and public policy in the UK' that I gave at the Oxford Centre for Christianity and Culture seminar series on 'Religion and Public Policy', held at Regent's Park College, Oxford, on 12 February 2008. In addition, and across the book, material is included from my unpublished paper on 'Whose justice from which perspective? Sex, blasphemy, religion and law: *The Satanic Verses* controversy in retrospect', which I gave at the Oxford Centre for Christianity and Culture's seminar series on 'The Idea of Justice – in Literature, Religion and Law', at Regent's Park College, Oxford, on 26 October 2004.

Thanks are also expressed to a number of newspapers and their publishers as copyright holders for permission to use, throughout the book, a range of materials quoted from their publications, full details of which are set out in the book's bibliography. These include: *The Baptist Times*; *The Church Times*; *The Financial Times*; *The Guardian*; *The Independent*; *Independent Television News*; *India Today*; *The Jewish Chronicle*; *The Observer*; *The Sydney Morning Herald*; *The Times*; *The Muslim News*; *The Sunday Times*; *Telegraph.co.uk*; *The People*; and *The Publishers Weekly*, as well as for a quotation reproduced by kind permission of the *The Telegraph and Argus*, Bradford. Acknowledgement is also made to the journalists and other writers published within these newspapers, as well as to religious leaders, personalities, politicians and members of the public whose perspectives are contained within reports that are summarized and referred to as sources of information, but without quotation (including also the newspapers *The Daily Mail*; *The Independent on Sunday*; *The International Herald Tribune*; and *New Life*).

Finally, in addition to those from whom specific copyright permissions have been sought and whose permissions are acknowledged above, with further details included in the bibliography of this book, I also wish to acknowledge the many other authors and editors of books, and the authors of journal, magazine and newspaper articles listed in the bibliography whose work I have either quoted within the generally recognized provisions for 'fair dealing . . . for the purposes of criticism or review', or else to whose work I have specifically referred as sources of information consulted in the course of the book. I also wish to thank the many others beyond those listed in the bibliography, but whose reporting of, and reflection upon, 'the Rushdie controversy', its 'entails' and issues later reprising or associated with it has, over the years, generally informed and challenged my own thinking.

If, in error, I have failed specifically to acknowledge the permission of any copyright holder for quotation of work that may fall outside of the generally recognized norms covered by 'fair dealing'; or have by mistake inaccurately or not fully represented or referenced any material originally written by anyone other than myself; then I offer my sincere apologies. If any such copyright holders were to bring the matter to my attention, I am also committed to rectifying any such failure in any future editions of this book that may be published.

Special Concerns

While all those named and referred to above are to be thanked for their work and acknowledged for the way in which it has informed my own work, the responsibility for this book and its contents remains mine alone. In the light of the passions that were kindled during 'the Rushdie affair' there are additional reasons for stressing this beyond the conventional ones alone.

When I began my original doctoral research in this area, a number of people close to me expressed some concern. Given the pain, passion, loss of liberty and of life involved in the controversy such concern was, and is, understandable. In truth, I have not myself been immune from occasional anxieties about how parts of my thesis, and now also of this book, might be read and interpreted by people on various sides of the controversy. However, as Appignanesi and Maitland stated in the Preface (1989: vii) to *The Rushdie File*, their edited collection of writings from the early days of the controversy:

> Fear, however intangible, is insidious and can impose silence where it is least desirable. The issues the Rushdie controversy has brought into the open need to be confronted, publicly argued, not swept under the carpet, if we are to live peacefully together in a multi-cultural world.

Together with such anxieties, there are also potential ethical concerns of which one needs to be aware in relation to a book of this kind. As Appignanesi and Maitland (1989: vii) said of their work in producing *The Rushdie File*, 'We were continually haunted by the tragic aspects of the affair – threats to lives, the lives lost; the perceived threats to communities.' In a context in which the issues translate into concrete matters of life and death, research and scholarship impose their own moral imperatives towards accuracy, fairness and care in stating the arguments that go beyond the norms of convention (see also Hanna, 1992).

Even with such awareness, there is still a danger that a book of this kind – which takes as its starting point a conflict involving the religious and social trauma of a group of people as well as an individual's loss of liberty and threat to life – can be open to the charge of being parasitical upon the suffering of others. Because of this, one can only justify an intervention of this kind because of a conviction about the importance of addressing the issues involved. But the seriousness of the issues with which this book is concerned means that these acknowledgements should close with an acknowledgement of the loss of many years of personal liberty for Salman Rushdie; the loss of life and injury experienced by a number of people of various backgrounds throughout the world who became caught up in the violent events that occurred around the controversy; as well as the passion and pain of many ordinary offended Muslims who felt their concerns had been misunderstood by the general non-Muslim public of the 'Western world', and who also felt betrayed by the liberal intelligentsia.

This book has no wish to be parasitical on any of this. It is written out of what has been, and will continue to be, an ongoing intellectual engagement with the issues that developed in the controversy itself, as well as with what might be called the 'entails' that have arisen from it over the past twenty years, and in relation to which the original controversy, as suggested in the title of this book, can be seen as 'a mirror for our times'. It is also written out of a personal, political and religious commitment to the social, political, cultural and theological project of life in a multicultural and multi-faith world, the future of which embodies the potential of so much threat and promise.

A Final Word of Thanks

In closing these acknowledgements, I would like to end with some personal thanks to Tom Crick and Rebecca Vaughan-Williams, and more recently to Kirsty Schaper, at my publishers, Continuum, for their help and support throughout the writing of this book.

I would also like to thank my wife, Margret Preisler-Weller, for her kind proofreading of the earlier drafts of the text. And, as always, my children, Katrina, Lisa and David, together with Greta, more than deserve thanks for their continued patience with a father and husband who disappears into his study more than he should to write about things which, though of importance for all our futures, are at the least no more important than the relationships that are close to hand and in which as human beings we can all too easily fall short of the mark.

Chronology of Key Events

'in the Mirror' of the Past Two Decades

Publication of Salman Rushdie's *The Satanic Verses*	1988 (26 September)
UK Attorney General clarifies that legal action cannot be taken	1988 (23 December)
Public burning of a copy of *The Satanic Verses* in Bradford	1989 (14 January)
W.H. Smith booksellers withdraws *The Satanic Verses* from sale	1989 (16 January)
Ten Muslim protestors shot dead outside Islamabad's US Embassy	1989 (12 February)
Five Muslim protestors killed in Srinagar, Kashmir, India	1989 (13 February)
Fatwa by the Ayatollah Khomeini proclaiming Rushdie apostate	1989 (14 February)
Rushdie issues apology for Muslim distress about the book	1989 (18 February)
Imam and his aide shot dead in Brussels, Belgium	1989 (29 March)
Bradford Council of Mosques issues a ten-point action plan	1989 (17 June)
In *In Good Faith*, Rushdie claims never to have been Muslim	1990 (4 February)
Rushdie claims to have embraced Islam	1990 (24 December)
Ayatollah Ali Khamenei reaffirms the fatwa as irrevocable	1990 (26 December)
Iranian Government undertakes not to implement the fatwa	1998 (24 September)
9/11 attacks on World Trade Center and Pentagon, USA	2001 (11 September)

Invasion of Afghanistan by the US and coalition forces	2001 (7 October)
Invasion of Iraq	2003 (20 March)
Employment Equality (Religion or Belief) Regulations, 2003	2003 (2 December)
11/3 bomb attack on the Madrid railway system	2004 (11 March)
Murder of Theo van Gogh in the Netherlands	2004 (2 November)
The play *Behzti* opens at the Birmingham Repertory Theatre	2004 (9 December)
Broadcast on BBC2 of *Jerry Springer: The Opera*	2005 (8 January)
7/7 bomb attacks on the London transport system	2005 (7 July)
'Face of Muhammad' cartoons published in *Jyllands-Posten*	2005 (30 September)
Racial and Religious Hatred Act, 2006	2006 (16 February)
Equality Act, 2006	2006 (16 February)
Salman Rushdie given a knighthood for 'services to literature'	2007 (15 June)
Inception of Commission for Equality and Human Rights	2007 (1 October)
Partial implementation of Religious and Racial Hatred Act, 2006	2007 (1 October)
Criminal Justice and Immigration Act, 2008 abolishes blasphemy	2008 (8 May)
Abolition of blasphemy and blasphemous libel comes into effect	2008 (8 July)

Introduction

A Look in the Mirror

'An Episode of Exceptional Significance'
The Controversy as Lightning Rod, Catalyst and 'Magnifying Mirror'

Writing in *The Church Times* (3.3.89) in the early days of what turned out to be one of the most long-running public controversies at the interface between religion, literature and law in modern British history, Douglas Brown commented in relation to 'the Rushdie affair' that 'We are living through an episode of exceptional significance in the history of thought, ideas, ethics, morals, politics.'

In 2008–9 we mark the twentieth anniversary of the beginning of that controversy – a controversy that this book argues can, in many ways, be seen as both a 'lightning rod' and a 'catalyst' that became paradigmatic for the issues of religion and public policy; of believing and belonging; of religion, art and values in contention; of legal rights and constraints; and of political representation and participation in a plural society. Globally, the controversy took place at a time of the shifting of economic, political and military tectonic plates when, with the fall of the Berlin Wall in 1989, the Cold War between 'East' and 'West' gave way to new conflicts emerging along cultural and religious lines. Domestically, it both marked and gave further impetus to the rise of individual and community self-identification on the basis of religion alongside, and sometimes in place of, ethnic, national and social-class factors.

The title chosen for this book was inspired by some words from the political scientist and the former Chair of the Commission for Racial Equality, Bhikhu Parekh, who in the early days of the controversy wrote both incisively and eirenically on it, arguing that: 'A political crisis is like a magnifying mirror reflecting some of the deepest trends and tendencies developing in society. A wise nation meditates on it, and uses it as a means for self-knowledge. The Rushdie affair has raised issues likely to preoccupy us for a long time' (Parekh, 1989b).

During the controversy, many Muslims objected to the use of the phrase 'the Rushdie affair' on the basis that it encouraged a focus on the person of the author. By contrast, Muslims opposed to *The Satanic Verses* wished to emphasize that their argument was with the *content* of the book, and also with some of the *reactions to their concerns*, rather than it being about an *individual* (or indeed about inter-state relations) albeit that the fatwa of the Ayatollah Khomeini had the effect of focusing it in these ways.

Thus many Muslims preferred to refer to 'the *Satanic Verses* controversy' rather than 'the Rushdie affair'. The latter was, however, a widely used phrase at the time, and it remains widely recognizable today. Because of this, the phrase appears in the title of this book. But the use of inverted commas around the phrase is intended to signal that it is used for these reasons rather than it being a reflection of the author's evaluation of the principal issues at stake, the exploration of which is what the book as a whole is about.

'Sound Bites' and Reflection

The controversy began to engage Muslims almost immediately following the publication of the book on 26 September 1988. But it remained relatively invisible to the wider public until a copy of *The Satanic Verses* was publicly burned in Bradford on 14 January 1989. This act, followed by the 14 February 1989 issuing of the Ayatollah Khomeini's fatwa on the author and his publishers, propelled the growing controversy into the wider media and the public sphere. Indeed, one could say that the controversy was partially *created* as a media event. For at least the next decade, the controversy became almost omnipresent in the news media. The effect of this on the substantive issues at stake was such that, at the height of the controversy, as Ziauddin Sardar and Merryl Wyn Davies (1990: 1) put it in their book *Distorted Imagination: Lessons From the Rushdie Affair*:

The 'Rushdie affair' became a matter of taking sides, defending positions and erecting barricades. So frantic has been the activity of defending high ideals from presumed onslaughts that it is questionable whether the opponents can any longer hear, much less understand, each other.

As noted in a 1989 statement made by the officers of the Inter Faith Network for the UK, 'There are difficult and divisive issues here which require more considered public debate in a calmer atmosphere as we develop the appropriate social framework for our life together in a multi-faith society' (Centre for the Study of Islam and Christian–Muslim Relations, 1989: 18–19). But in the fraught atmosphere of the times, it was difficult to engage in the kind of reflection that Parekh called for.

Both the existence of the fatwa issued by the Ayatollah Khomeini and the threat that it posed to the life of the author, Salman Rushdie and those of his publishers, as well as the media's insatiable demand for 'soundbites' and media events, made measured reflection very difficult at the peak of the controversy. However, the twentieth anniversary of its outbreak provides a good opportunity to review the incidents, issues and debates of the original controversy in the light of some historical perspective, while also utilizing them to illuminate aspects of subsequent incidents and developments that have, especially in the opening years of the twenty-first century, reprised some of the key themes of the original controversy, albeit in new and different ways.

A Flavour of the Times

Some Contemporary Sources: Newspapers and Edited Collections

In exploring its theme, the book takes as its starting point especially the opening years of the controversy, 1988 and 1989. These two years were packed with developments, issues and debates that subsequently proved to be paradigmatic for the ensuing two decades. This book tries to give a 'contemporary feel' of those times by extensive quotation from, and/or reference to, newspaper reports of the time. In doing so, it uses the events and arguments of these years as a lens through which to view what later developed, both in relation to the controversy itself, and also in relation to what became increasingly clear might be the wider 'entails' and implications of the controversy.

The book begins by charting the key outlines of that controversy and of the actions and reactions that developed as part of it. It does so by trying to provide a 'flavour' of the times, through summarizing the then contemporary events by reference to reports in, and quotations from, a range of national broadsheets (especially, but not only, *The Guardian* and *The Independent*) and religious newspapers (including *The Muslim News, The Jewish Chronicle* and *The Church Times*). It is, of course, appreciated that reference to newspaper sources is not, in itself, necessarily a means of accessing the factuality of historical events. But what it does provide is something of a 'collage' feel for the times.

As it proceeds, the book draws upon, and refers to, edited books and special editions of journal and magazines, published at the time and which contain important source materials about the controversy. Among those publications of the time are: Ahsan and Kidwai, eds. (1991), *Sacrilege Versus Civility: Muslim Perspectives on The Satanic Verses Affair*; Bowen, ed. (1992b), *The Satanic Verses: Bradford Responds*; Centre for the Study of Islam and Christian-Muslim Relations (1989), *The Rushdie Affair: A Documentation*; Cohn-Sherbook, ed., (1990), *The Salman Rushdie Controversy in Interreligious Perspective*; Commission for Racial Equality (1990b), *Free Speech: Report of a Seminar*, and Commission for Racial Equality (1990c), *Law, Blasphemy and the Multi-Faith Society: Report of a Seminar*; *Discernment: A Christian Journal for Inter-Religious Encounter* (1990), *Focus on the Salman Rushdie Affair* (special issue); *Impact International* (1990), special issue; Islamic Foundation (1989), *Focus on Christian–Muslim Relations (The Rushdie Affair – Responses and Reactions)*; and MacDonogh, ed., (1993), *Rushdie Letters: Freedom to Speak, Freedom to Write*.

Even at the height of the controversy, amidst all the action, reaction and comment, a number of more extended and reflective contributions were written from a variety of authorial perspectives. For a wider than Muslim perspective, these included books by: Easterman (1992), *New Jerusalems: Reflections on Islam, Fundamentalism and The Rushdie Affair*; Pipes (1990), *The Rushdie Affair: the Novel, the Ayatollah, and the West*; Ruthven (1991), *A Satanic Affair: Salman Rushdie and the Wrath of Islam* (revised and updated edition); Semminck (1993), *A Novel Visible But Unseen: A Thematic Analysis of Salman Rushdie's The Satanic Verses*; Weatherby (1990), *Salman Rushdie: Sentenced to Death*; Webster (1990), *A Brief History of Blasphemy: Liberalism, Censorship and the Satanic Verses*; and Weldon (1989), *Sacred Cows: A Portrait of Britain, Post-Rushdie, Pre-Utopia*.

But there were also a number of books and booklets written by Muslims at that time. However, with the possible exception of Akhtar's (1989c) *Be Careful With Muhammad! The Salman Rushdie Affair*, these did not generally receive so much prominence in the wider public debate at the time. They included Anees (1989), *The Kiss of Judas: Affairs of a Brown Sahib*; Deedat (n.d.), *How Rushdie Fooled the West: 'The Satanic Verses', Unexpurgated*; Mazrui (1989), *The Satanic Verses or a Satanic Novel? The Moral Dilemmas of the Rushdie Affair*; Mehdi (1989), *Islam and Intolerance: Reply to Salman Rushdie*; Mustapha (1989), *An Islamic Overview of The Satanic Verses by Western Writers*; Omer (1989), *The Holy Prophet and the Satanic Slander*; Pidcock, ed. (1992), *Satanic Voices Ancient and Modern*; Qureshi and Khan (1989), *The Politics of The Satanic Verses: Unmasking Western Attitudes*; Rashadath (1990), *The Satanic Conspiracy*; Sambhli, ed. (1990), *Our Campaign Against 'The Satanic Verses' and the Death Edict*; and Sardar and Wyn Davies (1990), *Distorted Imagination: Lessons from the Rushdie Affair*.

Some Contemporary Sources: Book Chapters, Journal and Newspaper Articles

Key book chapters of the time dealing with aspects of the controversy appeared in the edited collections referred to above, while articles were published in newspapers and in magazines, and in a range of journals in varied disciplinary fields including Political Science; Literature; and Race and Ethnic Relations; as well as in interfaith, Christian and Muslim religious publications.

With an emphasis on the earlier period of the controversy (1989–1992), though including some later work, these included pieces such as those by Akhtar (1989a), 'Whose light, whose darkness?'; Akhtar (1989b), 'The Liberal Inquisition'; Akhtar (1990b), 'Is freedom holy to Liberals?'; Akhtar (1990c), 'Art or literary terrorism?'; Azm (1991), 'The importance of being earnest about Salman Rushdie'; Bader (1992), '*The Satanic Verses*: an intercultural experiment by Salman Rushdie'; Boyle (1990), 'Freedom of religion, freedom of expression – Salman Rushdie case'; Chryssides (1990), 'Fact and fiction in the Salman Rushdie affair'; Cottle (1991), 'Reporting the Rushdie affair: a case study in the orchestration of public opinion'; D'Costa (1990), 'Secular discourse and the clash of faiths: "The

Satanic Verses" in British society'; Dossa (1989), 'Satanic Verses: imagination and its political context'; Durant (1990), 'From the Rushdie controversy to social pluralism'; Dyson (1990), 'Looking below the surface'; Goddard (1991), 'Stranger than fiction: the affair of The Satanic Verses'; Green (1990), 'Beyond The Satanic Verses: conservative religion and the liberal society'; Hartley (1989), 'Saving Mr. Rushdie?'; Hulmes (1992), *The Satanic Verses: A Test-Case for Pluralism*'; Impact International (1988a), 'Anti-Islam's new find "Simon Rushton" aka Salman Rushdie'; Impact International (1988b), 'Quote, unquote Satanic Verses'; Jones (1990a), 'Rushdie, race and religion'; Jones (1990b), 'Respecting beliefs and rebuking Rushdie'; Kerr (1989a), 'What *The Satanic Verses* mean in Brick Lane'; Kerr (1989b), 'The Satanic Verses and beyond'; Knönagel (1991), 'The "Satanic Verses": narrative structure and Islamic doctrine'; Lewis (1991), 'Behind the Rushdie affair'; Maitland (1990), 'Blasphemy and creativity'; Malak (1989), 'Reading the crisis: the polemics of Salman Rushdie's "The Satanic Verses" '; Mazrui (1990a), 'The Satanic Verses or a satanic novel? The moral dilemmas of the Rushdie affair'; and Mazrui (1990b), 'Witness for the prosecution: a cross-examination on *The Satanic Verses*'.

Both Tariq Modood and Bhikhu Parekh contributed a number of thoughtful pieces to the debate. These included Modood (1989), 'Religious anger and minority rights'; Modood (1990a), 'The Rushdie affair: texts and contexts'; Modood (1990b), *Muslims, Race and Equality in Britain: Some Post-Rushdie Affair Reflections*; Modood (1990c), 'Muslims, race and equality in Britain: some post-Rushdie affair Reflections'; and Modood (1990e) and 'British Asian Muslims and the Salman Rushdie affair'. Parekh's contributions included Parekh (1989a, 1989d), 'Between holy text and moral void'; Parekh (1989b), 'The mutual suspicions which fuelled the Rushdie affair'; Parkhe (1989c), 'Liberal versus religious fundamentalism'; Parekh (1990a), 'The Rushdie affair and the British press'; Parkhe (1990b), 'The Rushdie affair and the British press: some salutary lessons'; and Parekh (1990c), 'The Rushdie affair: the research agenda for political philosophy'.

Other essays included: Mozaffari (1990), 'The Rushdie affair: blasphemy as a new form of international conflict and crisis'; Mullen (1990), 'Satanic asides'; Newell (1992), 'The other God – Salman Rushdie's new aesthetic'; Newton (1992), 'Literary theory and the Rushdie affair'; Piscatori (1990), 'The Rushdie affair and the politics of ambiguity'; Robinson (1992), 'Reflections on the Rushdie

Affair – 18th April 1989'; Shepard (1992), 'Satanic Verses and the death of God – Salman Rushdie and Najib Mahfuz'; Simawe (1990), 'Rushdie's *The Satanic Verses* and heretical literature in Islam'; Spivak (1990), 'Reading The Satanic Verses'; Sprigge (1990), 'The Satanic novel: a philosophical dialogue on blasphemy and censorship'; Unterman (1990), 'A Jewish perspective on "the Rushdie affair"'; Werbner (1996), 'Allegories of sacred imperfection: magic, hermeneutics, and passion in *The Satanic Verses*'; and Wright (1990), 'The Rushdie controversy: the spread of communalism from South Asia to the west'.

During the early days of the controversy, Salman Rushdie himself wrote the keynote essays 'Is Nothing Sacred?' (Rushdie, 1990b, 1990c) and 'In good faith' (Rushdie, 1990d), as well as a number of other pieces such as 'Choice between light and dark' (Rushdie, 1989a); 'Bonfire of the certainties' (Rushdie, 1989b); 'Please, read "Satanic Verses" before condemning it' (Rushdie, 1989d); 'Open Letter to Rajiv Gandhi' (Rushdie, 1989f); 'Why I have embraced Islam' (Rushdie, 1990e); and 'One thousand days in a balloon' (Rushdie, 1991b).

Works about Rushdie, as well as on his larger body of work have included those by Brennan (1990), *Salman Rushdie and Third World: Myths of the Nation*; Dhawan and Taneja (1992), *The Novels of Salman Rushdie*; and Harrison (1992), *Salman Rushdie*.

Some later general pieces reflecting upon the controversy include those by: Afshari (1990), 'The poet and the prophet: the iconoclasm of The Satanic Verses'; Asad (1990), 'Multiculturalism and British identity in the wake of the Rushdie affair'; Baumann (2001), 'Cross-faith conflict and interfaith community in Britain: from the "Rushdie Affair" to the present'; Bennett (1994), 'The Salman Rushdie affair in Anglo Indian perspective'; Boyd (1997), 'Blasphemy: verbal offense against the sacred, from Moses to Salman Rushdie'; Fischer and Abedi (1990), 'Bombay talkies, the word and the world: Salman Rushdie's Satanic Verses'; Fong (2004), 'Satanic v. Angelic. The world welterweight fight: Rushdie takes on hegemony!'; Fowler (2000), 'A sociological analysis of The Satanic Verses'; Hebert, D. (1993), 'God and free speech: a Quaker perspective on the Satanic Verses controversy'; Hussain (2002), 'Misunderstandings and hurt: how Canadians joined worldwide Muslim reactions to Salman Rushdie's The Satanic Verses'; Kane (2006), 'Embodied panic: revisiting modernist "religion" in the controversies over Ulysses and The Satanic Verses'; Kuortti (1997), 'Dreams, intercultural identification and The Satanic Verses'; Kuortti (1999), ' "Nomsense": Salman Rushdie's The Satanic Verses'; O'Neill (1999), 'Multicultural liberals and the Rushdie affair: a critique of

Kymlicka, Taylor, and Walzer'; Parashkevova (2007), ' "Turn your watch upside down in Bombay and you see the time in London": Catoptric urban configurations in Salman Rushdie's The Satanic Verses'; Pipes (1998), 'Salman Rushdie's delusions, and ours'; Ramachandaran (2005), 'Salman Rushdie's The Satanic Verses: hearing the postcolonial cinematic novel'; Slaughter (1993), 'The Salman Rushdie affair: apostasy, honour, freedom of speech'; Weiser (1993), 'Varieties of censorship and response in The Satanic Verses'; and Zucker (2008), 'Roth, Rushdie and rage: religious reactions to Portnoy and the Verses'.

A Note on Method and Language

This book is not, as it might have been, based upon direct interviews with Salman Rushdie and/or the other principal actors in the controversy, Muslim or otherwise. That is a project that could still usefully be carried out. Securing the retrospective reflections of the key participants who are still alive would complement, in a more biographically informed way, what this book has set out to do. What the present book does do is to take materials and reports published in English during the early years (and especially the first two, 1988 and 1989) of the controversy and use these as the 'raw materials' for the arguments that it then develops about the future of multiculturalism in the light of the two decades that have since passed.

The engagement with, and use of, English language materials alone is a limitation that needs to be acknowledged, especially given the global reach of the controversy at the time. However, this arises both from the author's limited linguistic skills, while also reflecting the fact that the English literature on the controversy is, in itself, voluminous, and that the epicentre of the controversy was located in the United Kingdom. But again, for a fully rounded view of the controversy in retrospect, it will be helpful if other work is undertaken that can reflect other linguistic – and hence also, cultural – perspectives on the controversy.

The Issues Reprised

As the book moves towards its conclusion about the implications of the controversy for the future of multiculturalism, it is argued that a number of more recent incidents and developments have reprised aspects of the original controversy and that these have echoed and/or further developed some of its 'entails'. These include the 2004 killing of the Dutch film-maker, Theo van Gogh; the 2005 'Cartoons' controversy around the Danish newspaper *Jyllands-Posten*; and the terror attacks of 9/11 (New York and the Pentagon, USA, 2001), 11/3 (Madrid, Spain, 2003), and 7/7 (London, UK, 2005).

These events have seen the generation of an increased public and political questioning of multiculturalism. However, during the same period, both in the UK and throughout the EU, laws and policies have been introduced to tackle discrimination on the grounds of religion and belief and against incitement to religious hatred, and also to undergird the promotion of a more inclusive society in which religious groups can at least potentially make important contributions to civil society.

Future Trajectories

The argument of the present book is that the subsequent trends and tendencies of the past two decades can be better understood by revisiting the 'magnifying mirror' provided by the original controversy; while the implications of both the original controversy, and of the later trends and tendencies, can be better evaluated within the historical perspective that is provided by the passage of twenty years.

As the words of the title suggest, the book argues that the controversy can be understood as 'a mirror for our times' in a way that is of relevance to academics, politicians, lawyers, artists, religious believers, as well as to all who are engaged with the twenty-first-century challenges that are posed by living with difference, freedom of expression and mutual respect; with exploring the relationship between religion and secularity; and with understanding and overcoming the threats posed by religiously-informed violence. Through the literary material itself, and in the range of actions and reactions to it, questions of justice emerge in a multifaceted way and from multiple perspectives.

These questions include those of justice for the author as a novelist living under a pronouncement of death, based on an interpretation of religious law by a religious leader located in another part of the world. They are also concerned with justice for Muslims whose sensibilities were wounded by the text (and perhaps even more so by some of the wider reactions and incomprehensions in relation to their original concerns), and who found that they could not use existing legal instruments to further their concerns, while simultaneously being criticized for turning to book-burning and public demonstrations as alternative means to advance their case. The questions and issues also touch on the relationship between rights and responsibilities, and between individuals and groups. They reveal the existence of differing value-systems that can inform contrasting and sometimes conflicting world-views.

Thus the controversy that developed around the book, *The Satanic Verses* and also, whether wanted by Muslims or not, the person of Salman Rushdie, ultimately became one that was about more than either the author or the book. Rather, it held in seed form profound and challenging issues involved in the relationship between justice, equity, sensitivity, and the provisions of law with regard to freedom of expression and constraints upon it; as well as issues of globalization; the claims of religion in relation to secularity and secularity in relation to religion; and issues to do with violence sanctioned by religion.

Chapter 1

The Contours of the Controversy

Salman Rushdie and *The Satanic Verses*

The Controversy as a Global Event in Religion and Politics

To many, 'the Rushdie affair' burst unexpectedly upon the late twentieth century as something of a throwback to an age that was thought to have long passed in the UK outside of Northern Ireland at least, if not in other parts of the world. In a piece in *The Guardian* (7.4.89) the veteran socialist politician, Tony Benn, noted how 'the Rushdie affair' had burst onto the scene, bringing arguments back into the contemporary world of geopolitics to do with religion that it was thought had faded into the past (see also Haynes, 1998). But because of the global canvas on which the controversy eventually came to be played out, it is sometimes almost forgotten that what lies at its heart is a text and a writer, both of which became not only a literary event, but also a social and political one.

Personal and Literary Histories

The Satanic Verses was published in London by Viking Penguin on 26 September 1988 (for examples of reviews, see Anonymous, 1989; Enright, 1989; Mills, 1989; Parameswaran, 1989; Wiens, 1989). As a writer who was already being widely studied and written about and enjoying critical acclaim (for example, see Dhawan, 1985), Rushdie had also already been in the wider public eye as a writer of some note, having won in 1981 the prestigious Booker Prize for literature for his

1980 book *Midnight's Children* (for reviews and other discussions see Durix, 1985; Karamcheti, 1986; Naik, 1985; Shepherd, 1985; Singh, 1985; Swann, 1986; Millward, 1994; Price, 1994; Islam, 1999; Ramsey-Kurz, 2001; Mijares, 2003; Fenwick, 2004; Gane, 2006; and Mezey, 2006).

By the time that *The Satanic Verses* was published, Rushdie was already no stranger to controversy connected with his work. For example, his Booker Prize-winning novel, *Midnight's Children* (Rushdie, 1981), had been the focus of some conflict with the former Indian Prime Minister, Indira Gandhi, who had threatened to sue Rushdie over some of the contents. The novel portrayed a child, with powers of extra-sensory perception, who was born on Indian Independence Day (see Batty, 1987; Dayal, 1992; Hawes, 1993). It dealt with controversial themes of religion and politics interwoven into the story of the partition of Pakistan and India, while his 1983 book *Shame* explored a fictional version of Pakistan (see Watson-Williams, 1984; Ahmad, 1991; Deszcz, 2004; and Teverson, 2004) and the disappointments and disenchantments encountered in connection with the attempt of post-partition Pakistan to form a state that would be informed by an Islamic and a Muslim identity.

Rushdie had himself been born into the history of partition, in India, on 19 June 1947, as part of an Anglophile Muslim business family. In 1961 he was sent from his home city of Bombay (now Mumbai) to Rugby School in England. At the end of the 1960s, after studying at Cambridge, he began theatre and advertising work, being responsible, among other advertising slogans, for the famous catchphrase 'naughty but nice', used to advertise cream cakes. In 1972 he wrote his first novel, *The Book of the Pir*, which was about a successful Muslim holy person. His first published novel, *Grimus* (1975), was a work of science fiction that was not very well received by the critics at the time (for retrospective discussions of the book, see Johanssen, 1985; Cundy, 1992; Syed, 1994). With his outspoken attack on the Falklands War, racism and the Conservative Government in his broadcast piece on 'The new empire within Britain' (1982), Rushdie increasingly became associated with the political Left and with anti-racism. In 1987 *The Jaguar Smile* was published, giving his personal portrait of the Sandinista revolution of Nicaraguan priests and poets. In the same year, he divorced his first wife Clarissa. He later married the American novelist Marianne Wiggins.

But it was primarily as a novelist, rather than as a political writer, that Rushdie made his mark, although his writing continued to resonate with a range of political themes (Rahman, 1991). Thus it became identified with genres such as 'Commonwealth Literature' and 'Post-Colonial Literature' (see Ashcroft, Griffiths and Tiffin, 1989; Needham, 1988–89; Srivastava, 1989), while his style of writing was associated with what became known as 'magical realism' (see Durix, 1985; Zamora and Faris, 1996).

The Satanic Verses: Islamic Tradition and Book Title

The Satanic Verses is a very difficult novel to attempt to summarize in any straightforward way. At one level, it can be seen as dealing with themes of migration and of exile (see Hewson, 1989; Nair and Battacharya, 1990), explored through fantasies that utilize historical elements (see Amanuddin, 1989; Aravamudan, 1989). As Parekh (1989a) says of Rushdie, 'He fantasises and redefines real, recognisable men and women and does not create wholly new characters and images', thus noting an aspect of Rushdie's style which has been remarked upon by many critics (for example, Durix, 1985; Amanuddin, 1989). J.P. Stern (1989) described the style of *The Satanic Verses* as a special genre of 'magical realism':

> The complex structure of Mr Rushdie's novel involves a huge panorama of myths known and unknown, air disasters spiralling in whirls of time and place, a seemingly inexhaustible supply of streams of consciousness, arcane references to Indian lore in contact or conflict with English customs, and direct as well as oblique references to the Koran, some of them clearly blasphemous and pornographic.

The very title of the novel comes from a story related by two early Muslim commentators, al-Tabari and Ibn Sa'd. In al-Tabari's version (a translation of which can be found in Guillaume's (1987: 165f.), *The Life of Muhammad: A Translation of Ishaq's Sirat Rasul Allah*. In that story, the Prophet Muhammad wanted to help the pre-Islamic people of the city of Mecca more easily to accept his monotheistic teaching. Therefore, according to the story of these 'satanic verses', following the Qur'anic Surah (Surat al-Najm, Qur'an 53: 19–30), known in English by the name of 'The Star' (and that deals with the topic of what were the female tribal deities of the Meccans), Satan put upon Muhammad's lips the words, 'These are the exalted swans [in other words, beautiful ladies] whose intercession is to be hoped for.' The story, then, has it that it was because of this that the Meccans joined Muhammad in prostration. But then it is said that the Angel Gibreel showed Muhammad his error and the so-called 'satanic verses' were replaced with what is now in the text and which, in the light of the indigenous Meccan practice of female infanticide, critiques the Meccans' worship of a female deity as being illogical.

The story was dismissed by a number of early Muslim authorities on the grounds that its chain of transmission (one of the grounds for the authority of Hadith) was weak. Hence it was not included in any of the six authoritative collections of the Hadith that were put together in the centuries following Muhammad's death. But there is a widespread Muslim perception that, in the history of Christian attacks on Islam – and especially those attacks that majored on attacking the integrity of Muhammad with the charge that he was a liar and imposter – the story has been used against Islam (see Ahsan, 1982, 1988, 1991). Thus Razi wholly rejected it, describing it as 'a fiction invented by apostates' that is 'unfounded' (quoted in Ruthven, 1991: 39).

The Book and its Referents

Like many of the references in the novel, those to the original story of the 'satanic verses' are likely to be lost on the average western reader, who does not have the cultural capital necessary to locate and understand them. But these same references are full of resonances and meanings for readers brought up within the Muslim cultural and linguistic universe. To mention only a few in order to give a flavour of the way in which the sanctities of Islam are dealt with by the author: Rushdie uses the name of Mahound, itself a corruption of the name Muhammad, used in Christian attacks on Islam, and Mecca, the holy city of Islam becomes Jahiliya – traditionally the name given to the time of 'ignorance' before the revelation of Islam, but among many modern Muslims seen now as being linked with a contemporary world system of arrogance, immorality and enmity towards Islam.

The main characters of the book are Gibreel Farishta and Saladin Chamcha. The character of Gibreel Farishta is a flamboyant movie-star of Bombay religious films. In Urdu, his name translates as Gabriel

Angel. Saladin Chamcha is an Anglophile making his living from adverts, named after a medieval victor over the Crusaders who restored Islamic rule in Egypt. Many of the crossed-over web of narratives in the book take place in the dreams of Gibreel. The book, in fact, begins with Gibreel and Saladin falling from a jumbo jet that has exploded over the English/French Channel after being hijacked by terrorists.

Both characters survive, with Gibreel acquiring a halo, while Saladin disintegrates into a Satanic half-man, half-goat, with a monstrous penis. Gibreel dreams about the brothel called 'The Curtain' in which prostitutes act out the parts of Mahound's wives. The clients of this brothel are said by the author to go round the so-called 'Fountain of Love' in its inner courtyard, 'much as the pilgrims rotated for other reasons around the ancient Black Stone' (Rushdie, 1988: 381), this being a reference to the Kaaba in Mecca, which lies at the heart of the Muslim ritual universe.

As indicated previously, it is not really possible completely to summarize the book. But hopefully these cameos will give a sense of its phantasmagoric flavour, and of the way in which it interweaves traditional references and pieties with speculative elements and, at times, a Baudelairean ribaldry. All of this raises the question of what Salman Rushdie was intending in writing this book. Of course, subjective motivation is notoriously difficult to uncover and identifying it is made more difficult when, in different contexts, writers offer differing explanations for their work. Such variety of explanation on Rushdie's part is, at least, understandable given the whirlwind of controversy in which he soon found himself at the heart. But also, it contributes to the difficulties of analysis. Before the publication of the book, in an interview with Madhu Jain (1988) of *India Today* Rushdie explained that he had an Islamic reference point because that was what he knew about, although he noted that issues to do with religion and extremism were potentially applicable to almost any religion.

Warning Signs

Several weeks before the publication of *The Satanic Verses* in India, Khushwant Singh, an Indian journalist and adviser to Penguin Books India, had read the book in typescript form and had telephoned Peter Mayer, the Chair of the Penguin Group, to discuss his concerns about it. Singh was sure that it would lead to considerable trouble. According to Singh (cited in Ruthven, 1991: 85), Mayer was appalled at his reaction to the book. It was also reported (in *The Independent*, 21.10.89) that, both before and after publication, Rushdie had been asked about what the notorious 'Mahound' chapter in *The Satanic Verses* was intended to mean and that he appeared reluctant to explain. However, in a letter (25.10.89) to the editor of *The Independent* newspaper, Rushdie claimed that any implication that he deceived Viking Penguin was wholly unjustified.

Singh's warnings were soon borne out. Riots over *The Satanic Verses* broke out in Mumbai and, in due course, in other places around the world. At the time of the publication of *The Satanic Verses*, India was experiencing an increasingly fraught situation of rising communal tensions and political instability. Following representations from the Muslim Members of the Indian Parliament, Syed Shahabuddin and Kurshid Alam Khan, on 5 October 1988, the then Indian Prime Minister, Rajiv Gandhi, banned *The Satanic Verses* in India under Section 11 of the Indian Customs Act, for being offensive to Islam. The banning came after Muslim outrage about the book had increased following an interview with Madhu Jain (1988) in *India Today*, in which Rushdie told Madhu Jain that 'the image out of which the book grew was of the prophet going to the mountain and not being able to tell the difference between the angel and the devil'. In such a context Shahabuddin (1988) characterized the book as 'literary colonialism' and 'religious pornography'.

Literary and Critical Responses

Precursors and Rumblings

In December 1988 (see *The Independent*, 21.2.89a), the Iranian literary newspaper *Kayhan Farangi* published a review of *The Satanic Verses*. While critiquing the book and its author, and warning of the kind of controversy that might ensue, this review did so in tones which were comparatively mild in comparison with what would follow.

Literary critics pointed out that part of the background to the controversy might relate to the fact that the novel does not have a long tradition in Muslim cultures as a recognized literary form and that there was therefore little understanding of, or sympathy for, the way in which a novel uses ideas. However, Rushdie was not the first Muslim author to have used allegory and satire in criticism of Islam. For example, the Egyptian writer Naguib Mahfouz (see Mosley, 2007) had also utilized this. In 1959 the Cairo daily newspaper *Al-Ahram* had published, in serialized form, *Awlad Haratina* (*Children of the Gebelawi*, or *Children of the Alley*), which was later printed in book form in the Lebanon. This presented Moses, Jesus and Mary as characters of the Cairo streets and portrayed the God of the Old Testament as dying. Following serialization the book was banned in Egypt and Mahfouz was threatened with arrest and trial because the novel's allegorical approach to history was seen as undermining religion.

Mahfouz was quoted (in *The Guardian*, 31.3.89) as commenting on that ban to the effect that 'What is between my novel and al-Azhar is a misunderstanding'. He then went on to explain that 'It is a question of how to read a novel or a work of art. As they read it, it is not a novel but history.' This was also an aspect of the issues as they later developed between Muslim opponents of *The Satanic Verses* and Rushdie and the artistic community who insisted that the book was fiction, not history. In relation to Rushdie, Mahfouz made the carefully crafted comment that he had not been able to read the book but had 'heard that it is not rooted in scientific criticism of Islam, but is *insolent* in its treatment of these things. But we must accept the freedom of authors. Only this is not a small thing. Freedom is not to do what you want. There must be some rules, if only from the conscience.'

The Satanic Verses was shortlisted for the Booker Prize. In late January 1989, it was runner-up in the Whitbread competition. In February and March 1989, the committee of the Nobel Prize for Literature was split over its evaluation of the book when, following the fatwa, the book's profile had been raised in such a way as to make it highly controversial, attracting a lot of comment and debate (Gardels *et al.*, 1989; Garvey, 1989). In an unprecedented protest (reported in *The Independent*, 15.3.89a) against the organization's refusal to condemn the fatwa, two members of the Stockholm Academy – Kerstin Ekman and Lars Gyllensten – withdrew from membership of the committee (*The Guardian*, 15.3.89).

Initially, Viking Penguin apologized for the distress the book had caused but stressed that a novel is a work of fiction. It therefore rejected calls from Muslim critics for the inclusion of a statement in the book (see *New Life*, 27.1.89). This, together with the voluntary withdrawal of the book from further publication, was one of the early Muslim demands prior to the escalation of the controversy into calls for the prosecution of the author and banning of the book that only later became the more common aims of the campaign against *The*

Satanic Verses. At the end of January 1988, as Salman Rushdie prepared to set out on a three-week promotional tour of the USA to which fifty thousand copies of the book had been sent in advance, Viking was reported (in *The Sunday Times*, 29.1.89) as saying of Rushdie that it was concerned for his safety. This was in the context of bomb threats having been received at Viking Penguin's New York office, together with a telephone message that stated that five hundred thousand dollars would be offered for the assassination of Viking's President, Marvin Brown.

Book-Burning, Fatwa and Literary Outrage

But it was the 14 January 1989 Bradford burning of a copy of *The Satanic Verses* and the 14 February fatwa issued by Ayatollah Khomeini that sent shock waves through the literary community and galvanized it into organizing protests on Rushdie's behalf, with the Muslim campaigners against the book being seen as threatening freedom of expression. On 15 February, a report in *The Guardian* (15.2.89a) cited Viking Penguin as apologizing through an anonymous spokesperson. In a statement, the spokesperson explained that neither the publishers nor the author had intended to offend and that the publishers were appalled about the loss of life that had, by this time, already become associated with the book in other parts of the world. However, entrenched positions were already being taken up by all sides in the debate, and on 16 February all Viking/Penguin books were banned by Iran.

On 15 February, Harold Pinter led a delegation of publishers, literary agents and writers organized by himself and the editor of *The New Statesman and Society*, Stuart Weir, to deliver a letter of protest to the then British Prime Minister, Margaret Thatcher. This condemned the fatwa and supported Salman Rushdie and all those involved in the publication of the book (reported in *The Independent*, 16.2.89a). Those endorsing the letter included Hanif Kureishi, himself of Muslim background and previously the subject of Muslim demonstrations because of his portrayal of homosexuality in the Pakistani community in his film *My Beautiful Laundrette*.

As reported in *The Guardian* (15.2.89b), a range of organizations in the publishing world expressed concern about the fatwa and the general climate that was now surrounding the book. Mark LeFanu of the Society of Authors saw 'enormous implications' in the fatwa and stated that 'One hopes that this sort of thing will not impair people's right to write as they wish, but I think it could.' Clive Bradley, the Chief Executive of the Publishers' Association, said that 'You cannot not publish a book because it will cause offence . . .' Like Anthony Burgess, Louis Baum, the editor of *The Bookseller* magazine, invoked the spectre of Nazi totalitarianism and called for resistance to the fatwa as a means of testing '. . . the best traditions of British publishing, as well as our profoundest western traditions'. In *The Independent* (17.2.89a) the views of a number of publishing-related organizations were quoted. These included the Booksellers' Association, which issued a statement warning that:

> We have to assume that any UK bookseller that decides to sell the book in the future might be vulnerable. We deplore without reservation threats of violence. According to the laws of this land the book has done nothing illegal. Tolerance should be allowed in the expression of ideas.

They also included the Arts Council, which described the fatwa as 'intolerable' and stated that it:

> . . . .believes absolutely in freedom of expression and believes that freedom should be defended to the utmost. The council also accepts that freedom of expression means the Islamic community should have the freedom to criticize Mr Rushdie's book. It is, however, intolerable that there should be threats of physical violence against Mr Rushdie and his publishers. The council urges on everyone the tolerance and understanding that are the hallmark of a free society.

International support for Rushdie and his publishers began to be organized from within the literary community. The freedom of expression campaign group Article 19 argued that 'Any denunciation of acts of the imagination by secular or religious authorities strikes at the very heart of freedom – the freedom to imagine. As such, the order seeking Mr Rushdie's death is the ultimate and most extreme form of censorship and must be universally condemned.'

As reported in *The Guardian* (23.2.89a), on 22 February eight hundred Dutch authors, artists, publishers and journalists called on the Dutch government to break diplomatic relations with Iran if the threat to Rushdie's life was not withdrawn. On the same day, which was also the day of the book's publication in the USA, a coalition of the US

branch of PEN, the Authors' Guild and the anti-censorship organization, Article 19, organized a meeting of writers in New York. Norman
Mailer, Tom Wolfe and E.L. Doctorow attended a reading from the
book on Broadway. Also on 22 February, the National Writers' Union
of America tried to deliver a letter of protest at the Iranian mission to
the United Nations. In addition, there were protests about the country's three largest booksellers – Walden Books, B. Dalton, and Barnes
and Noble – because they had decided not to keep the book on their
shelves.

An International Committee for the Defence of Salman Rushdie was
formed with the active involvement of the writers Harold Pinter,
Margaret Drabble and Antonia Fraser. It had the support, among
others, of the Society of Authors, the Publishers' Association and the
National Union of Journalists. It published a pamphlet arguing for
the abolition of the blasphemy laws (The International Committee for
the Defence of Salman Rushdie and His Publishers, 1989). It also issued
a statement which was launched with twelve thousand signatures and,
as reported in *The Independent* (2.3.89a), aimed to gain one thousand
names for a global petition calling on world leaders to denounce the
threat against Rushdie and his publishers. The statement was initially
published under the title of a *World Statement*. Its signatories included
fifty Muslim writers – from Pakistan, Bangladesh and India, as well as
Britain. Supported, among others, by Graham Greene, Samuel Beckett
and Harold Pinter, it was printed in *The Guardian* (2.3.89). In the face
of the Ayatollah Khomeini's fatwa, the statement's signatories associated themselves with the publication of *The Satanic Verses* because of
their wish to uphold the right of freedom of opinion and expression as
set out in the Universal Declaration of Human Rights.

Nuance and Surprise

As reported in *The Independent* (24.2.89a), the participation of
Muslim writers in *The World Statement* had been prefigured by other
support for Rushdie from among black and Asian authors in Britain
when more than eighty leading Asian artists, writers and academics,
including Muslims among them, had issued another statement defending Rushdie. The statement, from 'Concerned Individuals of Asian
Origin' (1989), was published as an advertisement in *The Guardian*
newspaper (25.2.89). While supporting Rushdie, it signalled a more
nuanced approach to the whole affair by setting it within a wider

context. Thus, alongside a condemnation of the fatwa, the statement also expressed concern about the stereotyping of Muslims in the media, and recognized that many Muslims had felt genuine hurt in relation to the contents of *The Satanic Verses*. Another group from within the minority communities called Black Voices in Defence of Salman Rushdie and *The Satanic Verses* was set up and supported by, among others, Hanif Kureishi and Homi Bhabha. Its statement, reported in *The Guardian* (3.3.89a), tried to articulate the tension experienced by black intellectuals over the controversy:

> We who have experienced forms of racial and cultural discrimin-
> ation, and have engaged with its social effects, can only deplore the
> anti-Muslim statements and anti-Third World sentiments that have
> emerged in the escalation of international tension. Such political
> positions are profoundly at odds with Salman Rushdie's own beliefs
> and the causes to which he has dedicated his entire writing life.
> Equally, we who have experienced the crippling orthodoxies and
> patriarchalism of our own communities, and have witnessed its
> attempts to stifle dissent and discussion, can never endorse demands
> for censorship and unquestioned conformity.

However, although the literary and artistic community was generally supportive of Rushdie this response was not uniform. In a piece called 'Home Thoughts' in *The Independent Magazine* the historian Hugh Trevor-Roper (1989) stated that, while he agreed that Rushdie's life should be protected and that he could neither in principle, nor for any pragmatic reason support extension of the blasphemy law, he felt that he could not offer sympathy to Rushdie because, 'After all, he is well versed in Islamic ideas: he knew what he was doing and could foresee the consequences.' Surprisingly, in view of his argument that Rushdie should be offered protection, Trevor-Roper went on to say, 'I would not shed a tear if some British Muslims, deploring his manners, should waylay him in a dark street and seek to improve them.'

Writing in *The Guardian* (22.4.89) about a regular Birmingham Writers' Lunch hosted by the author David Lodge, Anne Devlin remarked that 'the most telling point' made in their discussions of the controversy was that while published authors all have a platform, 'the Muslims demonstrating have no platform', and that 'Street demonstrations are therefore a legitimate form of expression for people who wish to voice their opinions and have no other means of expression in public.'

At a seminar of the Writers' Guild of Great Britain in London (and reported in *The Guardian*, 27.2.89d), a 'senior Penguin editor' (who was said to have been speaking 'in a personal capacity') admitted that 'All of us regret the misery caused and the deaths that have occurred ... If there were a way to keep the book in print and prevent further loss of life, and if the way to do that is print some form of apology, then maybe we should do that.' However, Mervyn Jones of the Campaign Against Censorship opposed this as a dangerous precedent and defended the right to offend. In *The Independent* (28.2.89a), it was noted that Penguin did, in fact, take some decisive action in the withdrawal of the book when it retrieved and pulped some paperback copies that had been exported to continental Europe following the discovery of one of these in Naville's bookshop in Geneva.

Fear and Decision

In spring 1989, *The Rushdie File*, a collection of articles and statements edited by Lisa Appignanesi (deputy director of the Institute for Contemporary Arts) and Sara Maitland (a journalist), was published by Fourth Estate. In the Preface to this book, Appignanesi and Maitland (1989: vii) point out that their book was originally intended to have been published by Collins but that 'When the book was delivered ... senior management at Collins found a variety of excuses for backing out of its publication.' Collins explained that they did not wish to exacerbate the situation for Penguin and their managing director also argued that the book was 'not objective' although, in a piece in *The Independent*, Sara Maitland (1989) claimed that Collins had originally been enthusiastic about it. *The Rushdie File* book project had begun, under the original name of *The Rushdie Dossier*, following a 19 April Institute for Contemporary Arts conference addressing the issues raised by the controversy.

In the light of Collins' refusal to publish, a spokesperson for the Institute was cited in *The Independent* (3.5.89) as expressing a deep concern about the impact that the fatwa appeared to be having on British publishing. In her *Independent* article, Maitland (1989) cited fear and a lack of corporate courage as lying behind this. Even after the small and new publishing company, Fourth Estate, offered to publish the text, Appignanesi and Maitland (1989, viii) commented that 'We experienced a further delay when the printers who had originally accepted to print this book inexplicably refused to honour their agreement.' That printer was Richard Clay, which was the largest printer in Britain and had actually printed *The Satanic Verses* itself. Six other British printers turned the job down before a Dutch printer was finally found.

In a letter (25.2.89) to the editor of *The Independent* newspaper, Ian McEwan pointed out that, when he appeared on BBC2's *The Late Show* to discuss 'the Rushdie affair', three out of the six panellists had received threatening reminders that their views would be monitored, while other British writers had, out of fear, declined the invitation to defend *The Satanic Verses*. This perception was confirmed by Fadia Faqir, a writer who also appeared on *The Late Show* and who said that she had received messages in which her attention had been drawn to the fact that what she said would be carefully monitored, the implication of which she took to be a warning. *The Independent* (3.3.89a) reported that Peter Sissons, a newsreader for Channel 4, had been put under 24-hour guard following threats received from a group calling itself the Guardians of the Islamic Revolution, who accused him of having insulted Imam Khomeini during an interview with the Iranian chargé d'affaires in London.

Another example of what Howard Brenton (reported in *The Guardian*, 16.4.89a) called 'the climate of fear that has settled over any discussion of *Satanic Verses*' can be seen in the story of the play, *Iranian Nights*, that Brenton had written together with Tariq Ali. The originally proposed title, 'A Mullah's Night Out', was changed close to the end of the writing of the play after the National Theatre turned it down. It was then due to have been staged at the Royal Court Theatre for a run of eleven nights, starting on 19 April, and afterwards to be screened by Channel 4 on 20 May. However, two actors withdrew, apparently because of concern for their lives.

The play dealt with the issues raised by 'the Rushdie affair', but also with tyranny and Britain's responsibility for religious intolerance and divisions within the Muslim community. When it eventually went ahead at the Royal Court, Ali and Brenton noted that a large proportion of their Royal Court audiences were Iranians, Asians, Arabs and Turks (who were people not often seen at the theatre in the UK) and that when four white women Muslim converts tried to interrupt, they were heckled by other Muslims in the audience. Nevertheless, as reported in *New Life* (14.4.89a), further evidence of 'the climate of fear' referred to by Brenton appeared when, in order to avoid giving the slightest pretext for offence, Gareth Jones, the writer of the BBC drama series *Shalom, Salaam*, decided to cut a scene which showed the Qur'an being handled impatiently.

In the run-up to the first anniversary of the publication of *The Satanic Verses*, pressures were building on Penguin both to scrap the book and to publish it as a paperback. Following a 13 September discovery of bombs in York, Peterborough, Nottingham and Guildford, in a 'Commentary' column in *The Guardian* (16.9.89a) the trade magazine, *The Bookseller*, argued that the paperback edition must go ahead on the grounds that not to do so would be seen as appeasing this violence. As reported in *The Independent* (25.9.89), against the background of these bombing attempts, and after the sale of two hundred thousand hardback copies, Penguin were still debating whether to move ahead with the paperback or not.

From Lobbying to Book-Burning and Demonstrations

The Novel and 'The Real World'

Debates about literary works often take place in a comparatively rarefied atmosphere, either among academics, or in literary circles. However, some literary work becomes highly contextualized in terms of its impact, and it soon became obvious that the debate about *The Satanic Verses* was not going to be the preserve of the metropolitan literati alone. On the contrary, as the events of the controversy unfolded, it became clear that books such as *The Satanic Verses* can have explosive effects from the world of international relations through to the politics of the local street.

Making Representations

The Muslim campaign against the book had begun with lobbying initiatives from a range of Muslim organizations. On 24 October 1988, the Islamic Society for the Promotion of Religious Tolerance held a seminar in London to discuss both *The Satanic Verses* and Martin Scorsese's (1988) film *The Last Temptation of Christ*. As reported in *The Jewish Chronicle* (28.10.88), the chairman of the Society, Hesham El-Essawy, had written a letter to Viking Penguin describing *The Satanic Verses* as 'insulting in the extreme to everything that the Moslems hold sacred' in that it depicts 'God as a balding man with dandruff, calls the prophet Abraham, the father of Jews, Christians and Moslems, a bastard, and views the prophet Muhammed with such contempt as has never been shown by any of the other enemies of the prophet'. In this phase of the controversy, the goal of the campaign was, as explained in a letter to *The Guardian* (23.1.89) by El-Essawy, not a campaign for censorship but for the publishers to insert an historical and factual erratum in the book.

Initiatives also came from the Maududist organization in India, the Jamaat-i-Islami. According to Malise Ruthven (1991: 92), Ahmed Ejaz of the Islamic Foundation in Madras contacted the Islamic Foundation in Leicester with news of the Indian Government's banning of the book. The Maududists aimed to use Saudi Arabia and the Islamic Conference Organisation to bring pressure to bear to get the book banned in Britain. There was precedent for such hope because, in 1980, Saudi Arabia had acted to prevent the screening on several European television networks of the controversial film, *Death of a Princess*, a 'faction' documentary about a princess executed for adultery in Saudi Arabia. The Saudi chargé d'affaires in London had criticized the film as an attack on Islam and on the way of life in Saudi Arabia. The British Ambassador was expelled and the British Government feared losing billions of pounds worth of export contracts during the four months of the crisis, the solution to which involved an agreement to set up a joint cultural relations committee to prevent possible future 'misunderstandings' (see *The Guardian*, 1.3.89b).

In terms of national political institutions and figures, the first signs of awareness of the strength of Muslim concern emerged when, on 1 December 1988, Ken Hargreaves, MP moved an early day motion in the House of Commons expressing regret for the distress caused to Muslims by the publication of *The Satanic Verses*. On 10 December, the Islamic Defence Council organized the first public rally in London. This was quickly followed by similar protest marches and rallies in other towns and cities. On 19 December, a delegation of ambassadors from Muslim countries called on the Home Secretary to protest against *The Satanic Verses*. As later highlighted in an *Independent* (24.2.89b) newspaper report, one of those ambassadors subsequently claimed that they had warned the Foreign Office about the likely impact of the book, and that what had later happened had proved them right.

However, the peaceful lobbying methods of these organizations met with little success and evoked few signs of sympathy on the part of either the publishers or the government. During the first weeks of December protest marches began to emerge in Lancashire. *New Life*

(3.2.89) reported on a peacefully conducted protest in Blackburn by around 5,000 Muslims, but which broke out into scuffles after picketing of bookshops selling the book in town. A petition of 14,750 signatures was handed to the mayor, the central library and a leading bookshop manager, calling for the book to be banned. There were also marches in Burnley and Hyndburn, where a petition calling for banning was also handed in to the mayor. In Accrington marchers carried banners saying 'Ban the filthy book' and 'Muslims unite to banish filth'. There was some Muslim discomfort about the disturbances associated with these early protests with, for example, Mr Ishmail Lorgat of the Blackburn Action Committee on Islamic Affairs apologizing to bookshop owners, shoppers and the police. However, it was also reported that Muslims in Peterborough had threatened to take violent action against bookshops if copies of *The Satanic Verses* were not removed from their shelves.

It was reported by *The Guardian* (15.2.89e) that, in Bradford, the City Council had appointed a reading panel of four staff to examine the book. Eventually, *The Satanic Verses* was withdrawn from Bradford library shelves and was made available only on request, with a warning sticker appended explaining that it was offensive to Muslims. The sticker stated that:

> This book is a work of the imagination. It does not claim to be a contribution to historical knowledge. Nevertheless it has caused great offence to Muslims in our community. The library regrets this. However, in a free society, the public library has an over-riding duty to provide its readers with the books they may require in order to judge for themselves, subject only to the law of the land. (*The Guardian*, 11.3.89a)

Bradford as a Cauldron for the Controversy

At this stage, though, despite mounting Muslim anger and the outbreaks of street protest in northern England, the general public in the UK was largely unaware of the ferment which was brewing around the book. This, by and large, remained the case until the opening months of 1989, when the northern city of Bradford became the epicentre of the campaign (see Bowen, 1992a, 1992b; Lewis, P., 1989, 1990).

The Muslim community of the UK is primarily composed of groups (see Robinson, 1988; Raza, 1992) which originated in the subcontinental countries of India, Pakistan and Bangladesh. In Bradford (see Barton, 1986) most of the Muslims came from just sixteen villages in the Punjab, and had emigrated when a Pakistan government-sponsored hydroelectric power project flooded their area in the early 1960s. Family, community and political ties with the sub-continent are still very strong and, as a result, it was not long before news of Rushdie's Indian interviews and of the lobbying against the book by Indian Muslim MPs began to reach the British Muslim community in Bradford.

Sher Azam (the then Chair of Bradford Council of Mosques) explained that the book had first been heard of in Bradford when 'We received letters from Hizb-ul-Ulama in Blackburn at the end of September, enclosing extracts from two Indian magazines; we also received cuttings from a Bradford man who had read the articles in India . . .' (quoted in Ruthven, 1991: 84). Portions of the book were translated into Urdu so that the local *ulema* could decide whether it was blasphemous. This they unanimously did, and concern began to grow within the community. A circular from Blackburn was soon issued urging people not to buy or read the novel and to 'Wherever possible gather in crowds and force these places not to sell such rubbish pleadingly' (quoted in Ruthven, 1991: 91). The circular concluded by urging imams to utilize the Friday mosque prayers to organize petitions to be sent to the Queen, the Prime Minister and the Home Office.

The Muslim magazine *Impact International* (1988a) had devoted a special issue to Rushdie and *The Satanic Verses*. It contained a piece entitled 'Quote, unquote Satanic Verses' (*Impact International*, 1988b) which collected together quotations from the book that were likely to be offensive to Muslims. These quotations were copied and, according to El-Essawy (reported in *The Guardian*, 16.2.89a), were circulated widely among Muslims. But in addition to the activity that it generated among existing Muslim organizations, the controversy led to the creation of some new organizations formed to focus Muslim activity around the book. Nationally these included the Islamic Defence Council, which took up a position against both the book and the fatwa (see Islamic Defence Council, 1989). On 11 October 1988, the UK Action Committee on Islamic Affairs had been founded and subsequently developed a wider agenda of action with regard to broader Muslim concerns about the relationship between Muslims and the UK state and society (see UK Action Committee on Islamic Affairs, 1993).

The Book-Burning

Eventually it was in Bradford where an action took place that brought the debates around the book to wide and controversial public attention. This was on 14 January 1989 when, during a public demonstration against the book, Sayyid Abdul Quddus burned a copy of *The Satanic Verses*. Although this event gained the media spotlight it was not, in fact, the first occasion on which a copy of the book had been burned. As reported in *New Life* (16.12.88), already in December, outside Blackburn Town Hall, religious leaders had called for the book to be burned as a distortion of Muslim history. Indeed, six weeks prior to the Bradford burning, on 2 December 1988, in a seven thousand-strong demonstration in Bolton, a copy had actually been set alight. On that occasion, though, the burning of the book had been ignored, whereas in Bradford there had been a pre-arrangement between the media and the protesters to cover the event.

The deliberate orchestration of this event has to be understood against the background of growing frustration among Muslims at their apparent inability to achieve their goals or even to achieve wide publicity for their case. For example, on 23 December, the Attorney General had given the legal opinion that no action in law was possible against the publisher of *The Satanic Verses*. By contrast, two days after the Bradford book-burning, W.H. Smith booksellers in the Bradford area withdrew *The Satanic Verses* from display on its shelves, although it remained on display and sale in its outlets in other parts of the country.

Although successful in achieving such localized responses from booksellers and in drawing wider public attention to Muslim strength of feeling about *The Satanic Verses*, the actual symbolism of book-burning was double-edged in its effect. The vividly evocative title – 'On Not Burning Your Enemy's Flag' – of one of the chapters of Richard Webster's (1990) study of the controversy and its roots, underlined the ambiguous and contextual nature of the symbolism involved. In the living memory of European history, book-burning is associated with Nazism. Writing in *The Daily Mail* (31.1.89) in his piece on 'The burning truth', Anthony Burgess cited Heinrich Heine's famous comment on the Nazi burning of books to the effect that when one starts with the burning of books it will soon lead to the burning of men and women. At the same time, he acknowledged that the law had ordered the burning of D.H. Lawrence's *The Rainbow* in 1916 and that the British customs authorities had burnt James Joyce's *Ulysses* in 1922.

Street Actions

Following the Bradford book-burning the Islamic Defence Council organized a meeting at the East London Mosque at which over a thousand Muslims were present. Rushdie's immediate response was to blame the trouble on an artificially organized campaign rather than a popular upsurge of Muslim opinion. But after the Ayatollah Khomeini's fatwa, the Muslim demonstrations in Britain continued and also intensified, with *The Independent* (25.2.89a) reporting that two thousand Muslims demonstrated outside Manchester Town Hall and called for the withdrawal of the book from the library. In Yorkshire, on 4 March, approximately two thousand Muslims organized by the South Yorkshire Muslim Action Committee marched in Sheffield, burning effigies and pictures of Salman Rushdie and calling for a ban on the book in Sheffield libraries. The libraries responded to this by inserting a warning slip that the book was offensive to Muslims. In Keighley, one thousand Muslims marched. At the end of March, it was reported in *The Guardian* (27.3.89) that three thousand Muslims demonstrated in Dewsbury, West Yorkshire and six hundred in Reading, Berkshire.

The British Muslim Action Front, organized by Abdul Hussain Chaudhary, mobilized support both in Britain and in Europe for what was intended to be the biggest demonstration in twentieth-century Britain. It was planned for Hyde Park in London on 27 May, but also taking in Parliament Square and Downing Street. Its demands included calling upon Penguin to cease publication of *The Satanic Verses* and to destroy all copies, as well as to extend the blasphemy laws in order to include Islam within their scope (for reports see *The Guardian*, 4.5.89, 5.5.89, 15.5.89, 27.5.89, 29.5.89; and *The Independent*, 27.5.89).

The march did not explicitly support Khomeini's fatwa, which the demonstration organizer, Abdul Hussain Chaudhary, insisted was a separate matter. But at the demonstration, police in riot dress intervened after Iranian and Iraqi factions fought and as disputes flared between the demonstrators and around forty counter-demonstrators from Women Against Fundamentalism, as well as with Nicholas Walter of the Rationalist Press Association and Barbara Smoker of the

National Secular Society. A Union Jack and an effigy of Rushdie were burned in Parliament Square. Banners were carried with slogans calling for the killing of Salman Rushdie (see *The Independent*, 28.5.89 and *The Guardian*, 29.5.89). The march ended in violent clashes and over one hundred arrests. The British Muslim Action Front said further marches had not been ruled out, but a strike of Muslim businesses was also being considered. *The Independent* (31.5.89) highlighted reports that the march had been funded by up to £1,000,000 from the Iranian Office for Islamic Propaganda run by Ayatollah Ahmad Jannati, although it was also reported that Abdul Hussain Chaudhary had denied this.

Local demonstrations continued, with a 17 June demonstration of around three thousand in Bradford that developed into fighting between white and Asian youths, followed by an outbreak of more generalized violence (see *New Life*, 23.6.89). As reported in *The Sunday Times* (2.7.89), this coincided with an upsurge in white violence using 'Rushdie' as a racial and ethnic taunt. *The Independent* (24.6.89) reported that a further demonstration was planned to take place in Dewsbury the following weekend. However, Douglas Hurd agreed to a request from Kirklees Council to ban both the Muslim march and a counter-demonstration being planned by the National Front at which police intelligence had warned that there had been plans to burn a copy of the Qur'an. *The Guardian* (11.7.89) reported that tensions in Bradford had grown, with gangs of white youths attacking isolated Muslim areas.

Other Actions

On 17 June, during the Muslim Eid festival celebrations, the Bradford Council of Mosques (1989) launched a ten-point plan of action (see *Muslim News*, 7.7.89a and *New Life*, 21.7.89a). The plan included picketing Viking Penguin as well as bookshops and libraries that stocked the novel; a national day of action; and a protest march from Bradford to London. Meanwhile, as reported in *The Guardian* (22.7.89a), the UK Action Committee on Islamic Affairs and the Muslim Action Front declared that they were awaiting the outcome of blasphemy court cases before organizing further demonstrations. At around the time of the first anniversary of the hardback edition, the Bradford Council of Mosques had announced (see *The Guardian*, 25.9.89) that it was stepping up its campaigning after reports that

Penguin was planning to issue a paperback version, a move that the Council had condemned as being a provocation.

Beginning on 30 September, the South African Muslim preacher, Ahmed Deedat, the President of the Islamic Propagation Centre International in Birmingham, organized a week-long speaking tour addressing meetings in London as well as in Bradford, Blackburn, Leicester, Glasgow and Birmingham (reported in *New Life*, 13.10.89). His organization stated that it neither supported nor denounced the fatwa (*The Independent*, 30.9.89), but Deedat denounced Rushdie (see *The Guardian*, 2.10.89) and wrote a short booklet entitled *How Rushdie Fooled the West* (Deedat, n.d.) that was published by the Islamic Propagation Centre. It quoted many of the controversial sections of *The Satanic Verses* and was reported (see *New Life*, 3.10.89) as having caused considerable controversy in the Leicester Muslim community after it was distributed door-to-door to many houses in the Beaumont Leys area of the city.

The Political and Legal Arenas

Blasphemy and International Law

In concert with continuing political activity at both street and political levels, Muslim organizations attempted to utilize the law in their campaign against the book. As a result the law also became one of the major terrains in the developing conflict. At the beginning of 1989, the Islamic Defence Council's barrister, Mr Ali Mohammed Azhar, lodged papers with the Bow Street Magistrates' Court with the intention of proving that Rushdie had infringed the existing blasphemy law. If necessary, he vowed to take the case to the European Court (see *New Life*, 3.2.89).

An international lawyer, Sajid Qureshi, was invited to the Middle East to discuss the basis upon which international legal proceedings might be started against Rushdie and his publishers. On 13 February, the Chief Metropolitan Magistrate, Sir David Hopkins, refused Muslim lawyers a summons against Rushdie and Viking Penguin for blasphemy and seditious libel (see *The Independent*, 14.3.89a).

Politics and Law

On 27 February 1989, under the leadership of Teddy Taylor, Conservative MP for Southend, a delegation of British Muslims from the Islamic Defence Council visited John Patten, MP, the Minister of State at the Home Office, asking for equal treatment under the blasphemy laws. Patten, however, explained that the government was not considering a change in the law – in other words, it was intended neither to extend nor to abolish the current law. This was later confirmed when the Home Secretary, Douglas Hurd, while addressing Muslims in Birmingham on 1 February, stated that there would not be any changes in the blasphemy law while simultaneously urging British Muslims to join what he called the mainstream of British society (reported in *The Independent*, 28.2.89b).

By 3 March, the then Prime Minster, Margaret Thatcher and the Foreign Secretary, Sir Geoffrey Howe were conceding that *The Satanic Verses* was offensive to Muslims. On 28 March 1989, a delegation of the Pakistani action committee against *The Satanic Verses*, the Tehrik Tahaffuzi-Namoos-i-Risalat, presented a memorandum to the Foreign Secretary seeking the banning of the book (see Ahsan and Kidwai, eds., 1991: 16). On 1 April, the Muslim Institute held a London conference on the controversy, at which its Director, Dr Kalim Siddiqui, defended the fatwa and outlined his view of the wider political implications of the affair for Muslims in Britain.

On 19 June, the High Court gave the Muslim Action Front leave to challenge the 13 February Bow Street Magistrates' refusal to issue summonses to Rushdie and Viking Penguin for prosecution on the grounds of blasphemous and seditious libel. At the same time, the presiding judge, Mr Justice Nolan, warned the organization against demonstrations, which he advised would be counter-productive (see *The Independent*, 20.6.89 and *Muslim News*, 7.7.89b).

The decision to allow an appeal was made in the light of a 1980 High Court ruling which stated that, in a case where the existence of an offence is disputed, both sides should be heard before a decision is reached as to whether an offence does exist in English law. However, the protesting Muslims were also warned that the weight of legal authorities appeared to be strongly on the side of those who argued that the law of blasphemy was applicable only to Christianity. As reported in *The Independent* (5.7.89), on 4 July, John Patten, MP wrote a letter entitled 'Muslims in Britain Today', issued in a press release (Patten, 1989a), to leading British Muslims. In this, among other things, he stated his view about the difficulties that would be involved in extending legal protection beyond Anglican Christianity.

At its conference on 11 September, the Union of Muslim Organisations stated that it viewed the continued publication of *The Satanic Verses* as the most important issue facing British Muslims. On the same day, the Conservative Member of Parliament, Neil Thorne, MP, called for the book to be withdrawn. On 16 December, the Association of Sunni Muslims underlined its determination to continue campaigning until the book was withdrawn and, as a sign of solidarity in their campaign against the novel, Muslims at mosques throughout the UK were asked to raise their hands (see Ahsan and Kidwai, eds., 1991: 17).

The Fatwa: Its International Context and Repercussions

Contextualizing the Fatwa

It was the drama of the Bradford book-burning that had initially brought the controversy to the attention of the majority of the British people and made it into a media story. But it was the Ayatollah Khomeini's fatwa, issued on 14 February 1989 against Rushdie and against those knowingly associated with the publication of *The Satanic Verses*, that intensified the controversy's 'lightning conductor' effect as it developed throughout the rest of 1989 and into 1990 and beyond. The fatwa was a sharp reminder that the controversy in the UK took place within, and was also profoundly affected by, a wider international context. Action and response therefore took place at an international diplomatic level as well as at national government and local street level, with the issue of the fatwa affecting all of these levels simultaneously (see Mozaffari, 1990).

As has already been noted, on 5 October, the Indian Government had banned *The Satanic Verses*. This was followed by a range of Muslim organizations attempting to secure a worldwide ban (see Ahsan and Kidwai, eds., 1991: 11–14). On 11 October, the World Assembly of Muslim Youth, based in Riyadh, Saudi Arabia and representing over five hundred Muslim youth organizations throughout the world, had condemned the book and demanded a global ban on it. On 5 November, the General Secretariat of the Organisation of the Islamic Conference, which links 46 Muslim countries, asked those states in membership with it to take strong action against both the author and the publisher if they failed to withdraw the book. On that same day, Bangladesh banned *The Satanic Verses*, followed on 22 November by the Sudan; on 24 November by the Republic of South Africa; and on 14 December by Sri Lanka. On 28 December, Oman blacklisted Penguin, followed, on 15 February, by Iran.

Sheikh Zahram Ibrahim of the Regent's Park Islamic Centre in London was reported (in *New Life*, 3.2.89) as saying that the aim was for governments to ban booksellers that handled any Penguin book. The book's international impact was far-reaching. In Pakistan, where Rushdie's family continued to live, daily demonstrations were held against the book and Pakistani government ministers claimed that the opposition, led by the Islamic Democratic Alliance, was using the affair for undermining democracy and the Pakistani government. On 12 February 1989, in urban centres throughout Pakistan, demonstrations were held against the book. In Islamabad, ten people were reported killed and over one hundred were reported injured during disturbances about the book that took place outside the US Embassy.

In India, on 13 February, a Muslim demonstrator was reported (in *The Guardian*, 15.2.89c) killed and more than one hundred injured in Srinagar. On 27 February, in further demonstrations in India, one Muslim was reported (in *The Independent*, 28.2.89b) killed and seven people injured. In the USA, on 28 February, in attacks thought to be linked to the controversy, two bookshops in Berkeley, California were bombed as was the office of the Riverdale Press, the headquarters of a New York weekly that had endorsed the book (*The Independent*, 1.3.89e).

Despite this turmoil, outside of the Muslim community very few people in the UK were really aware of the book's international impact. Even after the impetus given to the controversy by the Bradford book-burning it appeared that the campaign was having little effect. Thus an editorial in the Asian newspaper *New Life* (3.2.89) expressed the opinion that, despite the book-burning, the anger of the Muslims involved in the campaign against the book was being ignored and that the issues involved might therefore go away. However, on 14 February 1989, events took a turn that ensured that the issue not only remained alive but intensified. This was when the spiritual leader of the Iranian Revolution, the late Ayatollah Khomeini, issued a fatwa in which he pronounced that Salman Rushdie was to be viewed as an apostate to Islam and should be punished by death:

I would like to inform all the intrepid Muslims in the world that the author of the book entitled *The Satanic Verses*, which has been compiled, printed and published in opposition to Islam, the Prophet and the Qur'an, as well as those publishers who were aware of its contents, have been declared *madhur el dam*. I call on all zealous Muslims to execute them quickly, wherever they find them, so that no one will dare to insult Islam again. Whoever is killed in this path will be regarded as a martyr . . . (quoted in Ruthven, 1991: 112)

Only three weeks prior to the fatwa Khomeini had already stated that a sentence of death would be appropriate for the producers of an Iranian television programme in which one of the women on the programme, when asked their opinion of Fatima, the revered daughter of the Prophet, had stated that she preferred a more contemporary role model, suggesting instead the star of a highly popular Japanese soap opera. The fatwa on Rushdie and those associated with the publication of *The Satanic Verses* was Khomeini's first public intervention in 'the Rushdie affair'.

Reactions to the Fatwa

A *Financial Times* editorial (16.2.89) suggested that it was doubtful whether the Ayatollah Khomeini was actively seeking a confrontation with Britain and suggested that the timing of Khomeini's fatwa suggested he was reacting to the deaths of anti-*Satanic Verses* demonstrators in Pakistan as much as to the book itself. In the light of the critical review of *The Satanic Verses* that had appeared three months previously in the Iranian cultural weekly *Kayhan Farangi*, there is evidence to support *The Financial Times*' interpretation. Khomeini and the ruling group in Iran would almost certainly have been aware of this review and of the book itself and yet no action had been taken and no statements were issued prior to February 1989.

From a secular political perspective the fatwa amounted to what *The Financial Times* editorial (16.2.89) described as 'a direct incitement to murder a British subject (or subjects) resident in Britain'. However, a fatwa is not, as it was sometimes incorrectly reported to be, an order. An anonymous London-based Iranian was cited (in *The Independent*, 16.2.89c) as arguing that matters of this kind are for an individual's conscience. In other words, as the Iranian authorities later insisted, Khomeini spoke not as a Head of State but as a *mujtahid*, in other words one of those who is qualified to interpret Islamic law. But if Rushdie were judged to have committed *fitna* or sedition, then the sentence would indeed be death.

However, there is in the Muslim world today an increasing debate about the historical meaning of this crime and about the contemporary interpretation and any implementation of the punishment associated with it. Thus, in Abdullah Saeed and Hassan Saeed's (2004) book, *Freedom of Religion, Apostasy and Islam*, the authors (who are, respectively, a Professor of Arab and Islamic Studies at the University of Melbourne and the Attorney General of the Maldives) argue from within a Muslim perspective that the law of apostasy and its punishment by death is untenable in the modern period, since it is in conflict with a variety of foundation texts in Islam that affirm freedom of religion, and they explore this through the example of Malaysia, as a Muslim majority but also multi-faith society.

Khomeini's first statement, then, though understood and presented by many as a verdict, was actually an opinion, albeit an authoritative one for Shi'a Muslims in particular. In a Channel 4 interview on 17 February 1989 (quoted in *The Guardian*, 18.2.89) Mr Mohammad Basti, the Iranian chargé d'affaires in London, stated that the fatwa was 'a religious command, not a political command' and that it was 'an opinion, a purely religious statement.' There were other indications, too, that at least some sections of the Iranian leadership did not want to let events spin out of control. In a sermon at Tehran University's prayer ground, President Ali Khamenei attacked Rushdie but went on to say that he might apologize for his mistakes and gain forgiveness (*The Independent*, 18.2.89a).

The British chargé d'affaires in Iran, Nicholas Browne, had a two-hour meeting with the Iranian Deputy Foreign Minister, Mohammad Javad Larijani at which it was several times underlined that the Ayatollah Khomeini's fatwa had been pronounced in his religious capacity rather than as head of the Iranian State. However, after Rushdie's expression of regret and diplomatic moves in the European Community, Khomeini reiterated the fatwa (see *The Guardian*, 23.2.89d) in a way that appeared to be a verdict, perhaps because Rushdie's expressions of regret following the first fatwa were taken as being tantamount to an admission of guilt.

Understanding the Fatwa

Although a part of the minority Shi'a branch of Islam, Khomeini's anti-colonial radicalism (see Moin, 1994: 64–94) also appealed to many Sunni Muslims. The fatwa has therefore to be seen in the context of the struggle that was taking place among Muslims in terms of the tension between the revolutionary version of Islam espoused by Khomeini (1981) and the Iranian radicals, and what Khomeini sometimes described as 'American Islam', by which he meant a depoliticized version of Islam that he believed could be found in Saudi Arabia and other Gulf states. The Saudi King has the honour of the title 'Keeper of the Holy Places' of Islam but, in 1987, more than four hundred people had been killed in violence between Saudi Arabian police and Iranian Shi'a pilgrims in Mecca.

Within Iran itself, after the Iran–Iraq war debacle, those identified in the West as 'pragmatists', such as the Speaker of the Iranian Parliament, Hashemi Rafsanjani, had been making some headway in their arguments for the development of more pragmatic international relations. In this internal context the fatwa could be interpreted as bringing pressure to bear upon such moves. However, after a visit to Tehran, the Lebanese Shi'a Muslim leader Sheikh Mohammed Hussein Fadlallah insisted that Khomeini's fatwa was not the result of radical counter-pressures. Fadlallah (quoted in *The Guardian*, 23.2.89b) said that 'There was no political dispute over this. Rushdie harmed Islam in a very flagrant way. We respond with dialogue to those who differ with us on an intellectual level. We do not enjoy the spirit of dialogue with those who insult our sacred symbols.' He added that the fatwa had functioned as a kind of shock tactic in that 'The West moved to publish this book in all Western countries without concern for Muslim feelings . . . Imam Khomeini's stand was important to control this plot.' Nevertheless, whether or not it was the original intention behind the fatwa, Khomeini clearly did use the affair to attack revisionists in Iran. In an hour-long broadcast on 22 February, Khomeini (quoted in *The Independent*, 24.2.89c) argued that:

> Those who still continue to believe that we must embark on revisions in our politics, principles and diplomacy and that we have blundered and must not repeat previous mistakes; those who still believe that extremist slogans of war will cause the West and East to be pessimistic about us and that ultimately all this has led to the country's isolation; those who believe that if we act in a pragmatic

way they will reciprocate and will mutually respect the nation, Islam and Muslims – to them this is an example.

The fatwa must also be seen in the context of the wider history of relations between Iran and the West generally. Relations between Iran and Britain, in particular, had been poisoned since the forced closure of the British Embassy in Tehran in 1979, in the wake of the Iranian Revolution and the upsurge of popular anti-Western activity. These relations had then deteriorated still further with the April 1980 armed takeover of the Iranian embassy in London and the subsequent SAS storming of the embassy. Britain, together with the USA, viewed Iran as a leading exporter of international terrorism. But Iran saw Britain as historically untrustworthy and guilty of interference in Iranian internal affairs. Britain was seen as 'the Little Satan' alongside the powerful 'Great Satan' of the USA (see *The Independent*, 22.2.89a).

The publication of *The Satanic Verses* was therefore understood as yet another chapter in the history of British involvement in Persian affairs which began with the British Empire's strategic interest in protecting Northern India from the Tsarist Empire's expansionist southern drive; Britain's involvement in setting up the Pahlavi dynasty; its occupation of the country during the Second World War; and its part in overthrowing Prime Minister Mohammad Mosaddeq in 1953. On 15 February 1989, which was a day of mourning about the book announced by the Iranian Prime Minister Mir-Hossein Mousavi, around a thousand Iranian demonstrators pelted the British embassy in Tehran, chanting 'Death to Britain' and 'Death to America', while the three diplomats and four support staff, including the chargé d'affaires, Nick Browne, tried to establish contact with senior Iranian officials (see *The Guardian*, 16.2.89b). Iranian Revolutionary Guards undertook to kill Rushdie.

A senior Iranian cleric, Hassani Sanei, offered a reward of one million dollars, later raised to three million, for any foreigner who killed what he called 'this mercenary of colonialism', to be paid from his Fifth of Khordad Foundation, and which was originally set up to care for people killed in anti-American demonstrations on 5 June 1963. However, the Tehran daily newspaper *Jomhuri Eslami* (*Islamic Republic*) was reported (in *The Independent*, 17.2.89b) as criticizing this financial reward as diverting attention from the religious nature of the fatwa, while the British publisher Robert Maxwell offered six million dollars for anyone who could 'civilize' Khomeini (see The Weasel, 1989). The controversy was thus beginning to poison the gradual restoration of normal diplomatic relations upon which Iran and the British Foreign Minister, Sir Geoffrey Howe, had agreed during 1988.

The initial British diplomatic reaction to the fatwa was relatively low-key with a Foreign Office spokesperson (quoted in *The Guardian*, 15.2.89a) saying only that the Ayatollah's words 'were a matter for serious concern', but the incremental movement that had previously taken place towards normalization was frozen. One factor that undoubtedly contributed to the initially muted response of the British Government was concern about how these events might complicate the diplomatic position with regard to Roger Cooper, a British businessman who had been held in prison in Tehran for three years, on suspicion of spying, but without charge or trial. Following the fatwa, the Iranian Information Ministry (reported in a *Financial Times* editorial, 16.2.89) had issued statements to the effect that Cooper had been given a long sentence for spying but that the final outcome in his case was still under consideration.

Another concern was that a stronger response might also jeopardize the efforts being made to release the British and Irish hostages held in Lebanon – Terry Waite, John McCarthy and Brian Keenan. Indeed, Sheikh Fadlallah warned that diplomatic attacks on Iran might lead to Iran freezing its good offices over the hostages, and it was reported (*The Independent*, 29.4.89b) that this had been confirmed by the Archbishop of Canterbury, who explained that, in the wake of the fatwa and the reactions to it, communications had become a lot more difficult.

Carrying out the Fatwa

On 26 February 1989 (see *The Guardian*, 27.2.89a) there had been anti-Rushdie and anti-British demonstrations in Beirut and the Beka'a Valley and soon after this the British embassy warned (reported in *The Guardian*, 9.3.89) British citizens to leave Lebanon. On 26 February, the Revolutionary Muslim Forces, claiming to speak for Islamic Jihad, for the Revolutionary Justice Organisation and for Islamic Jihad for the Liberation of Palestine, explicitly linked the position of the hostages with 'the Rushdie affair' and claimed that a group in Lebanon had been commissioned to kill Rushdie before March 15 (as reported in *The Guardian*, 23.2.89b). In Damascus, Ahmed Jibril, the leader of the Popular Front for the Liberation of Palestine – General Command, vowed to kill Rushdie (as reported in *The Independent*, 6.3.89a and *The Guardian*, 6.3.89a). In Libya, Colonel Mu'ammer Gaddafi (reported in *The Guardian*, 7.3.89) supported Iran's position in the controversy.

By 9 March, there were reports (highlighted in *The Guardian*, 10.3.89a) in the Spanish *Efe* news agency that a seven-strong hit squad had been assembled in Madrid and had set out to rendezvous with suppliers in Britain, France and Germany, although it was also reported (*The Guardian*, 11.3.89b) that the Spanish interior ministry, the German Government and British police said that they had no knowledge of this. Ian Gelderd of the Institute for the Study of Terrorism was reported in *The Guardian* (16.2.89c) as acknowledging that a lone individual might try to kill Rushdie. But he judged the most likely threat to Rushdie's life to be from an armed cell among the radical supporters (either among students or people on visitors' visas) of Khomeini in Britain.

The possibility of an organized attempt on Rushdie's life was consistent with a previous history of such activity in Britain. For example, in 1986, a Kensington video shop that sold anti-Khomeini literature and videos had been bombed, killing an Iranian exile and injuring thirteen other people. In July 1987, the Guardians of the Islamic Revolution had exploded a car bomb, injuring Amir Hussein Amir-Parviz, the London-based representative for the exiled pro-monarchy National Movement for Iranian Resistance. Also, in October 1987, the Iranian oppositionists, Mohammed Ali Tavakoli-Nabavi and his son, Noureddin, were shot dead at their Wembley flat in London.

Diplomatic Responses

In contrast to the British Government's initially low-key response, a European Community Foreign Ministers' meeting revealed an increasingly strong and united European feeling about the fatwa (as reported in *The Independent*, 21.2.89b). Therefore, on 20 February, in concert with other (then) European Community (EC) countries, while stopping short of completely cutting diplomatic relations, Sir Geoffrey Howe withdrew all accredited British diplomats from Tehran and expelled from Britain the Iranian chargé d'affaires as well as Iran's one other accredited diplomat (reported in *The Independent*, 22.2.89b).

Iran responded by recalling its EC ambassadors and chargés d'affaires for consultations. Strengthened by EC support, Sir Geoffrey Howe (quoted in *The Guardian*, 22.2.89) stated in the House of Commons that, 'Before normal relations can be restored, Iran must meet her obligations, in particular by renouncing the use or threat of violence against citizens of other countries.' The Dutch Foreign Minister, Hans van der Broek, cancelled a visit to Tehran and, as reported in *The Independent* (22.2.89b), from outside of the EC (as it was at that point), Sweden also recalled its ambassador while the Austrian President, Kurt Waldheim, rejected the death threats, but also criticized the book for insulting Islam.

The Soviet Union stated that it had no plans for publication. The chair of the Soviet State Publishing Committee, Mikhail Nenashev, explained that while Soviet policy allowed criticism of religion, it prohibited work that would be offensive to religious or national feelings. Sir Geoffrey Howe sent a letter (reported in *The Guardian*, 25.2.89a) asking the Soviet Foreign Minister, Eduard Shevardnadze, to exert any pressure that he was able to bring to bear concerning the fatwa. In the context of Khomeini's attempt at a spiritual outreach to President Gorbachev (highlighted in an *Independent* editorial of 28.2.89), on 26 February Shevardnadze met with Khomeini and, although the affair was not raised at their meeting, it was discussed with Iranian ministers (reported in *The Independent*, 1.3.89a). A commentary by *Tass* (see *The Independent*, 2.3.89b) critiqued the western press for presenting the issues in simplistic terms and it was reported in *The Guardian* (4.3.89) that the Soviet Union was seeking to broker a solution.

Elsewhere, outside of Europe and the Islamic world, it was reported (in *The Guardian*, 23.2.89d) that Otto Jelinek, the Revenue Minister of Canada, had been put under guard after he received death threats following his refusal to ban *The Satanic Verses*. It was also reported (in *The Guardian*, 27.2.89b) that the Japanese Foreign Minister, Mr Sosuke Uno, while stating that what he called 'incitement to murder' could not be tolerated, also said, 'We believe that the proper considerations should have been given to the Islamic people' by Rushdie, implying the book should not have been written in the way in which it was. Japan, in fact, was the only leading non-Communist country to retain its ambassador in Iran (see *The Independent*, 27.2.89a). In Hong Kong, Muslims put adverts in English-language newspapers calling for the book to be banned there and, on 26 February, 1,500 Muslims demonstrated at a protest service.

In relation to Iran itself, it was reported (in *The Independent*, 24.2.89c) that on 23 February, 115 of the 270 members of the Majlis (Iranian Parliament), called for a break in diplomatic relations with Britain and, on 25 February, Iran cancelled a British trade fair that had been planned to take place in Tehran, hitting hopes of British industrial involvement in Iran's post-war reconstruction (see *The Guardian*, 1.3.89a). On 28 February, the Iranian Parliament voted to break ties with Britain if the British Government did not change its position within a week.

In response, on 2 March, the British Government turned down a meeting proposed by Iranian officials to 'explain the background' to the Majlis resolution, arguing that nothing would be gained from such a meeting without the fatwa being lifted (reported in *The Guardian*, 3.3.89b). However, in a BBC World Service interview on the same day, Sir Geoffrey Howe stated that he wished to emphasize that neither the British people nor the government greatly liked the book, pointing out that, among other things, it had compared Britain to Nazi Germany. This statement, which was followed by Prime Minister Margaret Thatcher's comments (in *The Guardian*, 4.3.89) that she understood the deep offence caused to Muslims by the book, led to an editorial expression of concern in *The Guardian* (4.3.89) entitled 'Rude as in rudimentary', as well as one in *The Independent* (6.3.89) entitled 'A false sympathy with Islam'. On March 7 (reported in *The Guardian*, 8.3.89) Iran cut diplomatic relations and, following this, a number of Iranians were expelled from Britain on security grounds.

More Marches and Bannings

Paralleling these international diplomatic upheavals, the street-level demonstrations and violence associated with the book continued throughout the world, with violence being initiated both by protestors and against them. It was reported in *The Guardian* (25.2.89b) that, in Mumbai, on 24 February 1989, and following Friday prayers, the police had opened fire on a procession of thousands of Muslims who had defied a ban on gatherings, and at least ten people were reported as killed and over forty injured. On the same day an effigy of Rushdie was burned outside the British High Commission in New Delhi, with protestors demanding an immediate ban on *The Satanic Verses*.

On 26 February, there was a bomb attack on the British Council library in Karachi, Pakistan, which killed a Pakistani security guard and which resulted in closure of the office (*The Independent*, 28.2.89b). Also, on the same day (and as reported in *The Guardian*, 27.2.89b) between eight and ten thousand Muslims protested in New York, chanting 'Death to Rushdie' and burning an effigy of him; while in India, on 26 February, Muslim organizations called for a strike by businesses in protest at the shooting of Muslim demonstrators in Bombay.

In the light of the fatwa and diplomatic activity by international Muslim organizations, governments throughout the Muslim world began to respond by banning the book. At the level of international diplomacy, Iran called upon the Organisation of the Islamic Conference to convene an emergency meeting. The Chair of the Conference, the Kuwaiti minister Suleiman Majid al-Shaheen, opposed this on the practical grounds of short notice. Although Khomeini's fatwa was not endorsed, it was declared that, in the absence of justice from the British legal system, Rushdie could be tried in absentia for the crime of *zandaqa*, which carries the death penalty.

On 1 March 1989, Kenya banned *The Satanic Verses*. In the Comoros Islands off East Africa, foreign newspapers containing extracts were ritually destroyed by order of the interior ministry (reported in *The Independent*, 6.3.89b). This was followed on 7 March by Thailand banning the book; on 13 March by Tanzania; and on 14 March by Singapore. With an Anglican Bishop, David Hand, as Chief Censor of its Censorship Board, Papua New Guinea banned the book from being imported (reported in *The Church Times*, 31.3.89).

On 16 March, the Organisation of the Islamic Conference met and considered the affair. While not endorsing the fatwa, it passed a resolution calling for the banning of Penguin publications in 45 Muslim countries in protest at Penguin's refusal to withdraw the book (see *The Guardian*, 17.3.89). This was in response to representations from Hojatoleslam Mohammad Ali Tashkiri from the Iranian Islamic Guidance Ministry who linked Rushdie, in his view an apostate, also with the evils of colonialism and atheism (*The Independent*, 14.3.89b). In significantly different tones, Saudi Arabia's Prince Saud al-Faisal, as spokesperson of the Foreign Ministers' meeting of the Conference, explained that they wanted to create communication and understanding between people of different beliefs and cultures, on the basis of an approach characterized by mutual knowledge and respect (*The Independent*, 15.3.89b).

On 22 March, Poland decided not to publish *The Satanic Verses* and on 15 June, Venezuela banned it. At its meetings in Cairo between 31 July and 4 August, the Islamic Foreign Ministers' Conference adopted a mandatory resolution, calling upon its member states to take all necessary steps, including economic sanctions, against Penguin and its holding company, Pearson.

Incitement?

In Britain, the Murabitun European Muslim Movement, which at the time claimed between two and five thousand members in Europe and South Africa, aligned itself with the fatwa but tried to distance itself from any implementation of it in the UK, with Mr Mahmud Lund explaining that 'The clear distinction here is that Rushdie is legally sentenced to death within the guidelines of Islam but he lives in a land where he cannot be legally punished in this way' (quoted in *The Guardian*, 24.2.89a). In the context of such statements, debate began around possible legal action against Muslims in the UK who supported the fatwa. The West Yorkshire Police were reported (in *The Guardian*, 16.2.89d) as having consulted the Crown Prosecution Service to see if the statement of Quddus, the Bradford book-burner and supporter of the fatwa, amounted to incitement.

At the turn of the century, 'incitement' was a common-law offence to 'persuade, encourage or command another person to commit an offence' and was punishable by an unlimited fine or imprisonment. If a murder were carried out, an inciter became liable to prosecution as an accessory to murder and therefore faced the possibility of life imprisonment. Recordings and newspaper cuttings, together with statements by Quddus, had been sent to the Crown Prosecution Service. Quddus had stated that:

> I totally agree with what Ayatollah Khomeini has said in public. Every Muslim blames Salman Rushdie. If any Muslim will get a chance, he won't avoid it and should not. Why not? He has tortured every Muslim. Why should people be brutally murdered and lose their lives and Salman Rushdie not pay? (quoted in *The Guardian*, 15.2.89a)

However, the Crown Prosecution Service concluded that there was not at that time enough direct evidence for a charge to be brought, emphasizing that public interest was a key factor in its decision (*The Independent*, 22.2.89c). In October 1989, following a Manchester Town Hall meeting at which Kalim Siddiqui asked for a vote on whether Rushdie should die, it was reported (in *The Independent*, 2.11.89) that consideration was being given to sending a report to the Crown Prosecution Service and a judge ordered the BBC to hand over its film of the events (*New Life*, 1.12.89).

Violence All Round

That violent deaths connected with the controversy could indeed occur in Europe as well as in other parts of the world was illustrated by the 29 March shooting to death of Abdullah Al Ahdal, the Director of the Islamic Centre and spiritual leader of Belgium's Muslim community and his aide, Salem el-Behir (see *The Guardian*, 30.3.89a). This occurred after a radio interview on 20 February, in which Mr Ahdal had refused to call for the book to be banned in Belgium.

Publishers abroad began to express concern and the German publisher Kiepenheuer & Witsch of Cologne postponed plans for an autumn publication in German. The publishers who were planning to bring out a Danish edition said they had received threats (*The Guardian*, 18.2.89). Nevertheless, in London Penguin had stated (reported in *The Independent*, 16.2.89e) that a paperback run of 125,000 copies would be in the shops by September. El-Essawy described this as provocative, especially after Penguin confirmed that there were no plans to put a disclaimer in the book. An American edition was published on 22 February. In Italy, there was (reported in *The Independent*, 6.3.89b) a fire in Padua at a bookshop owned by *The Satanic Verses'* Italian publishing company, Mondadori. In England, it was reported (*The Guardian*, 11.3.89a) that publishers were, in general, reluctant to be quoted as expressing an opinion. In Germany, a consortium of fifty publishers was formed to publish a German edition that finally came out in the middle of October (*The Independent*, 15.10.89).

Violent reactions continued, with bomb attacks on a British cultural centre and the vice-consul's car in Ankara, Turkey. Back in Britain, a Dillon's bookshop in Gower Street and Collets Penguin bookstore in Charing Cross Road in London were firebombed, apparently because they stocked the book (reported in *The Independent*, 11.4.89). Collets said it was likely that their Charing Cross Road shop would cease stocking the book, the staff having previously decided to stock it but not display it. Their international bookshop had already ceased to stock it following death threats to staff at Foyles bookshop that had also led to it deciding to withdraw the book. On May 13, an arson attack on the Penguin Bookshop in the King's Road, Chelsea was suspected as being linked with 'the Rushdie affair'. It was also reported by the United Press Institute (in *The Independent*, 29.4.89a) that British diplomats in Europe were given extra security measures after a number were named in a death list sent to the Foreign Office from a group called the Defenders of Islamic Purity.

But there were also violent attacks upon Muslims. The office of the Bradford Council of Mosques was broken into and suffered vandalism while Sher Azam of the Council of Mosques experienced threatening phone calls and anonymous mail threats (*The Sunday Times*, 2.7.89). A firebomb was thrown at the Regent's Park Mosque and Islamic Cultural Centre complex in London. It hit a wall in its residential area and caused minor damage but hurt no one. In May, a Cypriot-born British citizen, Hratch Tchaderjian, was jailed for three years after pleading guilty to the bombing, which he said (reported in *The Independent*, 13.5.89) had been carried out as a gesture in support of Salman Rushdie. In a burglary at the offices of the Council of Mosques in Bradford, paint was poured onto a typewriter and the message 'Leave Salman Rushdie alone – or else' was left, and El-Essawy received three anonymous death threats (reported in *New Life*, 24.2.89a). At a more general level, many ordinary Muslims at the time experienced hostility and incomprehension from the wider public.

On June 3 1989 Ayatollah Khomeini died, aged eighty-six. President Ali Khamenei, aged forty-nine, was nominated to become Leader of the Revolution by the eighty-three member Assembly of Experts. On 5 June, amidst the mourning of crowds of two million people in Tehran, eight people were killed and hundreds injured in the crush and heat (reported in *The Guardian*, 6.6.89). After the funeral, Rafsanjani (*The Guardian*, 9.6.89) stated the position that the fatwa could not be withdrawn. On 16 June, the Associated Press reported (in *The Independent*, 17.6.89) that three more Iranians, two students and a businessman, were being expelled from Britain on security grounds, taking the total number of expulsions to twenty, out of the approximately 25,000-strong Iranian community in Britain.

On 13 August, Maulana Ziyaul Qasmi, the convenor of the International Islamic Mission, initially appeared to encourage Muslims to abduct Rushdie to an Islamic country, but then stated that Muslims should not take the law into their own hands (reported in *The Guardian*, 14.8.89). However, attacks on bookshops in Britain resumed in the run-up to the first anniversary of the book's publication. On 3 September Liberty's of Regent Street, London, was lightly damaged by a bomb and a woman sustained serious leg injuries, with another woman and two men being treated for shock. An anonymous warning had been received connecting the blast to *The Satanic Verses*. A spokesperson for the shop said that they did not currently stock the book, although a Penguin shop had been inside the store until two months prior to the blast. The Liberty's bookshop attack was followed on 13 September by an explosion at a Penguin bookshop at Coppergate in York (*The Independent*, 15.9.89). Police warnings to nine other forces with Penguin bookshops in their areas resulted in home-made bombs being defused in Guildford, Peterborough and Nottingham (*The Guardian*, 16.9.89b).

Sher Azam (quoted in *The Guardian*, 15.9.89) made it clear that 'We condemn this action and this is not part of our strategy. Despite the insults and slurs against Islam, we will continue to campaign within the law.' However, these attacks, at around the time of the first anniversary of publication, appeared to be aimed at bringing pressure to bear on Penguin not to publish a paperback. They highlighted the around £2,000,000 that had been spent by the company over the past year on security measures following threatening letters that had been posted to the home addresses of Viking Penguin board members. In the light of this, Sir Robert Lusty, formerly of Hutchinson, suggested that a consortium of publishers should print the paperback, although other publishers proved reluctant to become involved (*The Independent*, 21.10.89).

It was reported (*The Independent*, 29.9.89) that among booksellers as well as publishers, opinions were becoming increasingly divided over *The Satanic Verses*. Fewer than half of the four hundred booksellers who replied to a survey gave their backing to Penguin, with 40 per cent stating they would not stock the book. On 13 October, the trade journal *The Publishers Weekly* (1989: 6) came out with an editorial that, while acknowledging that 'members of the PW staff could not agree on a common position', nevertheless concluded:

> In the end, however, it seems to us that, as a sober decision taken on the purely economic merits of the case – the question of freedom of expression no longer being at issue – Penguin would be well advised to consider honour satisfied at this point, and to do its best to resume a normal life: without a paperback.

Even so, it was reported that it appeared that Penguin's Chief Executive, Peter Mayer, seemed 'determined to go ahead' with publishing a paperback, although by that time *The Satanic Verses* was known among some Penguin staff as 'that damned book' (*The Independent*, 21.10.89). In an interview with *The Tehran Times* towards the end of August, the Iranian Deputy Foreign Minister, Mr Mahmoud Vaezi, had said that leaving aside the question of the fatwa, relationships with the UK could be mended if the UK could convince the Iranian

Parliament that the UK Government would be respectful of Islamic values and principles. At the time, the British Foreign Office response was to state that 'If Iran wants to improve relations it is for her to make the first move. We do want normal relations, but we will not accept Iranian intervention in our internal affairs' (reported in *The Guardian*, 23.8.89).

The Continuing Controversy

Continuing Legal Effects

Vigils, protests, lobbying and campaigning continued. From 8 to 12 January 1990, a five-day vigil of Muslim representatives from all over Britain was held outside the London offices of Viking Penguin and a letter to the company was published, setting out Muslim demands. On 21 January, a gathering of 200 Muslim leaders organized by the International Muslims Organisation resolved to campaign against the book. On 3 February, the winter conference of the Union of Muslim Organisations held in Gwent, Wales, resolved to campaign for the extension of the blasphemy laws to cover Islam. On 16 February, the UK Action Committee on Islamic Affairs organized a Solidarity Day of Prayer and Dedication in memory of the Muslims who had been killed in February of the previous year during the protests against the book held in Islamabad, Bombay and Srinagar.

On 27 February 1990, in the High Court, Counsel for the British Muslim Action Front argued the case for the equality of Islam before the law and applied for a summons against Viking Penguin for causing public disorder. On 9 April, giving judgement on this case, the Queen's Bench Divisional Court dismissed the application for summonses under Section 4(1) of the Public Order Act, 1986. In the meantime, Lord Hutchinson and Lord Harris urged that British Muslims should be prosecuted for their protests over *The Satanic Verses*.

On 10 April, the British Muslim Action Front sought leave to appeal to the House of Lords on the question of protection for Islam under the current blasphemy laws. On 28 April, speaking on BBC Radio 4, Rushdie expressed surprise that no Muslim had been prosecuted for threats against him (see Ahsan and Kidwai, eds., 1991: 19–20). On 25 May, the High Court refused the British Muslim Action Front leave to appeal to the House of Lords against the judgment that the blasphemy law applies only to Christianity. On 16 July, the Muslim

Institute held a conference in London on the affair. On 2 August 1990, the Foreign Secretary, Douglas Hurd, in an intended gesture of conciliation towards Iran, reiterated Britain's respect for Islam. By 28 September 1990, Iran and Britain had again resumed diplomatic relations, although the agreement made no mention of the fatwa which, on 10 February 1990, had been re-affirmed by the Ayatollah Ali Khamenei, Iran's new supreme leader.

By 3 January 1991, the Home Office Minister, Angela Rumbold, was meeting with a delegation of the UK Action Committee on Islamic Affairs and speaking of the Government's attempt to find a way forward in terms of legal provisions to protect religious sensitivities. However, nothing specific was proposed. And the fatwa continued to have reverberations beyond 'the Rushdie affair' itself. Thus it was reported (in *The Guardian*, 2.5.90) that a school project on Iran was ended in the context of concerns arising from the fatwa. It also continued to have a wider effect upon the publishing world. Even as late as 11 February 1991, the Oxford University Press decided not to proceed with plans to include a passage from Rushdie's *Midnight's Children* in a book on teaching the English language, on the grounds that it might have been viewed as offensive to Muslims.

Rushdie's 'Conversion'

Rushdie's (1990d) essay 'In Good Faith' was his first developed attempt to respond to Muslim criticisms in a considered way, although the Muslim commentators Ahsan and Kidwai (1991: 18) evaluated it as 'a long, malicious piece.' Within 'In Good Faith', Rushdie stated that he had never regarded himself as a Muslim. In late 1990 and early 1991, a series of somewhat confusing events took place in which Rushdie initially appeared to have reached some form of rapprochement with a group of Muslim leaders, only then to draw back from it.

On 24 December 1990, Rushdie announced that he had embraced Islam and adopted a new position as a Muslim. It was stated that this had been done in the presence of the Egyptian Minister for Awqaf and a number of other Egyptian officials. As a part of his embrace of Islam, Rushdie stated that he would not publish a paperback edition of *The Satanic Verses* or permit its translation into additional languages 'while any risk of further offence exists' (quoted in Ahsan and Kidwai, eds., 1991: 21).

British Muslim leaders gave a cautious welcome to these reports while, at the same time, calling for the withdrawal of the hardback version of the book. However, on 26 December, Ayatollah Ali Khamenei restated the fatwa and even stressed its irrevocable nature. Sheikh Jamal Manna of the Islamic Cultural Centre, London, who was present at the meeting with Rushdie, stated that the book was offensive and called for the withdrawal of the hardback version. The UK Action Committee on Islamic Affairs pointed out that, from their perspective, Rushdie had not dealt with what they saw as the central issue – namely the book's withdrawal, which they saw as a 'religious duty' for Rushdie as evidence of a genuine penitence for the offence it had caused.

On 28 December, in an article in *The Times* entitled 'Why I have embraced Islam', Rushdie (1990e) tried to explain his reasons for this apparently dramatic turn of events. He stated that the Egyptian scholars did not find his book offensive and that totally to withdraw the book would be to betray his readers since it was not intended as a deliberate insult to Islam. On 29 December, the UK Action Committee on Islamic Affairs gave a press conference at the Islamic Cultural Centre in Regent's Park, London, at which they stated that they believed Rushdie's reported embrace of Islam was a ploy to get him off the hook and that he gave no serious evidence that his conversion was genuine. They therefore vowed to continue their campaign until the book was totally withdrawn, an unqualified apology was offered to Muslims, and payment for damages was made to an Islamic charity.

On 31 December, on the *Sunday* programme on BBC Radio 4, Rushdie claimed to have been blessed by the Egyptian officials and scholars he had met with and to have an invitation to meet with Sheikh Gad el-Haq Ali Gad el-Haq, the Grand Sheikh of al-Azhar in Cairo who, at the beginning of the controversy, had condemned the book. Rushdie also sought to justify and reaffirm his conversion (see *The Independent*, 29.12.90). However, on 1 January 1990, an Egyptian Government spokesperson said that Rushdie's claim to have an invitation to visit Egypt was 'absolutely without foundation' (in Ahsan and Kidwai, eds., 1991: 23).

These developments caused considerable confusion and some dispute among Rushdie's erstwhile supporters, with some believing that he had revealed himself an opportunist. On 4 January, Francis Bennion (quoted in Ahsan and Kidwai, eds., 1991: 23) dissociated himself from Rushdie, saying that he was 'not worth defending'. Several other members of the Committee for the Defence of Salman Rushdie were also reported to have been angered, including the playwright Arnold Wesker. Their reactions to this were particularly interesting in the light of El-Essawy's 'Open Letter' to Rushdie (referred to in *The Guardian*, 7.3.89), which had commented that Rushdie's fellow writers who were supporting him 'to the last drop of their ink' seemed to be the ones who were 'driving you into a position of enforced martyrdom. For them, freedom of expression has become a fetish. To them that alone is sacred.'

In a phone-in programme on 6 January on London's Sunrise Radio, Rushdie (quoted in Ahsan and Kidwai, eds., 1991: 24) insisted that the hardback version of the book 'should remain around as the basis of a serious analysis and discussion' and, in a 17 January interview with Akbar Ahmed in *The Guardian* (17.1.90), he stated that he wanted to meet with the UK Action Committee on Islamic Affairs to talk about the book. In the Sunrise Radio interview Rushdie had also offered, if a fund were to be set up, to contribute money for the families of those who had been killed in protests against *The Satanic Verses*. Later, however, Rushdie recanted on this embrace of Islam, pleading the pressures upon him that came about through the experience of isolation.

A bizarre twist occurred (reported in *The Guardian*, 24.7.90a, 18.8.90) in August 1990 when a Pakistani video film called *International Guerillas*, which portrayed Rushdie as a drunk and a murderer of Muslims, and featured a hunt for Rushdie, was initially banned from distribution by the British Board of Film Censors (*The Guardian*, 7.9.90). This was an action that appeared to Muslims as a double standard until Rushdie himself supported the lifting of the ban.

Rushdie's Further Publishing

During this confused period, Rushdie began publishing again. *Haroun and the Sea of Stories* (1990a) was written for his son (for reviews see, for example, Blishen, 1990; Donoghue, 1990; Applebaum, 1991; Durix, 1993; and Riordan, 1990, and for articles see Aji, 1995; Baena, 2001; Coppola, 1991; Flower, 1991; Bongartz and Richey, 2001). It managed to retain a lightness of spirit despite the lifestyle Rushdie had been forced to adopt, living in safe houses and constantly being moved. Rushdie's (1991a) *Imaginary Homelands: Essays and Criticism, 1981–1991* was a collection of his short pieces over the previous decade (for reviews see, for example, Dhondy, 1991; Kanga, 1991). This was followed by *The Wizard of Oz: An Appreciation* (Rushdie, 1992) and by *East, West: Stories* (Rushdie, 1994) a collection of stories on the theme suggested by its title (for review, see Bhabha,

1994). His book *The Moor's Last Sigh* (1995) caused some uproar in India among Hindu nationalists, but it was shortlisted for Rushdie to win the Booker Prize for a second time (for reviews see, for example, Bradbury, 1995; Kemp, 1995; Walters 1995; Wood, 1995; and for articles, see Henighan, 1998; Baker, 2000; Burningham, 2003; Didur, 2004). However, although he was a favourite to win, he was in the end not successful with this.

During this period, increasing evidence began to come to light to suggest that the specifically political and diplomatic dimensions of the controversy might eventually find a mutually agreed resolution in terms of the relationship between Iran and Britain. While the fatwa could be withdrawn, and this continued to be a sticking point in the negotiations between the European Union and Iran (see *The Guardian*, 23.6.95), the Iranian Government increasingly communicated the message that, as a state, it would not seek to implement the fatwa. This eventually allowed for some relaxation of the security measures surrounding Salman Rushdie, and Rushdie began gradually to emerge into public life with a number of appearances at public events such as lectures, book-signings and conferences.

No solution was reached in relation to the fundamental issues involved, but only a modus vivendi in international relations and some of their domestic consequences. Thus the affair rumbled on until, on 24 September 1998, the Iranian Government (by now headed by the Ayatollah Khatami) formally differentiated the Iranian state from the Ayatollah Khomeini's fatwa, stating that it would do nothing either to further or hinder its implementation. As a result of this, diplomatic relations between the UK and Iran were restored to full ambassadorial level.

At the same time, the fatwa remains in place since it can only be rescinded by Khomeini himself, who has since died, or by a higher authority, which is unlikely given Khomeini's standing as the spiritual leader of the Iranian Revolution. Also, from time to time, concern has broken out again as, for example, when the Ayatollah Khameini has continued to denounce Rushdie as a *mortad*, or apostate, and as *mahdour al-damm*, or someone whose blood may be shed. And, of course, in even more recent years, the wider context of problematic relations with the Iranian Government has continued in the context of the United States' response to the development of Iran's nuclear programme.

In his private life, following his divorce from Marianne Wiggins in 1993, Rushdie married Elizabeth West in 1994, being divorced again in 2004. In 2004 he married the Indian actress Padma Lakshmi, but in June 2007 it was announced that a divorce was planned. Rushdie, meanwhile, continued to publish. In 1993, his Booker Prize winner, *Midnight's Children*, won the 'Booker of Bookers' award for the best novel to have received the award during the first twenty-five years of the prize. In July 2008, the novel also won the 'Best of the Booker' prize, which commemorated the fortieth anniversary of the award.

In 1999, his book *The Ground Beneath Her Feet* became the basis for a song that Rushdie co-wrote with Bono of the rock group U2. This was followed in 2001 by *Fury* (see Brouillette, 2005). His *Imaginary Homelands* collection of non-fiction essays was followed up in 2001 by the collection *Step Across This Line: Collected Non-Fiction, 1992–2002*. In 2005, his book *Shalimar the Clown* was published and in 2008, *The Enchantress of Florence*.

In 2007, Rushdie had begun a five-year period of one month in every year at Emory University in the USA as a Distinguished Writer in Residence. On 15 June 2007, Rushdie was given a knighthood by the Queen for 'services to literature', henceforth becoming known as Sir Salman Rushdie. Many Muslims felt that this official recognition of Rushdie was a calculated slight of their feelings, while a number of countries with Muslim majority populations, including Iran and Pakistan, formally protested.

In relation to the fatwa itself, the possibility of an individual seeking to carry it out is likely never to completely vanish while Rushdie is alive. In relation to the wider issues surrounding the publication of *The Satanic Verses* and that lie at the heart of this book, these issues have continued to echo and reverberate over the past two decades, reappearing in new guises and contexts. The original events around publication of *The Satanic Verses*, including the reactions and counter-reactions surrounding it that will be explored in the following chapter have, in retrospect, proved themselves to have been a watershed. As the title of this book suggests, in those events and controversies, it is possible to find 'a mirror for our times'.

Chapter 2

Actions and Reactions in the Controversy

Muslim Concerns
Understanding in the Round

In order to understand what lay at the heart of the Muslim protests that led to 'the Rushdie affair', it is necessary to go beyond superficial comments on 'Muslim fundamentalists' or indeed a more sophisticated analysis of the positioning, through the controversy, of Iran in relation to the Muslim world, in order to uncover and discuss the roots of Muslim concerns. The roots of these concerns must be understood before a proper understanding of the particular and varied Muslim responses to the controversy can be gained, and also before any adequate analysis of the reactions to, and 'entails' of, the controversy can be undertaken.

In contrast to the perceptions of a number of other than Muslim commentators, it is important to understand that the outrage and hurt, and the sense of powerlessness to which these gave rise, were not something manufactured by Muslim 'extremists' or by the fatwa of the Ayatollah Khomeini. While the interventions of Khomeini, and the action of Islamist groups, undoubtedly did seek to capture and channel the energies so released, the outrage and hurt experienced formed part of the genuine emotional orientation of many Muslims.

Outrage

In a *Guardian* piece entitled 'Whose light, whose darkness?', the Muslim philosopher Shabbir Akhtar (1989a) argued that an evaluation

of *The Satanic Verses* as blasphemous should, for the Muslim conscience, be an uncontroversial matter and that 'Anyone who fails to be
offended by Rushdie's book *ipso facto* ceases to be a Muslim.' While
Akhtar's attempt to argue that this outrage is a necessary consequence
of Muslim belief and identity might be viewed as an overstatement,
there is little doubt that outrage was widespread within the community
(see *The Independent*, 18.2.89b).

But it was the vehemence and drama of this Muslim outrage that was
difficult for many of a secular outlook to understand. In a *Guardian*
(9.5.89) piece on 'The liberal taboos', Hugh Hebert observed that 'the
central puzzle the Rushdie affair sets for the liberal mind is how reasonable men and women can be so incensed by a work of the imagination, a fiction, that his book is burned and its author is put in genuine
fear of his life.' In an interview in *The Guardian* (27.2.89c) with the
journalist Paul Martin, Zaki Badawi – now deceased, but at the time
the head of the Muslim College in Ealing and Chair of the Imams and
Mosques Council UK – tried to explain the nature of the offence as
perceived by Muslims by making the startling analogy that:

What he has written is far worse to Muslims than if he's raped
one's own daughter. It's an assault on every Muslim's inner being.
Muslims see Muhammad as the ideal on whom to fashion our lives
and conduct, and the Prophet is internalised into every Muslim
heart. It's like a knife being dug into you – or being raped yourself.

In trying to convey the sense of shock and outrage which they experienced in relation to the novel, Muslims frequently utilized sexual
imagery. Thus the Tanzanian Muslim scholar Ali Mazrui (1989: 3)
recalled that when he was in Pakistan he had heard the book compared
to child abuse in reverse:

It's as if Rushdie had composed a brilliant poem about the private
parts of his parents, and then gone to the market place to recite that
poem to the applause of strangers, who invariably laughed at the
jokes he cracks about his parents' genitalia – and he's taking money
for doing it.

This dramatic imagery highlights the depth of Muslim reaction to the
contents of *The Satanic Verses* that often proved difficult for Westerners
to understand. Reflecting on this as a Muslim from the Arab world,
the Syrian writer Rana Kabbani says that 'The Salman Rushdie affair

has brought home to me the immense, perhaps unbridgeable, gulf between the world I belong to and the West,' although Kabbani had also noted that:

> No one should suppose that Islam and the Occident coexisted amicably until Rushdie came along to sour the relationship. On the contrary, there has been tension between them since the seventh century when Islam emerged as a political and ideological power able to challenge Christianity. (Kabbani, 1989: 1)

Historical and Political Context

Many social commentators, historians and theologians, Christian, Muslim and secular, have traced the history and reflected on the contemporary significance of the centuries of tension and sometimes conflict between Islam and the West/Christendom (see Said, 1978; Webster, 1990; Hussain, F., 1990). This tension has its roots in the military conflicts and expansionisms of the respective spheres of influence of the religions, including the initial rapid spread of the Islamic Empire that had been perceived by European Christendom as a threatening military conquest and the later brutality of the European Crusades to the Holy Land followed, in the nineteenth and early twentieth centuries, by the colonialism of the European powers in the Arabic heartlands of Islam.

During this latter period, and in the decolonization of the second half of the century, Muslims had responded to this ancient antagonism by means of either attempts at modernization or by means of Islamic resistance to all non-Muslim ideologies, whether of culture or religion, of capitalism or of socialism (Smith, 1957). More recently, this Islamic resistance has also led to opposition to the nationalism that created the modern nation states in which European-educated and oriented elites were installed and maintained in political power with the support of either the communist 'East' or the capitalist 'West'.

At the 27 May 1979 anti-*Satanic Verses* Muslim demonstration in Westminster, London, Shabir Khan of Nottingham was quoted in *The Guardian* (29.5.89) as saying: 'You have people here who may not have prayed for years, but the Rushdie book has brought them together to their religion' and that 'these young people have been brought up in Britain, and they are reacting against your system. It is more than the book now, it is about the West and Islam.' In this statement one can see a brief, but prescient, insight into the roots of developments that eventually led to the 7/7 bombings of London transport and the growth of political concerns about the Islamist radicalization of young Muslims, and in which a community-based approach to multiculturalism had begun to be held at least partially responsible for allowing a situation of 'parallel lives' to develop, which undermined social cohesion, and for creating an environment in which radicalization could more easily take place. However, quite apart from the question of 'modernist' radicalization, in speaking of the vast majority of ordinary Muslims, Rana Kabbani (1989: 2) commented that:

> Muslims understand that history can determine present emotions because that is how they feel themselves. Unlike Westerners, they are, for the most part, too poor and insecure to afford the luxury of individual feelings: instead their reactions to events are strongly shaped by communal memories.

Thus, even where a strongly religious vision of the world is absent, the sense of Islam as a locus of cultural belonging and pride can be a strongly communal one. This communal sense contrasts strongly with western individualism and these communal memories are highly sensitive to the fund of derogatory images of Islam that can be found within the 'Western' and Christian traditions.

Islamophobic Tradition, Sexuality and Honour

Two main sets of images have been used in Christian attacks on Islam. On the one hand, there has been the more populist tradition of insinuations about the person of the Prophet Muhammad and his alleged sexual proclivity and, on the other, the more theological tradition of accusations that his message was a Satanically-inspired deception. It was these two sets of images that Muslim critics of *The Satanic Verses* argued were deliberately reprised in the imagery used by Salman Rushdie.

For the prophet character in *The Satanic Verses*, Rushdie (1988: 93) used the epithet 'Mahound', which he describes as the 'devil's synonym' and which had also been used in medieval Christian apologetic attacks on Islam. Rushdie (1988: 366) says of Mahound that 'after his wife's death Mahound was no angel' and that his beard turned 'half-white' in a year because he slept with so many women. Sarah Maitland

(1990: 124–5) has pointed out that the sexually explicit nature of the novel was one of the main reasons cited by Muslims for the intensity of their rage.

Rushdie's implied criticism of the position of Muslim women was deeply resented (see *The Independent*, 25.2.89b). For example, the whorehouse is given the name of 'the *Hijab*', the name of the covering garment worn by Muslim women today and which itself, much later, became a symbol of contention in the development of political agendas relating to social cohesion following statements made by the Labour Government Minister Jack Straw, MP about the niqab, a form of the hijab that entails almost full face covering (see BBC.co.uk, 5.10.2006). But while this might be seen as a matter for legitimate public debate, including debate among Muslims themselves, Rushdie's inversion of the symbolic meaning of the hijab was seen not as contributing to debate, however uncomfortable, but as something that was deliberately provocative and insensitive.

Not only this, but the whores of 'the *Hijab*' were said to have assumed the names of the Prophet's wives in order to attract 300 per cent more business and the women of 'the *Hijab*' appoint Baal, a poet, as a make-believe husband to provide them, in turn, with sexual services. Thus, as the book (Rushdie 1988: 381) puts it, 'When the news got around Jahilia that the whores of The Curtain had each assumed the identity of one of Mahound's wives, the clandestine excitement of the city's males was intense . . .'

In Islam, Muhammad's family is *ahl-al-bait* (the first family) and his wives *alwaj-e-mutahire* (the sacred wives of the Prophet). Rushdie, however, transformed the Muslim imagery of 'the *Hijab*' and the wives of the Prophet from something connected with honour, modesty and purity into its opposite. According to Muslim revert Gai Eaton, the offensive effect of this was equivalent to that of portraying the Virgin Mary as a whore (*The Guardian*, 15.2.89d). Furthermore, when Rushdie (1988: 381) wrote that '. . . on many days a line of men curled round the innermost courtyard of the brothel, rotating around its centrally positioned Fountain of Love, much as pilgrims rotated for other reasons around the ancient Black Stone', he linked his transformed hijab imagery with imagery drawn from one of the so-called Five Pillars (or fundamental beliefs) of Islam – the *hajj*, or pilgrimage, which Muslims should undertake if at all possible at least once in their lives, and a part of which entails pilgrims circling the Kaaba in Mecca.

From a Muslim perspective, this was not perceived to be dissent or a critique of Islam but was experienced simply as insulting. Eaton commented (in *The Guardian*, 15.2.89d) that 'Salman Rushdie, who was brought up in Islam, knows exactly where to put the needle in. Western readers very often don't see this.' He explained that the general portrayal of the prophet figure in the novel had provoked 'more outrage than I have ever known.' In a *Guardian* (1.2.89) interview with the newspaper's religious affairs correspondent, Walter Schwarz, reported under the title 'Shame is the spur', the Saudi Arabian Hashem El-Essawy of the Islamic Society for the Promotion of Tolerance argued that 'The book isn't a danger to our religion, which has suffered far worse attacks. The danger is in the insults to believers which read as if they are deliberate. Insults like that generate anger in a community that already feels unpopular in Britain because of its religion.' In a *Guardian* (24.11.89) interview with the journalist Hugo Young (1989), Kalim Siddiqui of the Muslim Institute said that 'This is going to run and run. It is a matter, if you like, of honour.'

In the context of South Asian cultural traditions prevalent among many Muslims with a South Asian background, *izzat* is a key idea. Wilson (1978: 31) explains that this is a 'multi-faceted' concept that can be translated as 'honour, self-respect and sometimes plain male ego' (Wilson, 1978: 5). It is strongly connected with sexuality and a family's *izzat* is usually perceived as being particularly located in its female members. Where *izzat* is transgressed and besmirched, then other family members feel both a great collective shame and a responsibility to uphold or reinstate what has been threatened. It is this thinking and tradition that often lies behind the practice of so-called 'honour-based killings' and the legitimation of other forms of violence against women, the more recent focus of attention on which has also underlined questions about the role of multiculturalism in the perpetuation of patriarchy.

In many ways, then, the basic reaction of the predominantly South Asian Muslim groups in the UK to 'the Rushdie affair' can be understood as related to communal *izzat*. Coupled with this is the longer-standing religious minority experience and consequent relative psychological insecurity that can be found in the South Asian Muslim traditions and movements as compared with Arabic-speaking Muslims for whom Islam is the predominant cultural heritage.

Finally, the particular outrage and hurt over perceived insults to the Prophet, while shared by Muslims of many ethnic and cultural backgrounds, needs especially to be understood in the context of the comparatively high personal status accorded to the Prophet in some particular South Asian expressions of Islam, especially among the

Barelwis (see Robinson, 1988). Significantly, as long ago as the 1940s, in the context of comment upon South Asian Islam in particular, the historian of religion, Wilfred Cantwell Smith (1946: 235), noted that 'Muslims will allow attacks upon Allah: there are atheists and atheistic publications, and rationalistic societies, but to disparage Muhammad will provoke from the most "liberal" section of the community a fanaticism of blazing vehemence.'

In the face of such wounds to their deepest sensibilities and in the light of what they have perceived as an attack on the whole basis of their religious identity as a group already disadvantaged in terms of ethnicity, many Muslims felt that the majority British society and the UK state responded with, at best, mere sympathy; more often with indifference; and all too often with outright hostility. Bhikhu Parekh (1989a), in his *New Statesman and Society* piece on 'Between holy text and moral void', pointed out that Muslims were reacting because they 'feel belittled and demeaned in their own and others' eyes, provoked and challenged to a fight both by the language and by the "outrageous liberties" taken with their collective sacred heritage.'

The sense of the holy in which Muslim concerns are rooted has become something that is difficult for many within the secular and humanist traditions to understand. Its centrality within 'the Rushdie affair' thus underscores one of the clusters of issues or 'entails' that arise from the controversy, namely, that concerned with the role of religion in the relationship between secularization, religious belief and plurality. These 'entails' in turn connect with the problem of mutual incomprehension between differing value systems within a plural society and, at the level of the societal response to such variety, to the relationships between law, ethics and plurality.

The Spectrum of Muslim Responses

Muslim Unity and Diversity

Together with understanding the sense of outrage shared by many Muslims, in order to assess the 'entails' of the controversy in a more rounded way, it is necessary to examine something of the range of responses to the controversy found among Muslim organizations and individuals in the UK. These responses were not, in fact, as uniform as has sometimes been suggested.

In a piece in *The Independent* (28.1.89), entitled 'Muslims divided by a faith caught in a period of change', Sarah Helm commented about a day on which Muslims gathered in London to demonstrate an apparent unity to the effect that, while 'There has been strong and unified criticism about the lack of a public platform for Muslims in Britain and the unfairness of a law which outlaws blasphemy against Christianity but not other religions', nevertheless, 'behind the public statements, the Muslim community is not as one over the book. While most practising Muslims would agree that it insults Islam, there are profound disagreements about the response.' She also noted that 'The most virulent protests have been sparked among the most deprived communities.'

Conspiracy?

In the context of the long history of strained Christian–Muslim relations and the effects of modern colonialism upon the Muslim psyche, explanation of *The Satanic Verses* as the product not only of an anti-Islamic tradition (see Qureshi and Khan, 1989) but also, and specifically, of an anti-Islamic conspiracy was widespread. In Iran, Rafsanjani told the Majlis or Iranian Parliament that the Ayatollah Khomeini had delivered his fatwa not just because of the book itself but also because it was the focus of what he saw as a plot against Islam (*The Independent*, 16.2.89d).

More darkly, this conspiracy theme linked with the undercurrent of antisemitism that can be found in some Muslim circles and which can often be connected with Muslim support for the Palestinian struggle against the state of Israel. For example, some Muslims thought it no coincidence that the Chief Executive of the Penguin publishing house was Peter Mayer, the son of Jewish refugees from Nazi Europe (reported in *The Independent*, 21.10.89). In a 22 February address to the students and instructors of religious seminaries which was broadcast on Tehran Radio and reproduced in *The Guardian* in an edited, abbreviated and translated form under the title, 'A challenge to the world-devourers,' Khomeini (1989) said of the Western powers' defence of Rushdie that:

> The issue for them is not that of defending an individual, the issue for them is to support an anti-Islamic current, masterminded by those institutions – belonging to Zionism, Britain and the USA – which, through their ignorance and hate, have placed themselves against the Islamic world.

Furthermore, Khomeini argued that it was within the will of God that *The Satanic Verses* should have been published at this time so that 'the world of conceit, of arrogance and of barbarism, would bare its true face in its long-held enmity to Islam.' In the UK, in an article on 'Islamic fundamentals' in *The Jewish Chronicle* (12.5.89), Jenni Frazer noted that, over the previous 18 months, the Board of Deputies of British Jews had referred to the Attorney General 87 cases of hatred against Jews found in Muslim magazines and leaflets. In Frazer's report, Ronald Nettler, Fellow in Muslim–Jewish Relations at the Oxford Centre for Postgraduate Hebrew Studies, noted that 'Islam today, especially in its fundamentalist form, sees its struggle with the Jews as a cosmic and fateful war.' In a *Guardian* (23.2.89b) report entitled 'Rushdie reaction may hit British hostages', Sheikh Fadlallah of Lebanon confirmed the existence and influence of this strand of thinking when he explained, after his visit to Tehran, that 'Rushdie's case is distinguished by the conviction of our Iranian brothers that Jewish elements are using him to work against Islam.'

In the UK, on ITV's *Hypotheticals* programme, the founder of the Muslim Parliament of Britain, Kalim Siddiqui, claimed that the Rushdie book was the product of an anti-Islamic literary conspiracy. Following the 27 May demonstration in London, in a piece by Sarah Helm called 'Muslim warning on campaign of civil disobedience' published in *The Independent* (3.6.89), Siddiqui was cited as having written to the Prime Minister arguing that the British colonial inheritance had played a significant part in informing the government's stance on the controversy. By contrast, in his interview with Paul Martin in *The Guardian* (27.2.89c), Zaki Badawi described as a 'pretence' the view that 'Rushdie is part of a great conspiracy, a fifth column to undermine Islam, with the book's publishers spearheading a Zionist imperialist conspiracy against the Islamic world.'

In Walter Schwarz's *Guardian* (1.2.89) piece 'Shame is the spur', El-Essawy was reported as saying of the book-burning that 'It was a human response, not a religious one', while in a *Sunday Times* (29.1.89) piece by Amit Roy and Iqbal Wahab, entitled 'How Rushdie lit a world Islamic fire', El-Essawy noted that 'It has awakened the sleeping demons of racialism in so many.' While banning of the book was on the agenda of a number of Muslim organizations, El-Essawy claimed in a letter to *The Guardian* (23.1.89) that his society did not advocate either the banning or burning of books, but aimed to develop understanding and, through it, tolerance. Although in many ways taking a different stance from El-Essawy, even Kalim Siddiqui underlined in a letter to *The Guardian* (21.3.89) that his position had not been in favour of banning the book, but rather for the author and the publishers voluntarily to withdraw it in the interests of good relations.

The Fatwa in Contention

There was also a diversity of views among Muslim leaders with regard to the fatwa. As has already briefly been noted (and reported in *The Independent*, 2.11.89) in the previous chapter, at a 21 October meeting of around three hundred Muslims in Manchester Town Hall, organized to celebrate the birth of the Prophet Muhammad, there were reports of chants calling for Rushdie's death following an address from Kalim Siddiqui. Interviewed later by Hugo Young (1989) in *The Guardian* (24.11.89) in a piece entitled 'Life, death and Mr Rushdie', Siddiqui denied having incited murder at the Manchester meeting but also said that he could not take responsibility for the behaviour of all Muslims in the country.

In fact, after Khomeini's death in June 1989, Siddiqui maintained that, although the fatwa would stand, Rushdie could come out of hiding if he stopped publication and donated money to a trust for relatives of those killed in the Indian and Pakistani demonstrations against the book, and said that he would be content to leave matters there and to persuade others of that. But even apart from the possibility of Rushdie's repentance, there were alternative Muslim responses to the fatwa. As Aziz Al-Azmeh (1989) summarized matters in the days following the fatwa:

> It is now evident that some Muslim leaders in Britain have been genuinely alarmed by the excesses of the past three days. It is hoped that this alarm will enhance the sense of reality which is inseparable from any sense of responsibility. Fundamental to this reality is the reality of difference, as of the distinction between outrage and the desire to annihilate books by banning them or authors by murdering them.

Some Muslims, such as the former pop star Cat Stevens, now known by the Muslim name of Yusuf Islam, initially argued that spending money and effort on campaigning would be likely to be counterproductive (see 'Letter to the editor' in *The Sunday Times* of 29.1.89). In the record of his *Guardian* (27.2.89c) interview of Zaki Badawi noted above, Paul Martin reported that, early in the autumn, Badawi had sent a memorandum to all mosques and imams, appealing for a low-key response to the book and its publishers, coupled with a boycott of purchases. In relation to the fatwa, Iqbal Sacranie of the UK Action Committee on Islamic Affairs pointed out that no Muslim leader of any wider influence in Britain had supported the fatwa, although the impression had been created that the Muslim community as a whole wanted Salman Rushdie killed (reported in *New Life*, 3.3.89a).

More guardedly, as reported in a *New Life* (17.2.89) piece entitled 'British Muslims oppose Khomeini order', Dr Mughram Al-Ghamdi, of the Regent's Park Mosque and Chair of the UK Action Committee on Islamic Affairs, was reported as noting that since experience had taught Muslims to be sceptical of media reports, what had actually been said by the Ayatollah Khomeini was not necessarily known. However, he also went on to explain that Islamic law does not apply where Muslims are a minority and that, even in Muslim countries, it is not for individuals to act outside the law. In concluding, he noted that violence was not condoned and that the campaign around the book had, sadly, been hijacked by 'mischief-makers'.

As reported by the then *Guardian* religious affairs correspondent, Walter Schwarz (*The Guardian*, 1.2.89), El-Essawy expressed his belief that the worst scenarios had been averted: 'We had all these calls from our people – some had shaved their heads and pledged to kill him. Of course they are extremists on the fringe, but our people warned us: if we don't do something someone will kill him and it will rebound on the whole community.' However, following the fatwa, in a *Guardian* (16.2.89c) report entitled 'Radical minority feared most as likely assassins', El-Essawy said, 'We regret very much the declaration of Khomeini, and anyone who carried it out would be guilty of murder, as stated in the Koran.' As reported in *New Life* (17.2.89), El-Essawy declared that such a response was not a religious one and also that it was likely to evoke sympathy for Rushdie. His own belief was that a disclaimer stating that the book was fictional, that it was not intended to offend, and that it misrepresented Islam, could still resolve the situation.

The Independent (24.2.89b) reported that the Rector of al-Azhar, the leading seat of Sunni Muslim learning, had issued a statement in which he attacked the book, but also stressed the need for toleration and moderation, while in *The Guardian* (3.3.89d) piece on Rushdie and Mahfouz, Kalim Alrawi reported that the Mufti of Egypt, Dr Tantawi, had stated that no Muslim could be killed without a trial. With particular regard to the threat to Rushdie's life, in his interview with Paul Martin, Zaki Badawi described the global Muslim reaction as 'very stupid' and recounted that in Nigeria he had sheltered Christian Igbos from slaughter and affirmed that he would do the same for Rushdie or for any other person facing persecution. *The Guardian* (27.2.89d) also reported a statement from the Imams and Mosques Council which said:

> Acts of violence or incitement to violence are a violation of the law and can lead to tragic consequences . . . However great the provocation and however deep our feelings of hurt and anger, we must refrain and oppose any action that might lead to a breach of the law.

In his interview with Martin, and speaking as a Sunni rather than a Shi'a Muslim, Badawi pointed out that, in any case, no individual Muslim has the power to sentence Rushdie to death and that:

> I must state with all the authority under my command that anyone who seeks or incites anyone to kill Rushdie is committing a crime against God and the Islamic Shari'ah. It is unacceptable in Islam to try someone in their absence. (*The Guardian*, 27.2.89c)

Badawi argued that even if someone is sentenced to death under sharia law only Islamically appointed authorities could legally carry this out, and that death would not even be a certain penalty, since 'The Prophet himself tolerated many people who left Islamic beliefs but were not considered dangerous to the fabric of the state. Those who were put to death were killed because of rebellion, not because of their beliefs.' Furthermore, Badawi stressed that even convicted apostates had opportunities to repent – many scholars arguing for three days' reconsideration in prison and others for even longer, in some cases up to a lifetime. He therefore concluded that 'Putting an apostate to death stems from tradition, not from the Koran itself.'

Apostasy and Treason in Islam

But it is not only a question of what states might themselves do with such laws: there is also the question of the way in which the law can have the effect of encouraging individual action and, in some cases, even appearing to legitimize it. Thus, as Saeed and Saeed (2004: 101) point out, 'although no one has been executed by the state under any of these provisions, religious extremists have killed some persons accused under them.' For example, since 1986, there has been a blasphemy law in Pakistan. While this has, on occasion, been invoked against Christians, there appears to be quite a lot of agreement among Pakistani government officials, legal advocates and leaders of a range of religious groups that these legal provisions are being abused for all kinds of purposes, including the furthering of personal grudges.

In 1992, the Egyptian intellectual Farag Foda was shot by people who accused him of apostasy. In 1993, apostasy charges were filed against the Professor of Islamic Philosophy at Cairo University, Nasr Hamid Abu Zayd. In 2001, this also happened to the Egyptian feminist writer, Nawal al-Saadawi. When, in Bangladesh, Taslima Nasreen criticized the Qur'an and Islamic law, a number of Bangladeshi religious leaders declared her, in a fatwa, to be an apostate and called for her execution.

Islam traditionally distinguishes between *dar al-Islam*, in which sharia applies, and *dar al-harb*, where it does not protect Muslims. This traditional distinction represents the classical Islamic way of dealing with the issues that arise from Muslims living in a non-Islamic society and state such as that of the UK. However, the Ayatollah Khomeini was a Twelver Shi'a and therefore could not be seen as automatically speaking for the majority, Sunni Muslims. Islamic juridical interpretation takes into account the Hadith as well as the Qur'an, and Shi'a and Sunni Muslims differ over which Hadith they accept as authoritative as well as over their relative significance. Furthermore, within Shi'a Islam there were those who saw Khomeini as the promised Hidden Imam of Twelver Shi'ism, the Twelfth Imam having been believed to have gone into hiding in 874 CE, with his awaited reappearance being held to be of eschatological significance.

However, as Malcolm Yapp (1989) pointed out in a piece in *The Independent* (22.2.89) on 'The hubris of the hidden Imam', prior to the Iranian Revolution, even the Shi'a Ayatollah Shariat-Madari thought that Khomeini was claiming a degree of authority beyond the appropriate limits. Yapp therefore concluded with respect to the fatwa that, even among the Shi'a, it would have been at least possible for another Shi'a Muslim to obtain a different opinion from another *mujtahid* (one viewed as Islamically qualified to interpret Islam), while a Sunni Muslim could consult a *mufti* of one of the four traditional Sunni schools of Islamic law and interpretation, and they would not necessarily all agree.

Yapp furthermore stressed that, even with a consensus, a *mujtahid*'s opinion on a point of law remained an opinion even if it was seen as authoritative, and that for it to be applied in a case under Islamic law, this would need to be done in the context of an appropriately convened and conducted trial. Therefore Yapp argued that Rushdie could, in terms of Islamic law, have legitimately appealed for a different Muslim opinion that would also be seen as Islamically valid. In fact, in connection with this, *New Life* (17.2.89) reported the Ayatollah Mehdi Rouhani, an exiled Shi'a leader, as saying of the fatwa that it did not have theological credibility. Nevertheless, Yapp's conclusion was that for Rushdie to have made an appeal to an alternative Muslim opinion could have had the effect of weakening his claim to be treated under the terms of English law, rather than Muslim law.

Muslim Views 'From Below'

The divergence of views among national and international Muslim figures was mirrored in local Muslim population centres across the UK. An *Independent* (18.2.89) newspaper editorial entitled 'Limits to Mutual Tolerance' noted that a survey conducted by the newspaper had shown that, alarmingly, many ordinary British Muslims, including those born and educated in the UK, had been willing at least to condone the call for Rushdie to be killed. In October of 1989, as highlighted in *The Independent's* (22.2.89) editorial on 'British law for Britain's Muslims', a survey for the BBC television programme *Public Eye* found that four out of five Muslim respondents wanted some action taken against Salman Rushdie, while a *Church Times* (27.10.89) piece on 'British Islam draws together' indicated that almost 30 per cent supported the fatwa, rising to 45 per cent of Muslims under twenty.

New Life (24.2.89a) reported that ordinary Muslims in Brick Lane in East London constantly expressed incomprehension about why their campaign seemed to have received so little sympathy since even Ibrahim (Abraham), who is honoured in common by Muslims, Jews and Christians, was vilified as a 'bastard'. On a visit to test the views of the ordinary citizens of Bradford, Martin Wainwright reported that many Muslims endorsed Quddus's support for the fatwa and emphasized that the average Muslim in Bradford was certainly aggrieved, while noting that, exceptionally, he also found some Muslims there who apparently thought of Salman Rushdie as a Sufi saint (*The Guardian*, 16.2.89f).

In Birmingham the picture appeared more varied. *The Independent* (18.2.89c) reported that in a Moseley mosque, a readiness to kill

Rushdie had been proclaimed. However, while united in their sense of outrage and offence about the novel, the Birmingham Central Mosque was divided on the issue of the fatwa. While the sense of outrage was shared, Muslims drew very different conclusions with respect to the implications of the controversy and the appropriate action to be taken in pursuit of their goals.

However, in closing this section, in order to gain a grounded understanding of the locus of these varied Muslim responses, it may be helpful to highlight the context of an interesting 'Open Letter' to Salman Rushdie penned by one Abdul Ali of the East End of London and sent as a letter to the editor (11.8.89) of the Asian newspaper *New Life*. In this, Abdul Ali pointed out that although Rushdie had been praised by the intelligentsia as an anti-racist, since the publication of *The Satanic Verses* the reality for Muslims on the streets was that racist attacks had dramatically increased and that Salman Rushdie's name had been invoked in connection with these attacks.

Abdul Ali pointed to the firebombing of a mosque in London, to the vandalization of a mosque in Darnall in Sheffield, and to those white youths who now chanted 'Rushdie, Rushdie' instead of 'Paki, Paki'. The letter concluded that, unlike Salman Rushdie's safe houses, working-class Muslims could not hide from the violence against them. In this way, the issues arising from the controversy were located in a grounded social and political context in which the already existing minority and disadvantaged position of Muslims in the UK was exacerbated by a controversy around a novel that had real social and political consequences and was not merely a matter of polite literary debate. Indeed, in the same issue of *New Life* as Abdul Ali's letter, there was an article reporting on the killing of 14-year-old Tahir Akram, who died of a ruptured neck artery after four white youths in a car fired shots into the air during an anti-Rushdie demonstration in Oldham, Lancashire.

Rushdie's Reactions

Civilization and the Freedom to Publish

On 12 October 1988, following the Indian Prime Minister's banning of *The Satanic Verses*, Salman Rushdie (1989f) delivered an 'Open Letter' to Rajiv Gandhi via the Indian Ambassador in London. In this letter, Rushdie questioned the Muslim Member of Parliament Shahabuddin's argument that no civilized society would allow the publication of such a book and turned that argument on its head to claim that 'The question raised by the book's banning is precisely whether India, by behaving in this . . . fashion, can any more lay claim to the title of a civilised society.'

Rushdie saw the banning of his book as evidence that 'it's the fundamentalists who now control the political agenda in India', arguing that 'the real issue is who gets the Moslem vote.' Rushdie also deployed, for the first time, his argument that the book was not 'a direct attack on Islam', stating that 'I have admitted no such thing, and deny it strongly.' He then went on to say that 'the book is not actually about Islam, but about migration, metamorphosis, divided selves, love, death, London and Bombay' and that it 'deals with a prophet – who is not called Mohammed – living in a highly fantasticated city' (Rushdie, in Appignanesi and Maitland, eds., 1989: 44).

Following the Bradford book-burning, Rushdie was reported (*New Life*, 20.1.89) as arguing that if the groups campaigning against his book were successful, then the same thing would soon start happening also with other books. Rushdie maintained that in a free society he could not accept being told that there are things that are 'off limits'. In critique, Bhikhu Parekh observed (1989a) that 'It was a pity that for months Rushdie contemptuously dismissed the protests of the Muslims.' Parekh went on to explain that 'His book was about them, and he owed them an obligation to understand their feelings, to explain his position, to argue with them, to do all in his power to mollify and hopefully win them over to his point of view.' Parekh argued that 'When a creative writer, conducting imaginative experiments and daring to think the unthinkable outrages, hurts or provokes others, he should be challenged, criticised, asked to explain himself and made to suffer his peers' criticism and the anger of hurt sensibilities.'

It was reported that, at the beginning of February, El-Essawy met Rushdie on a train and put to him the idea of inserting a historical disclaimer into the novel as a way to bring peace in this dispute (*The Guardian*, 7.3.89). According to El-Essawy, Rushdie's reaction was 'You want me to apologise. I will not apologise. I said what I said and I will never stand down.' Later, El-Essawy wrote an 'Open Letter' to Rushdie, delivered through Viking Penguin, in which he referred to this incident, stating that 'The half-apology that you later offered was quickly accepted by this society and myself as a full one' but that by then it was too late. In this letter, El-Essawy said to Rushdie that 'I do not think that it will make you happy to stay where you are and watch people die' and appealed to him as copyright holder to stop the book's further publication. In this he was supported by Norman Lewis (1989), one of the signatories to the World Statement of the International Committee for the Defence of Salman Rushdie and his Publishers. Despite continuing to uphold the principle of free speech and publication, in a letter (7.3.89) to the editor of *The Independent*, Lewis stated that he had come to the view that because of the conflict and violence surrounding the book it would be to the credit of the author and of the publisher if the book were, at that point, voluntarily withdrawn.

Living in Hiding

Salman Rushdie went into hiding under police protection the day after the fatwa (see *The Guardian*, 15.2.89a). Initially he was with his then wife Marianne Wiggins, who was reported as saying that he was terrified by the fatwa and that, in all the circumstances, he should now stay in hiding guarded by Special Branch. It was later reported (in *The Guardian*, 18.2.89) that Rushdie and Wiggins were under 24-hour guard from at least six officers at a cost of around £150,000 a year. It was also reported that he was housed in safe houses operated by Special Branch and MI5 and moved every few weeks (*The Independent*, 24.7.89). As early as 16 February, experts in relation to Islam as well as terrorism experts were being quoted in *The Independent* (16.2.89g) as saying that Rushdie may need protection for the rest of his life.

On 21 February a telephone message claiming to come from the Guardians of the Islamic Revolution warned international news agencies in London that they might attack British targets if Rushdie did not come out of hiding (*The Independent*, 22.2.89c). On 3 August 1989, what appears to have been two bombs, which were perhaps being primed, went off in the Beverley House Hotel in Sussex Gardens, Paddington, London. The previously unknown Organisation of the Mujahadeen of Islam claimed responsibility, stating that it was an operation against Salman Rushdie (reported in *The Independent*, 5.8.89).

An Apology and The Silence

As already noted, in a sermon in Tehran during Friday prayers on 17 February 1989, President Ali Khamenei (as reported in *The Guardian*, 18.2.89) suggested that if Rushdie repented and apologized to Muslims and to the Imam, then it was possible that the people would pardon him. On 18 February, Rushdie (1989c) issued a statement in which he said:

> As author of *The Satanic Verses* I recognise that Moslems in many parts of the world are genuinely distressed by the publication of my novel. I profoundly regret the distress that publication has occasioned to the sincere followers of Islam. Living as we do in a world of many faiths this experience has served to remind us that we must all be conscious of the sensibilities of others. (Rushdie, 1989c, in Appignanesi and Maitland, eds., 1989: 120)

Although this was a conciliatory move, the wording was careful and it was not precisely an apology, but rather was a statement of regret about the way in which Muslims had taken offence at the book. In addition, Rushdie did not offer to withdraw the book or make any other tangible concession. The Iranian authorities made it clear that his statement had fallen short of the public repentance required for a pardon and, on 19 February, Khomeini renewed the fatwa, declaring that 'Even if Salman Rushdie repents and became the most pious man of time, it is incumbent upon every Muslim to employ everything he has got, his life and his wealth, to send him to hell' (quoted in Appignanesi and Maitland, eds., 1989: 122).

A series of interviews with ordinary Muslims in Southall, Spitalfields, Moseley and Bradford, reported in *The Independent* (18.2.89b), revealed a variety of views about whether Islamic law might allow the possibility for Rushdie at this stage still to apologize and save his life and/or whether any such possibility that might have existed was now past. On 26 February, the Bradford Council of Mosques issued a statement saying that 'The Council of Mosques reaffirms its stand on the withdrawal from circulation of *The Satanic Verses* and its continued campaign until such time as the publishers agree to withdraw the book with an apology to all Muslims' (*The Guardian*, 27.2.89d).

Following Rushdie's disappearance from public view the controversy rumbled on continuously, issuing, in ways outlined in the previous chapter, into bursts of activity and sharp debate at 'critical incidents' in its development. The author's own next public comment came after Sir Geoffrey Howe criticized *The Satanic Verses* in a radio interview, following which Rushdie made a ten-minute telephone call to the office of the Liberal Democrat Leader, Paddy Ashdown, MP, in which he thanked Mr Ashdown for his support and expressed concerns about what now appeared to be signs of the British Government beginning to distance itself from the book (*The Guardian*, 4.3.89). After this, Rushdie maintained a period of withdrawal from media comment until a 19 July press conference of the International Committee for the Defence of Salman Rushdie and His Publishers, through which he made his first public statement since going into hiding in February, and in which he claimed to have received messages of support from Muslims that might indicate the possibility of reconciliation (*The Guardian*, 20.7.89).

On 1 September, *Granta* published a three-verse poem by Rushdie (1989g), entitled '6th March 1989', in which he attacked his critics. This poem, too, was subject to a banning call from Sher Azam of the Bradford Council of Mosques. In late September, *New Life* (29.9.89) reported that Rushdie had threatened to sue Penguin for breach of contract if they did not soon publish the paperback edition. Later on, in his 1990 piece on *In Good Faith*, Rushdie wrote that:

It has been a year since I last spoke in defence of my novel *The Satanic Verses*. I have remained silent, though silence is against my nature, because I felt that my voice was simply not loud enough to be heard above the clamour of the voices raised against me. (Rushdie, 1990d in Rushdie, 1991a: 393)

But in this essay, Rushdie attempted to clarify his authorial intent and approach in relation to a number of matters that had been highlighted by critics of *The Satanic Verses* as being at the heart of their concerns. To take an example of this, with regard to the already mentioned use of the word 'Mahound', Rushdie explained that:

I must have known, my accusers say, that my use of the old devil-name 'Mahound' would cause offence. In fact, this is an instance in which decontextualization has created a complete reversal of meaning. A part of the relevant text is on page ninety-three of the novel. 'To turn insults into strengths, whigs, tories, Blacks all chose to wear with pride the names they were given with scorn; likewise, our mountain-climbing, prophet-motivated solitary is to be found in the medieval baby-frightener, the Devil's synonym: Mahound.' Central to the purposes of *The Satanic Verses* is the process of reclaiming language from one's opponents. (Rushdie, 1990 in Rushdie, 1991a: 402)

He then went on to give other examples of this approach, including in relation to the very notion of 'the satanic verses' themselves, and explained his approach both to religion in general and to Islam in particular, and in relation to his own personal history and current positions. But in doing so, he concluded that 'The controversy over *The Satanic Verses* needs to be looked at as a political event, not purely a theological one' (Rushdie, 1990 in Rushdie 1991a: 410). And it is to political actions and reactions within the controversy as it played out in the UK that we now turn.

Political Reactions

Keith Vaz and the Issues

The forms that Muslim protests took against *The Satanic Verses* have to be understood in the context of the relative political powerlessness experienced by Muslims within the UK society and state. In the absence at the time of a Muslim Member of Parliament (MP) from a mainstream political party or an effective Muslim minority party, Muslim concerns were identified with, and taken up by, a handful of non-Muslim MPs who took a particular interest in their cause, including Keith Vaz, the Labour MP for Leicester East.

As a practising Roman Catholic, Vaz had previously taken a stand (see *New Life*, 9.9.88) against Martin Scorsese's (1988) film, *The Last Temptation of Christ*. In the context of 'the Rushdie affair', Vaz defended Muslims in Britain for having in general acted with diplomacy and calm. Also, with regard to the famous incident of the burning of a copy of *The Satanic Verses* that had so outraged many intellectuals and politicians, Vaz pointed out that prior to that event six MPs had symbolically burned a copy of the 1988 Immigration Act on the steps of the Home Office even though the action entailed elected MPs burning copies of a law that had been passed by Parliament (Vaz, 1989a).

Following Vaz's (1989b) article in the traditional left-wing Labour newspaper *Tribune*, and reproduced in *New Life* (14.4.89c) under the title 'Godless Labour', *The Guardian* (27.3.89) suggested that he might be deselected over the issue, although, in the face of this criticism, the chair of Vaz's constituency party said that Vaz had the support of party members (*New Life*, 31.3.89). In his article, Vaz (1989b) challenged the Labour Party about what he saw as the contrast between its support for black issues all over the rest of the world, but not for those near at hand, which he argued had come about because the party had not really understood the hurt that had been caused to Muslims in Britain. Vaz was also quoted as saying that if the issue of racism is on our own doorstep:

> Then the issue becomes embarrassing. It becomes distasteful. It becomes uncivilised. It becomes regrettable. Burning books. Burning effigies. You can support us at election time. You can join us. But please don't come to us if you want support from us. Don't come to us if you are affronted and afraid. Keep away. (in *The Independent*, 22.7.89)

Bradford Politics

The Bradford Labour MPs Pat Wall and Bob Cryer were in an electorally exposed position, having only small majorities in their constituencies. Pat Wall, the then Bradford North MP, who had once been closely linked with the Militant Tendency, said of *The Satanic Verses* that 'I don't like it very much. I found it confusing. I don't think it has got any continuity and I find the language pretty offensive – perhaps I am old-fashioned in that' (*The Guardian*, 16.2.89e). He presented concern for the 15 per cent Muslim vote in his constituency as a principled socialist position while condemning Khomeini's 'extreme language' and his 'monstrous regime of murder and torture'.

In a letter to *The Guardian* (23.1.89), Max Madden, the then Labour MP for Bradford West, pointed out that in the pluralistic Britain of many cultures and faiths, freedom of speech needs to be evaluated in a context in which many ethnic and religious minorities feel that their perspectives are neither adequately represented nor sufficiently understood. In this context, Madden suggested to Viking Penguin that Rushdie might agree to a short statement of Muslim critique of the book being placed in the book or in bookshops stocking the book, with the ultimate aim of creating 'circumstances where Muslims have some effective way of presenting and explaining their views to the public' rather than the media 'just filming the marches and the book burning'. He also urged Rushdie to debate with Muslim critics on national television and he tabled an amendment to a Parliamentary motion seeking time to debate the issues involved in the controversy, including the issue of the reform or repeal of the blasphemy laws.

However, together with Bob Cryer, MP for Bradford South, neither Madden nor Wall supported calls for the banning of the book. They therefore faced resignation calls from Sher Azam, who urged them to fight by-elections on the issue. Following a conference of Muslims in Bradford, in March 1989, Sher Azam stated that, while traditionally the majority of working-class Asian Muslims had voted for the Labour Party, which they had seen as most likely to defend the interests of immigrants and minorities, Muslims were now likely to switch their vote if the Labour Party would not help (*The Guardian*, 27.3.89).

So far as the wider local scene of Bradford was concerned, the Conservative Bradford Council leader, Eric Pickles, said the main non-Muslim reaction had been one not so much of anger as of puzzlement (*The Guardian*, 30.3.89b). Yasmin Alibhai reported that 'Salman Rushdie' had become a term of abuse in Bradford school playgrounds (*The Church Times*, 27.10.89). The Monday Club distributed leaflets entitled *Civil War in Bradford?* that demanded an immediate end to immigration and Frank Kelly, the secretary of the local branch, saw the Muslim talk of violence as the result of years of surrender to Muslim demands by the local authority, and denounced the book's withdrawal from Bradford library shelves. Current and past controversies connected in Bradford when it was reported in *The Independent* (27.10.89) that Ray Honeyford, the former Bradford head teacher of Drummond School and contributor to *The Salisbury Review*, who had been at the heart of an earlier local controversy bearing upon Muslims in the city, was warned off from giving a planned lecture on 'The Rushdie Affair' to a private supper party of members of the Pudsey Conservative Association and organized in the premises of the Bradford Golf Club.

View(s) from Westminster

The positions taken by national politicians in both the Conservative and the Labour Parliamentary parties were quite varied. Thus, as early as 11 December 1988, Ken Hargreaves, MP had moved an early day motion in the House of Commons, expressing regret for the distress caused to Muslims by the publication of *The Satanic Verses*. Following the December 1988 demonstrations against the book, Blackburn Labour MP Jack Straw had requested the Lord Chancellor to extend the terms of the blasphemy laws beyond Christianity. On the Conservative side Sir Teddy Taylor, the Southend Conservative MP, led a delegation of the Islamic Defence Council to see John Patten at the Home Office to press for the blasphemy law to be extended (*The Independent*, 28.2.89b). Neil Thorn, the Conservative MP for Ilford South, a constituency with around ten thousand Muslims, agreed to present a petition to Parliament calling for the book to be withdrawn.

On 10 May the Union of Muslim Organisations, with the assistance of Gary Waller, MP, arranged a meeting at the House of Commons for Conservative Members of Parliament. Tim Yeo, MP, Neil Thorne, MP and Hugo Summerson, MP attended and Gary Waller supported an amendment to the Public Order Act to include incitement to religious hatred as an offence (*Muslim News*, 9.6.89). By contrast, following the 27 May 1989 march on Westminster, the Tory MP for Halesowen and Stourbridge, John Stokes, was reported as saying, 'I cannot understand why they allow immigrants to parade and riot in large numbers outside the Houses of Parliament or anywhere else. No other nation would be so supinely tolerant. The British public will not stand for this disgraceful behaviour. Those who settle here must obey our laws and customs' (in *The Independent*, 29.5.89).

Among Labour MPs nationally, the pattern of response was much more varied than that of the Bradford Labour MPs and their attempts at conciliation of Muslim concerns. For example, Salman Rushdie's own constituency (Islington South and Finsbury) MP, Chris Smith, put down an early day motion urging the Home Secretary to ensure Rushdie's safety (*The Guardian*, 16.2.89d). This was also signed by Michael Foot, MP, the former leader of the Labour Party, and by Mark Fisher, the Shadow Arts spokesperson. Following the fatwa, in the Commons debate on the recall of diplomats from Tehran, Smith argued that 'freedom to write is not only one of the elements of democratic society, but is the best guarantee that we have of the free and full development of individual cultures and religions, including the Muslim community in this country' (*The Guardian*, 22.2.89).

Michael Foot (1989) developed his ideas in an article entitled 'Historical Rushdie' (published in *The Guardian*, 10.3.89b) in which he defended Rushdie's book from the charge of stirring up trouble and pointed to the historical record of religious killings. Foot spoke of 'the Montaignes, the Jonathan Swifts, the Voltaires, the Salman Rushdies who knew that if such insanities were to be stopped, they must be mocked in the name of a common human decency with a claim to take precedence over any religion'.

When, with the assistance of Keith Vaz, MP, the Union of Muslim Organisations arranged a meeting for Labour Members of Parliament, only Keith Vaz and Jim Marshall, MP (also from Leicester) from the Commons attended, with Lords Bonham-Carter and Buckmaster from the Lords (*Muslim News*, 9.6.89). By June, however, in an article in

New Life, Alf Lomas, MEP for London North East, was calling on the publishers and author not to publish further copies as the best way of trying to reach a resolution of the issues (Lomas 1989). Eventually, Alistair Darling – at that time the Labour Party race relations spokesperson (and at the time of writing in 2008 Chancellor of the Exchequer) – wrote a letter asking Viking Penguin not to publish a paperback version of the novel. The leader of the black caucus in the House of Commons, Bernie Grant (MP for Tottenham), argued that the book had become an excuse for racists to legitimise anti-Muslim attacks and that the book should therefore be withdrawn (*The Independent*, 22.7.89), although the Labour Party Black sections outside the Commons disagreed with that position.

The absolutism of Foot's secularist attack upon religion contrasted with the position taken by the Labour Party Deputy Leader, Roy Hattersley, who wrote an article in *The Independent* entitled 'The racism of asserting that "they" must behave like "us"' (1989). In this piece, Hattersley defended Rushdie's rights as an author, stating they were 'absolute and ought to be inalienable', but he also made clear that 'The proposition that Muslims are welcome in Britain if, and only if, they stop behaving like Muslims is incompatible with the principles of a free society.' Hattersley also critiqued the writer Fay Weldon's (1989: 32) defence of the 'uniculturalist' vision of the USA which, he argued, had in any case never entirely corresponded with reality.

Michael Foot responded with a letter to the editor of *The Independent* (24.7.89) in which he argued that the right to burn books should never be conceded on the basis that the relative tolerance that exists in Britain was because religious authorities no longer had absolute rights and that this, in fact, was to the benefit of all in the society, including its religious and ethnic minorities. As a convinced secularist, Foot identified the main problem as being religious bigotry, which he argued needs constantly to be challenged in the name of a shared humanity.

The Labour MP Gerald Kaufman took a line similar to that of Roy Hattersley in an article in *The Independent* entitled 'So-called liberals for whom some are more tolerable than others' (Kaufman 1989). In this, he defended general liberal positions with regard to freedom of expression, but at the same time he stated clearly that 'What I cannot accept is the implication that it is somehow anti-democratic and un-British for Mr Rushdie's writings to be the object of criticism on religious, as distinct from literary grounds' and that Pakistanis and Bangladeshis, by asserting themselves in 'fashions not immediately regarded as attractive to conventional notions ... are regarded as having crossed some kind of line that they ought to stay meekly on the other side of.'

The generally low level of representative political support for the Muslim position can be seen from the very poor level of response to a May 1989 survey of MPs' views conducted by the Bradford Council of Mosques and reported in *Muslim News* (22.9.89). As many as 96 per cent of Conservatives and 88 per cent of Labour MPs did not respond at all, meaning that only 50 out of a total of 650 MPs of all parties responded. Analysing the positions of those who did respond, positive responses were categorized as 'strong' (those supporting Muslim demands for withdrawal of the book, or who had tabled or supported motions on Muslim concerns), 'mild' (those supporting changes to legislation, either extending blasphemy law or under the Public Order Act) or those offering 'some' support (in other words, understanding the book's offensiveness, but not proposing any specific action).

Ten MPs (three Conservative, five Labour, one Social & Liberal Democrat and one Social Democrat) were classified as 'strong supporters'. Eleven MPs (four Conservative, six Labour, one Social & Liberal Democrat) were classified as 'mild supporters'; and fourteen MPs were seen as offering 'some' support (five Conservatives, eight Labour and one 'Other'), while twelve MPs upheld the absolute right to free speech. Max Madden commented on the opening months of the controversy that 'This has been the loneliest 12 months of my political life' (*The Independent*, 22.7.89) and that:

> There has been a frightening degree of intolerance which has been expressed to me by some within the Labour Party – thankfully, a very small number . . . They have echoed the sort of racialist views which are to be found widely outside the House of Commons. . . . If they do like *our* way of doing things; if *they* do not like *our* laws; if they aren't prepared to behave themselves, then maybe some of *them* should be sent back and some of *them* shouldn't be allowed in. (*The Independent*, 21.7.89a)

Madden argued about the controversy that 'It is about a symbolic controversy in which lots of other Muslim fears and anxieties and aspirations are tied up. . . . It's all about how Britain is going to develop as a multi-racial, multi-faith country. If it is to develop in that way, then it is absolutely vital that it be on the basis of a secular society where all religions are respected.'

In the political reactions to the controversy and the Muslim concerns

within it, then, the debates among representative politicians underlined the 'entails' arising from the controversy that are concerned with
the relationship between ethnicity, nationhood, plurality and religion;
the relationships between religion, freedom and the law; and those
concerned with the role of religion in a secularizing and plural society.
In their varied reactions, the positions taken up by elected politicians
generally reflected broader social reactions and it is to these reactions
that the following section turns.

Media and Social Reactions

Editorial and Columnist Outrage

Editorial comment in the major national newspapers provides one indication of the range of general social responses to the controversy among
significant sectors of the non-Muslim general public. A significant proportion of the editorial and political comment in the popular press was
full of outrage against Islam and Muslims. However, in Muslim perception this was simply consistent with a long history of misrepresentation
and animosity towards Islam. In relation to this, however, Shabbir
Akhtar's (1989a) *Guardian* article defending fundamentalism as intel-
lectually respectable declared that 'there can be no doubt concerning
the media's endorsement of an operative veto on any exploration of
the intellectual grounds for fundamentalist options in religion.'

Reflecting on the role of the media in the controversy, Parekh
(1989a) pointed out that until the copy of *The Satanic Verses* was
burned in Bradford 'no national newspaper published the offending
passages, invited Muslim spokesmen to write about the book, or
made a sympathetic attempt to read it with their eyes. Liberal opinion
came down on Muslims like a ton of bricks, ridiculing them and
asking if such barbarians deserved to be citizens of "civilised" society.'
Summarizing what he judged to be the poor reporting of the Rushdie
affair, Parekh (1989b) argued that:

> The influence of racism and anti-Muslim feeling should not be
> underestimated. The bulk of influential public opinion in Britain
> tends to dismiss most Muslims as fundamentalists and funda-
> mentalism as a new form of barbarism. Thus they are infantilised,
> ridiculed as illiterate peasants preferring the sleep of superstition
> to liberal light, and placed outside the pale of civilised discourse.

In a piece in *The People* (19.2.89) entitled '20 ways to spot a mad mullah', Peter Cliff included such observations on the Muslim community as:

> Teenagers are not allowed to marry for love. One 16-year-old Bradford schoolgirl won a fight to stay in council care rather than return to Pakistan for an arranged marriage . . .; Beating children for not learning the Koran properly is part of the fanatics' creed. Sheffield police closed a mosque because the religious instructor beat his children so savagely . . .; Some Muslim leaders have boasted that Islam will eventually wipe out Western culture and 'take over the world'.

Khomeini himself occasioned a lot of lurid description. Even some of the more cultured commentators on the controversy, such as the Nigerian novelist and film-maker Wole Soyinka (1989), referred to Khomeini as 'a sick and dangerous man'. The editorial columns of newspapers such as *The Guardian* and *The Independent* were more measured but sentiments not too dissimilar from those expressed by the popular press could nevertheless be found, albeit expressed in more moderate language. *The Independent*'s editorial 'Limits to Mutual Tolerance' (18.2.89) stated categorically that 'Islam is not a tolerant religion and makes no pretence of being so.' *The Independent* followed this up with an editorial (21.2.89) entitled 'Too tolerant for too long', which complained that the governments of Britain's European Community partners had reacted 'more rapidly and more firmly than the British government'. It praised the Archbishop of Canterbury's statement on the fatwa, going on to say that 'It is for those who lead Britain's Muslims to respond with tolerance and maturity to the Archbishop's direct appeal and to ensure that their zealots obey the law of the land – not the dictates of a bloodthirsty medieval bigot.'

In 'British law for Britain's Muslims,' *The Independent*'s editorial (22.2.89) called upon the Home Secretary to prosecute Muslims who supported the fatwa, stating that 'It is clear that some Muslim leaders in this country do not understand their obligation to obey the law of the land.' The editorial commented that 'So far, because of the profound emotion felt by Muslims, it seems to have been decided that to try to enforce the law would make matters worse.' While acknowledging the arguments for this position, the editorial went on to warn that 'If the belief spreads that Muslims enjoy a privileged position compared with anyone else, incalculable harm will result.' When Viking was rumoured to be considering postponing or even abandoning its original plans for an autumn launch of the paperback version of *The Satanic Verses*, an editorial appeared in *The Independent* (27.2.89) entitled 'Viking Must Stand Firm', urging the publishers not to make 'any concession which represented a surrender to pressure'. It argued that:

> It is an illusion of cultivated liberal opinion – a category which embraces most publishers – that fellow human beings are at heart reasonable and can be won over by compromises. Religious funda-mentalists, of whatever faith, are at heart unreasonable; it is in their nature to believe that the end justifies the means.

Interestingly, however, the editorial also stated that 'The insertion of some words of explanation and/or regret by the author' would not represent the kind of 'significant concession' that they would wish Viking to steer clear of. However, an editorial in *The Independent* (6.3.89) entitled 'A false sympathy with Islam' cited Sir Geoffrey Howe's expression of concern about *The Satanic Verses* while its editorial (*The Independent*, 20.5.89) on 'Dangers of the Muslim Campaign' supported John Patten's call for greater integration, and warned that the price of ignoring this could be that, for Muslims, educated opinion and feeling could turn against them.

In Bradford, the local newspaper the *Bradford Telegraph and Argus* tried to maintain coverage and provide a forum for the expression of community anger. But it also (as reported in *The Independent*, 15.3.89c) had its own security concerns in the context of controversy. This was because its ownership by the Westminster Press meant that it was commercially linked with Viking Penguin through the holding company Pearson. It had therefore posted a security guard on duty at the entrance to its buildings.

Attempts at Understanding Muslim Concerns

On the whole, while there were exceptions, editorial and journalistic comment in both the popular and the quality press supported Rushdie and attacked the Muslims' protests. Nevertheless, there were some press pieces that did try to move beyond simplistic dichotomies. For example *The Guardian's* editorial 'Beyond the threat' (25.2.89) tried to examine some of the wider issues arising from 'the Rushdie affair' in the light of Douglas Hurd's speech at the Birmingham Central Mosque. It pointed out that, reduced to a tabloid front-page headline, the central thrust of Douglas Hurd's speech meant that if Muslims were not going to behave in a 'British' way, then they should not live in Britain. The editorial went on to explore the controversy's ambiguity in terms of support for a principle of freedom that does not, at the same time, wish to give succour to racist sentiments.

Such a stance was similar to the approach taken by the heterogeneous campaigning group, Voices for Salman Rushdie, which consisted of a diverse group of individuals including Tony Benn, MP, Gita Saghal, Hanif Kureishi, Hilary Wainwright and eighteen organizations. They issued an 'Open Letter' to the editor of *The Guardian* (25.5.89) in which they sought both to support Rushdie's right of free speech, while also opposing any manipulation of the controversy by either racists or fundamentalists. They also went on to call for the disestablishment of the Church of England as a precondition for a more genuinely plural society to be developed in Britain. This, in turn, raises the question of the role taken up in the controversy by the established Church and by other Christian Churches in Britain, and it is with this that the following section is concerned.

Christian Reactions

The Established Church of England

Robert Runcie, the Archbishop of Canterbury and Primate of the Church of England at the time of the outbreak of 'the Rushdie affair', issued a statement soon after the Ayatollah's fatwa was pronounced. In this, Runcie clearly stated that 'Only the utterly insensitive can fail to see that the publication of Salman Rushdie's book has deeply offended Muslims both here and throughout the world. I understand their feelings and I firmly believe that offence to the religious beliefs of the followers of Islam or any other faith is quite as wrong as offence to the religious beliefs of Christians' (Runcie, 1989).

Runcie then went on to condemn 'incitement to murder or any other violence from any source whatsoever', declaring that he could 'no more accept such incitement from those who claim to speak in the name of Islam than . . . from anyone who claims to speak in the name of Christianity'. He also appealed to Muslim leaders in Britain to 'urge their followers to have regard to the expression of profound regret that

Salman Rushdie has issued . . . and to contain their anger within the bounds of the law.'

Both in 1981 and 1985, the Archbishop had supported proposals to extend the offences of blasphemy and blasphemous libel in order to bring within their scope religious traditions other than Christianity. These proposals had been made by a working group (General Synod, 1981) established to advise him on the Law Commission's (1981) consultative working paper on the blasphemy laws, the work of which had later been extended to include consideration of the Law Commission's (1985) final recommendations. The working group's own final recommendations were published in the General Synod (1988) report on *Offences Against Religion and Public Worship*. However, in the context of 'the Rushdie affair', Runcie did not explicitly call for the equalization of the blasphemy laws, although a report by Sandra Barwick in *The Independent* (21.2.89d) suggested that while his statement might not explicitly have done this, it did implicitly do so.

As the controversy developed further, Lambeth Palace's involvement built upon its liaison with the Anglican Diocese of Bradford and with its Bishop, the Rt Revd Roy Williamson. The Church of England's Bradford Diocese had, for a number of years, been served by a chaplain appointed with a specific brief for race and community relations. The post holder during the time of the controversy was Philip Lewis, a former Church Missionary Society missionary in India, and author of the book *Islamic Britain: Religion, Politics and Identity Among British Muslims* (Lewis, 1994a), and a number of articles and reviews on 'the Rushdie affair' (see Lewis, 1989 and 1990) and on the Muslim community in Bradford.

During the week in which the fatwa was pronounced, while letting it be known that he found the fatwa 'abhorrent', it was reported in *The Church Times* (24.2.89) that the Bishop of Bradford brought forward an already planned private meeting of representatives of the Muslim, Christian, Hindu and Jewish traditions in order to try to address the issues raised by the affair. The Bishop reported that at this meeting Muslim leaders had emphasized their respect for British law. The blasphemy law and legal position of minorities were discussed and, in a joint statement, all the representatives said they understood Muslim outrage at a publication 'which seemed to rejoice in irreverent and scurrilous comments about the most revered figures in the Islamic tradition' (*The Baptist Times*, 2.3.89). It was also reported in *The Guardian* (23.2.89c) that Muslim leaders endorsed plans for a city forum for the exchange of views that was to be coordinated by the Bishop of

Bradford, although Liaquat Hussain, Secretary of the Council of Mosques, had warned that religious leaders could not control the expression of feelings at street level.

In the wake of the violence that followed the 17 June demonstrations in Bradford, the Bishop called for a reappraisal of some of the Muslim community's approaches in the light of the tensions emerging in Bradford. He stated that he now believed that 'There is a real chance that these protests may be counter-productive and serve only to isolate the Muslim community' (*The Guardian*, 20.6.89).

In response, as reported in the *Bradford Telegraph and Argus* (20.6.89), a statement issued by the Council of Mosques countered that 'Muslims do not have access to the higher seats of power, and the majority community and its institutions are defiant of our needs and aspirations.' Also, Sher Azam of the Council of Mosques pointed out that the Bishop had not referred to the peaceful Muslim demonstrations over the past 18 months and argued that the Bishop 'does not fully recognise what it is like for a minority with no privilege or position of power which the majority take for granted' (*The Guardian*, 20.6.89). In these ways the religious powerlessness and disadvantage of the Muslim community were contrasted with the relatively privileged access to political decision-making and the machinery of the state enjoyed by the established Church of England, and as reflected in the blasphemy laws themselves.

In Manchester, the Church of England Bishop of Manchester, the Rt Revd Stanley Booth-Clibborn, and some other Church leaders met with Muslims for an 'exchange of ideas' out of which it was agreed that the question of changes to the blasphemy laws would be put on the agenda of a forthcoming Northern Church Leaders' Conference. Eventually, the Bishop of Manchester called for abolition, saying, 'It must go. It is outdated and it must go. It is hopeless to have a law which simply protects one religion, and in particular the Established Church ... The real debate is about whether it should be replaced. My own view is that it should not' (*The Church Times*, 31.3.89). Among other Anglican Bishops, the Rt Revd John Taylor, the Bishop of St Albans, called for the withdrawal of the book on the grounds that it had caused social harm within the UK and that to proceed with publishing a paperback version would compound the situation.

At a national level the Archbishop of Canterbury asked Muslims to meet him at Lambeth Palace. At this meeting it was agreed that a joint Anglican–Muslim working party should be set up to examine the legal issues involved in the protection of religious sensibilities in contemporary British society. The Lambeth Palace official charged with setting up this working group, John Lyttle, became a centre of controversy when he intervened to call for the postponement of *The Blasphemer's Banquet* television programme. This was due to be presented by the controversial poet Tony Harrison and was scheduled for broadcast on BBC1 on 31 July (see *The Independent*, 31.7.89) as a part of *Byline*, the personal view documentary series. Mr Lyttle's intervention was made on the grounds of the programme's potentially inflammatory nature for Muslims, in particular with regard to the late Ayatollah Khomeini. When they learned about the nature of the programme, it was reported in *New Life* (11.8.89) that the owners of the restaurant featured in it expressed concerns about the use of their restaurant and they planned to sue the BBC for giving inadequate information on how the film would be used. However, an *Independent* editorial (31.7.89) on 'Dissent and fundamentalism' attacked Lyttle's intervention, contrasting it with the Archbishop of Canterbury's earlier and more robust statement about the responsibility for bloodshed that lay with fundamentalists of all religions.

The BBC turned down Lyttle's request and the programme was broadcast (see *The Guardian*, 1.8.89). As broadcast, it was set in a Bradford tandoori restaurant to which guests, including Rushdie, Voltaire, Molière and Byron – all of whom had been accused of blasphemy – were invited. It included images of Shi'a Muslims, which taken out of the context of a proper understanding of Shi'a Islam would be likely to be perceived as lurid confirmations of the kind of stereotypes of Iranian Islam already noted in connection with the popular press's editorializing on Khomeini. *The Guardian* (2.8.89) reported that the Bishop of Bradford regretted that, instead of showing pictures of the smiling Muslim children he was familiar with, the programme had focused on 'revolting scenes of Muslim fanatics teaching their children to hit their heads until they bled'.

Commenting on these Church of England interventions, the religious affairs correspondent of *The Independent*, Andrew Brown, noted in a piece (3.8.89) on 'Disarming the zealot with tea, cakes and conversation', that 'Bishops and archbishops seem to be popping up all over the place to defend the feelings of the Muslim communities.' Brown viewed this as odd since he argued that Islam and Christianity were theologically at odds and that Anglican 'sensibilities' are highly tentative in contrast with the certainties of Islam. Brown reflected that one way of trying to understand this apparently strange rapprochement would be to proceed on the basis that '. . . it is essential to ignore what people are saying if you wish to understand their motives: merely to ask whom they are trying to please and what they are trying to protect.'

Brown acknowledged that, due to its established status, the Church of England '. . . in its parish network has an unrivalled intelligence-gathering capability'. He speculated that inviting Muslims to Lambeth Palace may be something which 'squares with the practice of the British establishment through the ages', namely that 'there is no better and more effective way of disarming a potential book-burner than to take him to tea at Lambeth Palace and draw him into the endless Anglican conversation.' Summarizing his reflections on the role of the Church of England in the controversy, Brown concluded that 'The integration of Muslims into whatever British society will become as a result may seem a curious service for the established Church to attempt for the nation. No one else, though, seems to be offering very loudly to do it.'

The Church Times editorial (24.2.89) on 'Islam and modernity' began with the words 'Many Christians will have found their mind divided over the fierce Muslim reaction to Salman Rushdie and his novel *The Satanic Verses*.' Liberal and radical Christians of all denominational traditions certainly found themselves slightly bewildered at what was happening in 'the Rushdie affair' and torn between conflicting solidarities. On the one hand, they wished to stand with the largely minority ethnic Muslim communities against the torrents of media abuse and outbreaks of physical violence which afflicted the Muslims in the days following the book-burning in Bradford and the Ayatollah Khomeini's fatwa. However, they could not agree that *The Satanic Verses* should be censored or its publisher or author prosecuted for blasphemy. They also felt solidarity with Salman Rushdie as an author who had been forced to live in hiding under armed guard, and who had been prominent in the anti-racist movement of the 1980s with his searing indictments of racism in the UK.

Ecumenical Christian Perspectives

One of the clearest articulations of this radical and liberal Christian perspective can be found in the response of the former British Council of Churches to the issues involved in the controversy. In its statement, the then British Council of Churches (1989) focused on the three aspects of the controversy's impact: the impact upon interfaith relations, community relations and international relations. The statement notes that the British Council of Churches had been 'greatly encouraged by the increasing co-operation between the different faith communities in Britain in many areas of shared concern.'

This was, perhaps, a tangential reference to the Faith Alliance for Human Rights and Racial Justice, which the BCC's Community and Race Relations Unit and Committee for Relations with People of Other Faiths staff had been instrumental in setting up and which had resulted in *The Manifesto for Human Rights and Racial Justice*, signed by a number of religious leaders from various traditions and endorsed by a range of national and local religious organizations. But, at the same time, precisely because of this encouragement, the statement also expressed 'grave concern at the damaging effect on inter-faith and community relations of the controversy'.

In wording which attempted to express sympathy for Muslim feelings, without endorsing the Muslim judgement on the book, the British Council of Churches went on to declare that 'We recognise something of the deep pain and hurt experienced by the British Muslim community because it believes that the Prophet of Islam has been dishonoured.' But the central note of the statement was an expression of hope that 'the difficulties created by this matter will act as a spur to further development of understanding, respect and common purpose, rather than the opposite.'

Perspectives From Other Christian Traditions

The Independent (6.3.89b) reported that, among Roman Catholic Christian responses, the Vatican newspaper, *L'Osservatore Romano* carried an unsigned article on 4 March 1989, condemning *The Satanic Verses* as blasphemous. Among the responses from within the Free Church traditions of England, there was a distinctive response by The Unitarian and Free Christian Churches that drew upon its own experience of religious discrimination and social and political exclusion due to its advocacy of freedom of thought. Its own theologically grounded arguments for freedom of conscience were the basis of the declaration on the controversy issued by the General Assembly of the Unitarian and Free Christian Churches (1989), through its Council, which stated that:

> Unitarians have a long history of promoting inter-faith understanding at international and national levels and are frequently to be found as active members of local inter-faith groups. They are keenly

aware of the distress felt when artistic expressions are believed to be offensive by particular communities, but believe that the extension of the law into religious disputes exacerbates tensions rather than resolving them. The abolition of criminal blasphemy rather than its extension to cover non-Christian groups is the preferred course.

Some Individual Christian Theologians

Among the Christian responses were also those of individual theologians working within the various Christian traditions. These included Keith Ward, who at the time was an Anglican Professor of History and Philosophy of Religion at King's College London (and who later became Regius Professor of Divinity at the University of Oxford) and Chair of the World Congress of Faiths, and who wrote a piece in *The Independent* entitled 'The violent gifts of modern Islam' (Ward, 1989). In this article, while pointing to the 'great and tolerant cultures' which developed under the rule of what 'has been a great and noble faith', Ward commented that 'We seem to see in the modern world the sad spectacle of the decadence of Islam.' Furthermore, he posed the question concerning Islam in Britain: 'Can it make a positive contribution to social harmony and human well-being?', giving the answer that 'At the moment it does not seem so.'

By contrast, Bishop Lesslie Newbigin saw the Muslim passion over *The Satanic Verses* as posing a theological critique to Christian lukewarmness. In a letter (21.2.89) to *The Independent*, Bishop Newbigin pointed out that the notion of blasphemy had become generally without meaning in British society because of a loss of conviction about the reality of the divine. Because of this, Christians had become generally used to blasphemy in relation to Christianity. In addition, on religious grounds, Christians should not respond in the way that the Ayatollah Khomeini had done because Christian faith finds its focus in one who accepted crucifixion on charges of blasphemy. At the same time, Newbigin noted that only God would know whether the silence of Christians on blasphemy against their own religion was because of religious indifference or was rooted in an understanding of their faith.

In connection with this, Shabbir Akhtar (1989a: 99) had already made the sharp observation that 'Christian tolerance may well be a virtue inspired by love for justice and forbearance. Yet too often it is found only in lands and epochs where the faith is dead or dying ... Could the real motives be indifference and apathy, themselves rooted in a loss of faith?' Commenting on what he saw as Christianity's corrosion by tolerance, Shabbir Akhtar (1989a) pointed out that 'Many writers often condescendingly imply that Muslims should become as tolerant as modern Christians,' but for Akhtar, 'Any faith which compromises its internal temper of militant wrath is destined for the dustbin of history, for it can no longer preserve its faithful heritage in the face of corrosive influences.'

Other Religious Reactions
Wider Reactions

Of course, alongside Christians of various traditions, and Muslims themselves (as the largest religious minority) in the UK, there are also significant numbers of Hindus, Sikhs, Jews and Buddhists together with smaller minorities of Baha'is, Jains and Zoroastrians.

Jewish Reactions

Like Christianity, Judaism shares common 'Abrahamic' roots with Islam. As Jenni Frazer (1989) noted in a *Jewish Chronicle* article commenting on Jewish–Muslim relations in the context of 'the Rushdie affair', 'For Anglo-Jewry, there is renewed consideration of the often strained relations between the two communities – where the dominant feature of their relations is conflict, rather than contact, and the shadow of the Middle East is a constant factor.' In this connection it has already been noted that, in a number of Muslim statements about the controversy, dark hints could be found suggesting that powerful global forces and interests were at work behind Rushdie – hints that seemed to point in the direction of a conspiracy theory in which Zionism played a prominent part.

In the context of the controversy, however, a number of leading Jews expressed feelings of solidarity with the Muslims in the face of the distorted treatment that Muslims felt they were receiving from the media. This is perhaps not surprising coming from a community which has itself suffered stigmatization from the wider society and a large proportion of whose members had also originally arrived as poor immigrants.

Muslims writing about the controversy have themselves seen parallels with the Jewish experience. Some have even gone so far as to argue

that Muslims have taken the place of the Jews in European demon-
ology, in the context of which they have expressed fears that the
enmity against Islam they believe to be focused through 'the Rushdie
affair' could lead to Muslims becoming the victims of a new Holocaust
in Europe. For example, in reflecting on the Muslim position in
Europe, Shabbir Akhtar (1989a) has said, dramatically, 'The next time
there are gas chambers in Europe, there is no doubt concerning who'll
be inside them.' This kind of perception was reinforced by some of the
reactions to Muslims which emerged during the Gulf War and, in
the light of revelations about the concentration camps for Bosnian
Muslims and campaigns of ethnic cleansing in Bosnia–Herzogovina, in
the eyes of many Muslims it has been proven to be not too far from the
truth (Kabbani, 1989).

As early as October 1988, the Chief Rabbi, Sir (now Lord) Immanuel
Jakobovits, (quoted in *The Jewish Chronicle*, 28.10.88), expressed
strong sympathy for the wounded feelings of Muslim believers. His
letter to the Islamic Society for the Promotion of Religious Tolerance's
conference on *The Satanic Verses* and Martin Scorsese's film *The Last
Temptation of Christ* stated that he 'deprecates not only the falsification
of established historical records but the offence caused to religious convictions and susceptibilities of countless citizens.' Jakobovits argued
that 'In a civilised society we should generate respect for other people's
religious beliefs and not tolerate a form of denigration and ridicule
which can only breed resentment to the point of hatred and strife', and
he later repeated his position in a letter (4.2.89) to *The Times*.

It is noteworthy that considerable controversy surrounded the Chief
Rabbi's stance on this issue (see *The Jewish Chronicle*, 10.3.89a), thus
suggesting that it did not entirely reflect a consensus within the community. With regard to the fatwa, *The Jewish Chronicle* (24.2.89b)
reported that Rabbi Rodney Mariner, the Convenor of the Reform
Synagogues of Great Britain, called the threat to Rushdie 'an obscenity',
while Dayan Isaac Berge of the London Beth Din thought it 'highly
irresponsible'. Rabbi Dr Jeffrey Cohen of the Stanmore Synagogue
spoke of 'a dividing line between the blessing of free speech on the one
hand and the pernicious effects of blatant misrepresentation of racial
and religious ideas and values on the other', warning that 'Fabrication
and distortion of history can cause great emotional damage and real
hurt to a race, religion or nation, which cannot retaliate in kind.
We Jews sympathise with the outrage felt by the Moslems, but our
response would definitely not be to over-react by calling for the
author's execution.'

A group of leading Jewish writers, including Arnold Wesker, Harold Pinter, Bernice Rubens, Frederic Raphael, Bernard Kops and Jon Silkin, issued a statement (in *The Jewish Chronicle*, 26.5.89) opposing the extension of the blasphemy laws on the grounds that this would 'involve an undesirable restriction on our precious freedom of inquiry and expression and an equally undesirable encouragement of dangerous fanaticism in our pluralist society.' But alternative views to those of the Chief Rabbi were not only expressed on the Reform and Liberal wings of Judaism. Rabbi Dr Normon Solomon (in *The Jewish Chronicle*, 10.3.89), an Orthodox Jew and a leading Jewish proponent of interfaith dialogue, held that the blasphemy law was a thing of the past which should not be resuscitated. The Chief Rabbi clarified that he had not advocated an extension of the blasphemy laws, arguing that:

> While I fully share the worldwide outrage at the murderous threat against the book's author, publishers and distributor, I stand by my view that the book should not have been published. What should concern us are not *religious* offences but *socially* intolerable conduct calculated or likely to incite revulsion or violence, by holding up religious beliefs to scurrilous contempt, or by encouraging murder.

Reflecting on the complex issues involved, in *The Jewish Chronicle* (10.3.89c), Chaim Bermant pointed out that while the Jews had suffered the burning of Talmuds there had been Jewish offences too. In 1233, the Montpellian Jewish authorities denounced Maimonides' *Guide to the Perplexed* to the Dominicans, who later burned it; in 1624, Uriel da Costa, a Jewish philosopher from the Netherlands, had his work burned by the Jewish community; and in 1656 Spinoza was excommunicated and had an attempt made against his life. In the light of this history, Bermant described the Chief Rabbi's position as 'the authentic Jewish voice of authentic Jewish intolerance'. However, it was reported by *The Jewish Chronicle* (17.3.89) that the Chief Rabbi's office said they had received more favourable responses than opposing ones and that they had received 'no protest from any organisation, be it Jewish or non-Jewish'.

On a symbolic level the Bradford book-burning had been highly problematic for Jews. In a *Jewish Chronicle* article (3.2.89) entitled 'Bradford burning evokes unhappy memories', Chaim Bermant argued that 'if the anti-Rushdie campaign has led to a backlash of anti-Moslem feelings – which it has – then Moslems have only themselves to blame', pointing out that the Bradford conflagration 'evoked painful memories of what book-burning led to in Nazi Germany'. Bermant went on to state that:

This may be an indelicate point to make by someone who is himself an immigrant, but it has to be made: the Moslems are abusing the very freedoms which have led them to seek, and obtain, a home in Britain. They are making things difficult for themselves; they are making things impossible for prospective immigrants, especially from the Moslem world.

However, in a letter (10.2.89) to *The Jewish Chronicle* responding to Bermant, Ibrahim Hewitt of the Islamic Organisation for Media Monitoring argued that there had been a lot of hypocrisy around the incident of the book-burning, and pointed out that the Nazis were able to mobilize anti-Semitism precisely because the authors of anti-Semitic books were allowed the kind of freedom that Rushdie's supporters were advocating.

The Jews are, of course, the religious minority with the longest historical presence in Britain. However, there are other religious minorities too. Representatives of these religions did not have such a public profile in their contributions to the controversy as have Christians, Muslims and Jews. Nevertheless, their reactions were also important within the total context of a religiously plural society.

Sikh and Hindu Reactions

Among Sikhs and Hindus it was reported that, in Bradford, a joint meeting between Hindu representatives of the Hindu Vishwa Parishad and the Federation of Bradford Sikh Organisations had called for a change to the current blasphemy legislation. Mohinder Singh Chana, the General Secretary of the Federation of Bradford Sikh Organisations, stated that, in the context of Britain now being multi-religious, the current legal position needed to be reviewed (in *New Life*, 10.3.89a).

Buddhist Reactions

One of the few pieces of sustained published argument to come from organizations or individuals of other than Christian, Jewish or Muslim religious traditions appeared in a statement issued by the Friends of the Western Buddhist Order, which opposed the extension of the blasphemy laws. Significantly, its argument was advanced on clearly religious grounds and so could not simply be dismissed as an expression of secularized religious sentiment. The FWBO's (1990) press release stated that 'Buddhists do not want the protection of any such law. Moreover, we would prefer that the blasphemy laws be scrapped altogether and removed from the statute books, as we consider them to be an impediment to our freedom of expression as Buddhists.'

The FWBO press release went on to express the concern that if the blasphemy laws were extended, then 'Buddhism itself may be deemed by some to be blasphemous and it would seem to be impossible to frame laws for the "protection" of the theistic religions which do not by their very nature have this effect upon non-theistic religions.' Finally, the statement concluded that 'to respond with anger to a disparagement of one's religious beliefs is entirely un-Buddhistic, indeed, from a Buddhist standpoint, profoundly irreligious. We as Buddhists therefore expressly reject any attempt to bring the rule of law, and therefore ultimately the application of force and coercion, to bear upon our religious beliefs.'

In fact, in a report in *The Independent* (27.2.89b), Dharmachari Kulananda of the FWBO went further than this and, in continuity with an argument advanced in the context of the *Gay News* trial by the Venerable Sangharakshita (1978), the founder of the FWBO, he noted that there can be contexts in which blasphemous utterances can be helpful in freeing individuals from the effects on their lives of belief in a vengeful deity.

Interfaith and Cross-Community Reactions

The Inter Faith Network for the UK

Together with the positions taken by religious organizations and leaders within individual religious traditions, a number of interfaith organizations took up stances in relation to the issues involved in the controversy. The Inter Faith Network for the UK, a national framework for interfaith cooperation and communication set up in 1987, found itself, in the days following the fatwa of the Ayatollah Khomeini, in the position of having to make some public response.

As an umbrella organization which, at the time, linked some sixty or so other organizations and groups involved in interfaith relations at local and national level the Network had not, until then, entered the public arena by means of issuing press releases. Indeed, until this point it had no mechanisms in place for speaking at short notice on behalf of its affiliated organizations. In addition, the difficulties involved in producing a statement were obvious in a body whose membership included both Muslim organizations themselves campaigning against the book and the Friends of the Western Buddhist Order whose position has just been outlined above. However, such was the seriousness of the issues involved that a statement was issued by the officers of The Inter Faith Network (1989), the full text of which is reproduced because of what, in retrospect, seems to have been its very balanced and nuanced treatment of the issues involved:

> The Satanic Verses contains passages which were bound to cause deep offence to Muslims. There have been peaceful protests from them about the book for many months and inevitably a sense of frustration has developed as time has passed. In this country the Muslim community is a minority. They are naturally concerned about attacks upon the integrity of their faith and its misrepresentation. Like others, they are also concerned at attitudes in a society which does not always appear sympathetic to religious values in the community or in family life.
>
> As in the case of other religious faiths, there is no single individual (here or abroad) who has the authority to speak for all Muslims. But in Britain, senior leaders of the community have at all times insisted that Muslim protests should avoid violence and should strictly observe the requirements of our laws. We wholly endorse this view.
>
> There is, in this country, a long and deeply cherished tradition of freedom of expression. It is not an absolute right: there is, for example, the law of libel. Freedom of expression creates a corresponding responsibility in the way in which this freedom is exercised. A tension faces us all between freedom, responsibility and the law: this is particularly true in relation to what is sacred in our lives.
>
> Within the faith communities themselves, there are differences of view about the appropriateness or practicality of legal sanctions against blasphemy and in protection of religious sensitivities. But there will be general agreement that if there is protection provided by the law it should apply to all religious communities.
>
> There are difficult and divisive issues here which require more considered public debate in a calmer atmosphere as we develop the appropriate social framework for our life together in a multi-faith

society. This will take patience, tolerance and commitment as we forge a shared vision of such a society.

Writing as an individual, one of the co-Chairs of the Network, the Anglican Bishop, Jim Thompson of Stepney, called for a reassessment of the blasphemy laws in the context of a multi-faith society. The Inter Faith Network followed up its officers' statement by holding two jointly sponsored seminars together with the Commission for Racial Equality. The first (Commission for Racial Equality, 1990c) was at Regent's College, London on 14 September 1989. According to the letters of invitation to this event, its purpose was to consider:

> ... the appropriateness (and practicality) of legal sanctions (including the law of blasphemy) or voluntary 'codes of conduct' to protect religious sensibilities in a multi-faith society, together with some of the more general questions of freedom of expression, personal responsibility and social values which arise in this field.

The very involved description of the seminar's purpose reflects the complexity and sensitivity of the issues involved in the controversy and the way in which it was felt to be important not to make any prior assumptions about how the issues should be approached, other than a common willingness to share in exploration together with people from a wide range of religious perspectives and professional disciplines. A second seminar organized by the Inter Faith Network (1991) and Commission for Racial Equality took place at the latter's offices on 24 October 1990, at which the focus was on possible alternative legal provisions for the protection of religious sensibilities.

World Conference on Religion and Peace

Another national interfaith organization that made a statement on the controversy was the UK and Ireland Chapter of the World Conference on Religion and Peace (WCRP). The officers of the WCRP wrote a letter to the editor of *The Times* (16.3.89) in which they put the controversy in its wider setting and then went beyond the Network officers' statement on the question of the scope of the blasphemy laws, expressing a hope that the inequality in the blasphemy laws as they were could be addressed through providing legal protection for religious minorities too, though without specifying the preferred form of such protection.

The controversy both caused and revealed significant underlying tensions in interfaith relations. For some involved in such groups, it was a very discouraging and depressing experience. However, as a result of the controversy, at the very least, all who were involved in interfaith relations needed to recognize what a serious challenge interfaith activity entails. Those who are fully committed to the project of building a multi-faith society were no longer able to talk glibly about its potential. After 'the Rushdie affair', serious participants in such a social and theological project and in interfaith dialogue knew that major issues were involved – and that this included issues that could indeed become literally matters of life and death.

The Commission for Racial Equality

In terms of cross-community bodies involving both religious and secular people, the controversy posed new and challenging issues for bodies such as the Commission for Racial Equality (see Day, 1990). At the early height of the controversy, the Commission issued a statement in which it expressed understanding for 'the hurt and pain caused to deeply held religious beliefs of Muslims' (Commission for Racial Equality, 1989). However, the statement also expressed concern about 'the harmful effect this whole controversy may have on race relations', condemning the fatwa as 'monstrous' and arguing that 'there are peaceful and constructive ways of resolving such disagreements' since 'Tolerance is demanded of us all in a pluralist society and those who identify with extremism on any side undermine the harmony so many are committed to achieve.'

Women's Organizations

It should be noted that much of the public inter-religious and community debate was conducted among males. This was, of course, not surprising since most public spokespersons for religious and ethnic community organizations have been male. However, it does mean that only half of the religious debate is usually brought into the public sphere and recorded and, as a consequence, that some of the gendered dimensions of the controversy have been relatively less visible.

The one significant exception to this was (as reported in *New Life*, 14.4.89b) the activities of women from various religious and ethnic backgrounds gathered in the group Women Against Fundamentalism (WAF). The group was launched on 6 May 1989 and included Southall Black Sisters, Brent Asian Women's Refuge, the Iranian Women's Organisation in Britain and Irish Women (see *New Life*, 7.7.89; Connolly, 1991). Women Against Fundamentalism is not a religious group, although it includes women from a range of religious and cultural backgrounds who have attempted to pursue an independent line from that of the male spokespeople of their communities. As Hannana Siddiqui, a member of WAF, put it:

> On 27th May 1989 when the Muslim fundamentalists marched through Central London against Rushdie, I was not there as a part of their demonstration, but as a part of the counter picket organised by Women Against Fundamentalism. . . . When I saw thousands of angry Asian male faces, it reminded me of . . . a culture and religion which intertwine to sanction and reinforce male power and domination . . . I shared this battleground with other women from diverse religious backgrounds. But we were all doubters and dissenters . . . I do not want men and mullahs to build my future. I want to create my own future in a world where women can choose to live as they please. I want a secular state without blasphemy laws which impose religious censorship. I support Salman Rushdie's right to write *The Satanic Verses* because his right to doubt and dissent is also my right to doubt and dissent. (Siddiqui, 1989: 2)

Reported in *The Guardian* (25.7.89), Pragna Patel of the group explained that 'We thought long and hard about whether to picket the anti-Rushdie demonstration. We did not want to be seen standing side by side with racists. But we felt that on this issue we could not prevaricate. If we are not to raise these things, who would?' In this one can see that Women Against Fundamentalism had been struggling against an undifferentiated view of their communities. Together with supporting Rushdie's right to publish they opposed the extension of the blasphemy laws, and were against separate religious schools, and also against state aid for Religious Education and Christian assemblies in schools. At the same time, issues in the politics of gender, ethnicity and religion are wider, and arguably more complex (see Ali, 1992), than the positions taken by this specific feminist group, as has been illustrated by the kind of debates that subsequently came to prominence two decades on in connection with the controversies surrounding the wearing of head coverings by young Muslim women.

'The Rushdie affair' therefore sharpened the challenges involved both in inter-religious relations and in questions concerning the reorganization of society to take fuller account of the present diversity of religious belief and practice amongst its citizenry. But it has also underlined the problems of dealing with the diversity within, as well as between, communities. This diversity is found in the varied responses and strategies proposed by different Muslim organizations and in gender and other differences within communities such as those highlighted by Women Against Fundamentalism.

The 'Entails' of the Controversy

Having in the previous chapter surveyed the contours of the controversy, and in this chapter examined some of the actions and reactions that are interwoven within those contours, it is possible now systematically to begin to identify some clustering of 'entails' that arise from the controversy and that both focus and contribute to wider contemporary debates on multiculturalism. These 'entails' are broadly linked in five clusters of issues.

The five clusters are concerned with: issues of social integration and identity in relationships between ethnicity, nationhood, religion and plurality; issues around religion and the secular; issues of culture, in terms of the relationships between values, art, education and plurality; issues of law, in terms of the relationships between law, ethics and plurality; and issues of politics, in terms of the relationships between politics, the constitution and plurality.

I would argue that these clusters of issues reflect the debates at the heart of *The Satanic Verses* controversy. In so doing, they act as a microcosm for wider questions that are, in the opening decade of the twenty-first century, being debated in relation to the nature and future of multiculturalism. Among the fundamental questions for which the controversy serves as a 'magnifying mirror' are: what is the relationship between religions, nationhood and the state? How far can various religions coexist in a society of many religions within a wider context in which secular, if not explicitly secularist, visions and values hold considerable power? What is the relationship between cultural and religious identity and social integration? What 'glue' might hold heterogeneous societies together? How far, and on what basis, can the concerns and values of minority cultural and religious communities be recognized and incorporated within the legal systems of the society?

Or how far does such recognition entail radical changes being made to that system if more than lip service is to be paid to meeting them? To what extent is it correct to call the UK or other European countries a 'Christian' country, a 'secular society' or a 'multi-faith society'? How adequately are the concerns of religious minorities represented by the mainstream political parties and what are the possibilities for the development of religiously based political organizations?

Chapter 3

Through the Looking Glass

The Controversy as Magnifying Glass
General and Specific Issues

At a time when 'the Rushdie affair' was in full flow, Clinton Bennett, a former Executive Secretary of the Council of Churches for Britain and Ireland's Committee for Relations With People of Other Faiths, wrote in an essay in a special edition of the Committee's journal *Discernment* (1990) that, in the light of what was shaping up to be a long-running issue, 'the insistent question I find myself asking is this – is it any longer about the book at all or has the book become a catalyst for other, perhaps even more crucial issues?' (Bennett, 1990: 10).

As Salman Rushdie himself expressed it, 'There are times when I feel that the original intentions of *The Satanic Verses* have been so thoroughly scrambled by events as to be lost forever' (Rushdie 1990 in Rushdie 1991a: 403). However, notwithstanding Rushdie's obvious frustration in relation to his authorial intention as a novelist, it is the argument of this book that the controversy around *The Satanic Verses* contained in microcosm many of the themes, issues and debates that have, twenty years on, come to form a large part of public, religious and political debate and consciousness in relation to religion and public policy. Thus it is argued that, with hindsight, one can understand 'the Rushdie affair' as having been an early 'lightning rod' for what were then only incipient issues, but have since become 'full blown' in relation both to the degree of the challenges posed and of the actions and reactions in relation to these.

Continuity and Discontinuity of the Issues

In the closing chapter of the book it will be argued that, on 'the other side of the looking glass' (which is also on 'the other side of terror/the War on Terror'), the issues as they originally emerged in direct connection with 'the Rushdie affair' have been reprised in ways that include some elements of continuity and some of discontinuity when compared with the incidents described in the first two chapters of this book, and some of the broader implications arising from them that are explored in this chapter.

These implications include aspects of the relationship between believing and belonging in the twenty-first century; religion, art and values in contention; issues of rights and restraints in relation to law; and matters to do with political representation in a plural society. Therefore, this chapter forms a 'bridge' between the specific issues that are linked directly to 'the Rushdie affair' itself and were highlighted in the first two chapters of the book; the broader ramifications of those issues which form the substance of the discussions in this chapter; and the way in which those issues are reprised on the other side of 9/11, together with the way in which all of this opens out into a consideration of wider questions around the future of multiculturalism.

Believing and Belonging in the Twenty-First Century

Faith, Culture and the Christendom Inheritance

Writing prior to 'the Rushdie affair', Christopher Lamb (1985: 13) pointed out that a plural society poses questions for people of all religions and none in that, 'For the first time in centuries Western Christians – indeed all people of whatever faith or none – are being compelled to make the difficult distinction between faith and culture.' For some, to be forced self-consciously to wrestle with issues surrounding the relationship of religion and culture is almost to call into question both religion and culture, so close has the relationship between them been.

Europe inherited from medieval Christianity a model of the *corpus Christianum* in which Church and society were coterminous and which involved, in various forms, a fusion of political and religious realities into a synthesis in which a religious monopoly provided a legitimization for the rules and in turn received their protection. Those who conceived of the *corpus Christianum* could see only a synthesis in which Church and society numerically coincided. This argument stood in a tradition that identified religious diversity with the dangers of anarchy and a threat to national unity. For example, Edwin Sandys, Archbishop of York under Queen Elizabeth I, had argued that religious plurality would be dangerous to the body politic:

> This liberty, that men may openly profess diversity of religion must needs be dangerous to the Commonwealth. What stirs diversity of religion hath raised in nations and kingdoms the histories are so many and plain, and in our times insuch sort have told you, that with further proof I need not trouble your ears. One God, one King, one profession, is fit for one monarchy and commonwealth. Let conformity and unity in religion be provided for; and it shall be as a wall of defence unto this realm. (Sandys, in McGrath, 1967: 1)

Thomas Arnold, in his *Principles of Church Reform* (quoted in Jackson and Rogan, 1962: 166), while upholding what he called 'the noble, the divine theory that the Christian nation of England was the Church of England', argued that this settlement could and should be 'stretched' to include other Christians, though on political grounds he excluded Roman Catholics. Arnold (in Jackson and Rogan, 1962: 167) argued that if there is no Christian majority then 'Christians have no right as such to press the establishment of their religion to the prejudice of the civil rights of others'; that if there is an equal distribution of religions, then this would 'be a reason why such a nation should separate itself in two, and the Christian and Heathen portions of it form each a state distinct from the other', but when the majority of a country is Christian then the state may 'justly become a Church' and 'the Heathen part of the population ought to be excluded from the legislature and encouraged, if it be possible, to emigrate to other countries, if they complain of not participating in the full rights of citizenship'.

Culture, Ethnicity and Belonging in 'the Rushdie Affair'

During 'the Rushdie affair', some secularized echoes of the main lines of Arnold's approach could be observed. For example, John Townend, MP for Bridlington (quoted in *The Guardian*, 29.8.90), stated that

'England must be reconquered for the English'. He argued that 'When Muslims say they cannot live in a country when Salman Rushdie is free to express his views, they should be told they have the answer in their own hands – go back from whence you came.' Townend went on to complain of what had happened to 'this green and pleasant land' due to immigration and what he called 'the pernicious doctrine of multi-culturalism', arguing with regard to the latter that 'The British people were never consulted as to whether they would change from being a homogenous society to a multi-racial society.'

Until 'the Rushdie affair', issues of 'culture' were often less significant, at least in terms of street-level racism, than were issues around skin pigmentation or 'colour'. However, even as early as the 1970s, Enoch Powell, MP, in his attack on the developing multicultural society, was primarily concerned with what he viewed as the potential erosion of the English 'way of life' rather than with differentiating people on the basis of 'colour'. Later on, thinkers around the Conservative journal, *The Salisbury Review*, attempted to rehabilitate the concept of 'nationhood' in the context of debate about the pluralist society. Positing this concept as the basis for social unity, they argued that the presence of large numbers of minorities with 'non-Christian' cultures and religions was fundamentally subversive of the nation and that ideas of multiculturalism and religious and cultural pluralism were alien constructs deriving from a flawed sociology. From more within the Thatcherite political mainstream, Norman (now Lord) Tebbit suggested that minorities might find his now infamous 'cricket test' difficult to pass on the basis that their real loyalties lay elsewhere rather than in England (*The Guardian*, 21.4.90).

As might have been expected, politicians and social commentators within that kind of tradition claimed that 'the Rushdie affair' had proved them to be right all along about the dangers of New Commonwealth immigration. After the controversy and, even more so, following the emergence of terrorist violence associated with Muslims and Islam, such questioning of multiculturalism as a viable basis for social cohesion in a plural society was not only limited to the political tendency of which Townend is a representative example. But an early indication of the coming changes in the tone and parameters of the debate can be seen in an *Independent* article with the significant title, 'Xenophobia as a survival mechanism', that was penned by the otherwise politically liberal columnist, Jill Tweedie (1989). Even more starkly, the novelist Fay Weldon (1989: 31) declared that 'Our attempt at multi-culturalism has failed. The Rushdie affair demonstrates it.'

Weldon's stark statement of obituary upon the social project of multiculturalism in Britain resonated with the more mildly expressed anxieties of liberal opinion, articulated even by Lord Jenkins, the former Labour Government Home Secretary and political architect of British race relations legislation, who commented in the light of 'the Rushdie affair' that 'In retrospect we might have been more cautious about allowing the creation in the 1950s of substantial Muslim communities here' (Jenkins, 1989). In view of Jenkins' original advocacy of the idea of 'integration' (in its original meaning, as opposed to 'assimilation', rather than in the meaning it has come to have in the context of the most recent social and political developments), this admission is highly significant and underlines just how deeply 'the Rushdie affair' has raised profound questions and issues.

Contested 'Imagined Communities'

Despite the variety of their provenance and expression, such critiques all tended to assume a view of society which expects that, ideally, it should be homogeneous. As argued by Benedict Anderson (1983), modern ideas of nationhood originally evolved around 'ethnicity', which is a concept that is the subject of a substantial social scientific theoretical literature (Bacal, 1991). As can clearly be seen in examples from the recent European history of the disintegration of ethnically diverse states such as the former Yugoslavia, ethnic diversity can – and often does – pose challenges to the concept of the nation state.

But there are also reasonably successful historical examples of how diverse ethnic belongings can be incorporated within the greater whole of loyalty to a unitary state and its institutions. As Fay Weldon (1989: 32) suggests, one of these might be the United States of America's model of the 'melting-pot' for integrating diversity, which has achieved at least some relative success. Even if in historical practice it is often difficult to achieve, ethnic plurality is, in principle, capable of accommodation. But while there is evidence for successful integration by means of relativizing ethnic identities, there has been a growing suspicion that religious identities might not be so easily relativized within overarching national identities.

For example, during 'the Rushdie affair', the Anglican Bishop, Jim Thompson argued that Fay Weldon's advocacy of the 'one flag' uniculturalist vision of the USA did not work in relation to the challenges posed by pluralities of religion 'because when God is robbed of specific revelation and given a national identity, religion becomes a propaganda tool, or a bland lowest common denominator which will not touch the soul of a child' (Thompson, 1989). In historical reality, religions have tended either to lay the foundation for building a social order (as in a theocracy) or to sacralize a pre-existing order with a degree of religious legitimation. But the question still has to be asked about whether there might be something about its absoluteness of religious commitment, its international character and its transcendent referents that, in the final analysis, suggests that having a primary religious identity may not be fully compatible with national identity.

In the course of constructing his theory of nation states as 'imagined communities', Anderson (1983) suggested that the nation state was a competitive concept for religion, secularizing previous ideas of primary belonging that were defined mainly in religious terms. Is there, then, perhaps a fundamental sense in which religions cannot allow the state to claim an ultimate value since this would be a usurpation of a loyalty which, in the perspective of religious traditions, should only be offered to that which is unconditioned and infinite? Perhaps, in principle at least, those religious traditions which will finally not allow themselves to be completely privatized are ultimately more difficult fully to incorporate into a common bond within national and state identities than are ethnicities.

In the context of twentieth-century globalization processes (Featherstone, 1990) and widespread migration, there has been a significant resurgence in the idea of religion as a primary identifying marker associated with culture, sometimes leading to what is often identified as 'communalism'. Writing in 1974 in an essay on 'Communalism and the social structure of religion', but perhaps with even more relevance today, Trevor Ling stated that 'Among the dangers to the peace of the world today religious communalism might appear to rank as one of the more serious' (1974: 59). In positing this analysis, Ling drew upon the leitmotif of Wilfred Cantwell Smith's *The Meaning and End of Religion* (1978) that had protested against the reification of what Cantwell Smith preferred to identify as 'cumulative traditions' into entities such as 'Hinduism' and 'Christianity'. Ling (1974: 61) argued that:

The fact that such terms have been invented and have gained currency is no guarantee that they refer to real objective recognisable entities, each possessing a sufficiently high degree of internal unity to justify the degree of external differentiation which the terms imply.

Furthermore, Ling (1974: 66) argued that such constructions of sharply defined religious identities 'arise out of concealed quasi-nationalisms, and they advance concealed quasi-nationalistic causes'. Concluding his 1994 essay on religion and politics in Britain since 1945, Gerald Parsons (1994b: 154) issued a warning that without an effort on the part of religious leaders and politicians, political parties and religious groups to 'understand the subtleties and complexities of the inter-actions to which their various commitments give rise . . . the alterna-tive is the reduction of increasingly complex issues to the convenient slogans of competing religious-cum-political pressure groups – a bleak and unhappy prospect indeed'.

'Integration', 'Assimilation' and 'Britishness'

The sharpness of the boundaries between these 'imagined belongings', as well as their relative importance, can vary. Thus, for example, more settled and affluent environments tend to promote more complex indi-vidual and group identification, while environments that are threaten-ing and poverty-stricken tend towards the simplification of identity. But the claimed primacy of religious identity over national loyalty among Muslims is precisely what both the secular commentators and authorities found difficult about 'the Rushdie affair'.

During 'the Rushdie affair', the difficulty for many of coming to terms with such an approach was clearly illustrated by the then Home Secretary, Douglas Hurd's speech in Birmingham Central Mosque on 'Race Relations and the Rule of Law' (Hurd, 1989); by the then Home Office Minister, John Patten's (1989a) letter to a number of leading British Muslims, released to the press under the title of 'Muslims in Britain Today'; and by his (Patten, 1989b) even sharper letter to mem-bers of the Home Office Advisory Council on Race Relations entitled 'On Being British'.

Douglas Hurd's speech had been planned prior to the fatwa, but was given special force by the context in which it was eventually delivered. In the speech, Hurd argued for greater integration in the light of the needs of the generation of Asians born in Britain. He argued that no ethnic or religious minority would develop if it cut itself off from the mainstream of social life. He agreed that protests by British Muslims against a book that they believed denigrated the Prophet were legitim-ate, but warned that there could not be a picking and choosing in obeying some laws and not others. Finally, he stressed that the rule of law, freedom of speech, and the toleration of a variety of opinions were ideals that everyone in the country was expected to respect.

A *New Life* editorial (3.3.89) entitled 'Misfired message' charged that Hurd's speech had backfired, arguing that it had confirmed racist stereotypes and belittled the attempts made by the Muslim community to become an integral part of British society. Muslim leaders reacted strongly to what Iqbal Sacranie described as being a 'provocation' to Muslims (*New Life*, 3.3.89a). This was because, at that point, in the UK, the only violence connected with 'the Rushdie affair' had been against Muslim property, as in the firebombing of Regent's Park Mosque. Melanie Phillips (1989) commented on Hurd's speech that its subtext was 'the British horror of separateness'.

Both of John Patten's letters raised questions about the relationship between a universal loyalty to a religious tradition and community and a particular loyalty to a civic society and state. In 'On Being British', Patten (1989b) stated that 'Being British means exactly what it says. One cannot be British on one's own exclusive terms or on a selective basis. Nor is there room for dual loyalties where those loyalties openly contradict one another.' Both Hurd's and Patten's themes were, in the following months, continually stressed by Government ministers.

In a 15 April speech to Anglo-Asian Conservatives in Coventry, and reported in *The Guardian* (16.4.89b), the then Home Office Minister Timothy Renton argued that South Asians should make a real effort to 'learn the norms and customs of British life'. In May, Renton (in *New Life*, 12.5.89a), while addressing a meeting of the Southern constituencies of the One Nation Forum (an organization for Asian Tories) in Reading, brought Eid greetings to Muslims. But he again argued for greater 'integration'. In principle, he distinguished such 'integration' from 'assimilation'. But in the way he referred to it, one could already discern outlines of the way in which the originally distinct meanings of these concepts in time became elided so that now, the meaning of the concept of 'integration' is perversely almost equivalent to that which the concept of 'assimilation' originally referred when Roy Jenkins' original vision of 'integration' was put forward as the basis of the bipartisan social policy orthodoxy that flowed from it.

Religion, The Universal and the National

But any religion that makes a universal claim and has an international membership brings with it an inevitable tension between nation-state formations and the universal community of that religion. This is all the more so the case where a religious community has a focus on an external geographical centre or centres. Historically, this tension has been a significant part of the Jewish experience in England (Cooper and Morrison, 1991) and it is sometimes resurrected today as part of anti-Jewish agitation in connection with questions concerning the relationship of Diaspora Jewry to the ideology of Zionism and the state of Israel.

On the basis of a Jewish history that is experienced at recognizing subtexts that are directed towards minorities, Rabbi Jonathan Magonet (reported in *The Jewish Chronicle*, 18.8.89) charged Mr Patten with 'bullying' and 'scaremongering'. Magonet noted that 'When you talk about dual loyalties to a minority group, what you are really telling them is: "Stay in line and don't make waves because we don't really trust you"', and that 'you're also sending a message to the wider community saying, "Don't trust them because they have other loyalties."'

In Christianity, the tension between belonging to a universal community of faith and belonging to a particular civil community has also been historically and theologically present. But with the emergence of Constantinian Christianity this tension was often obscured in European history, although it could still be seen in the medieval struggle between the Papacy and the Emperor. However, the tensions were again obscured due to the post-Reformation development of so-called 'national Churches', of which the Church of England was a specific example. With the rise of nationalisms and the fragmentation of Western Christendom in the Reformation period, the basic approach of Constantinianism took on nationalistic forms in the shape of state or national Churches.

As Klassen (1981: 22) argued, the Protestant Reformation did not fundamentally challenge the basic Christendom approach except in so far as it made its scope national rather than universal. This is because, in clearing the way for the ascendency of the government over the Church, the Lutheran Reformation was 'simply reversing the Roman claim that the Church should have primacy over the Government' and 'the symbiotic tie between the two remained in place'. Thus the Catholic ideal of Christendom harmoniously ruled by Pope and Emperor was replaced by the Lutheran pattern of *cuius regio, eius religio* or the 'nationalized religion' of the Elizabethan English settlement.

In Reformation Northern Europe Roman Catholicism was therefore frequently under suspicion from, and sometimes opposed by, the

Protestant governmental 'powers that be', not simply on the grounds of theological doctrine, but also because Roman Catholics were perceived to pose an extra-territorial threat to the precursor formations of the modern nation states. This was because Catholic Christianity entailed loyalty to a Church that extended across national boundaries and also involved Roman Catholics in a close relationship with the diplomatic power and influence of the Papacy.

In modern times, similar fears concerning the relationship between religious groups and external powers have also been seen in parts of the world such as China, where religions or ideologies other than Christianity have been in the ascendency and the Christian community, founded by externally based missionary organizations, has often been perceived as being too much under the influence of foreign powers. During 'the Rushdie affair' similar fears came to the surface in the UK, in which strong anxieties about Muslims being 'the enemy within' were reinforced by concerns, on the one hand, about the influence bought by the oil wealth of Muslim countries and, on the other hand, about the development of an Islamicist radicalism that has been perceived as all the more threatening since the seismic shocks of 9/11, 11/3 and 7/7 which will be examined in the closing chapter of this book.

Whereas in Europe both Protestant and Catholic Churches saw a gradual acceleration in the degree of separation of spheres between Church and state (although in predominantly Orthodox areas of post-Communist Europe this process has been to some extent reversed), in Islam the ideal of a universal *ummah* integrating religion, law and politics is still a strong and vibrant idea, especially for those Muslims inspired by the ideologies of Qutb (see Tripp, 1994) and Maududi (see Nasr, 1994). In relation to Iran, although national and Islamic motives have often coincided, for Khomeini the notion of nationhood was, at root, a secular Western perversion and if it came to a conflict of a conventionally defined 'national' interest and the interest of Islam, Khomeini would always choose Islam.

Indeed, in contrast to the widespread secular perception, from an Islamic perspective it can cogently be argued that the formation of the modern nation states and the operation of modern secular ideologies have led to just as much, if not more, human suffering as have states founded upon religion. The phenomenon of the secular nation state can hardly be uncritically glorified in a century that has seen it give birth to Nazism and the gas chambers, and Stalinism and the gulags. Seen in this light, the basis of the nation state can understandably seem no less dangerous than religious fanaticism.

The Muslim critique of the nation state in fact poses important questions to English society and the British state, in which Muslim values interrogate the adequacy of secular ideologies where religions and religious concerns are relegated to the private margins of society. In the context of 'the Rushdie affair', the Christian theologian Lesslie Newbigin underlined some of the question marks which, from within religious perspectives, can be placed against the nation state. Newbigin pointed out that, with the twentieth-century apotheosis of the nation state:

> The symbols of sacredness now clustered the nation. Blasphemy against God became a meaningless idea; but treason against the state becomes the ultimate crime. Men who die in defence of their religion are ignorant fundamentalists; men who die in defence of their nation are heroes. (Newbigin 1990: 13)

As Haider Reeve (1989), an indigenous English convert to Islam, stated in an article in *The Guardian*, the fatwa 'does not signify a declaration of war; it is an overlap of two totally different systems', since Britain 'is unfamiliar with the concept of temporal authority being vested in religious bodies. It is a while since pope held sway over king in Europe'; while Iran 'in accordance with the principles of Islam does not in theory recognize the concept of nation-states. Religious and temporal authority are combined in one leadership.'

It was, of course, particularly in the light of the Ayatollah Khomeini's fatwa and the apparent eagerness of some Muslims to execute that fatwa themselves that the Muslim position became particularly vulnerable to charges about lack of civil loyalty. This is because Muslims who actively or tacitly supported this course of action appeared to be appealing not so much to the tension between a universal religious community and a particular nation state as to the right of the Iranian state to interfere in the internal affairs of the British state. Such suspicions were further reinforced during the Gulf War over Kuwait in which Muslims were suspected by many of being potentially, if not actually, disloyal. As Philip Lewis, writing in the early years of 'the Rushdie affair' pointed out, 'Muslims in Britain have still to work out a pattern of relationship with the wider Muslim community – Ummah – which does not suggest that their agenda is being dictated by external Muslim powers' (1990: 34).

There is, however, evidence that, while affirming their international community in the *ummah*, even during the early years of 'the Rushdie affair', Muslims were beginning to recognize something of the force of critiques about their relationship with external political powers. For example, in his background paper to a national Muslim conference of 29 April 1990, called by the Bradford Council of Mosques, Asaf Hussain, author of *Beyond Islamic Fundamentalism* (Hussain, 1992), argued strongly that 'foreign funding produces foreign mouth-pieces which do not address the problems confronting the Muslim community in Britain' (quoted in Lewis, 1990: 34). By contrast with a Muslim stance that finds its points of reference outside of the country, the (now deceased) Muslim leader Sheikh Zaki Badawi (in *The Guardian*, 27.2.89c) pointed out that:

> Muslims who have come to live in Britain have come to a tacit concordat to obey British law. Only if the secular authorities prevent them carrying out their individual Islamic duties – like praying – does our teaching allow them to disobey.

But by demanding recognition primarily on the basis of religious identity, Muslims have been posing fundamental questions to British society. In a cultural milieu in which ethnicity, nationality, class and lifestyle had (arguably until the impact of 'the Rushdie affair') been seen as the major determining factors of individual and corporate identity, for a group to define itself primarily in terms of religious identity represented a major break with the prevailing social ethos. It was therefore perhaps not surprising that secular people of good will were somewhat taken aback to find that many Muslims were insisting that they did not want to be dealt with as an 'ethnic minority group' or in terms of 'race relations' considerations. Thus, one of the questions that 'the Rushdie affair' put on the agenda was whether the *corpus Christianum* – which was *de jure* represented by the continuation of the establishment of the Church of England – had been replaced *de facto* by a *corpus Saecularum* that, perhaps, like the *corpus Christianum*, could only conceive of its modification or removal as necessarily leading to anarchy and chaos.

In a society in which religious and cultural pluralization continues apace, when the questions around unity and fragmentation in civil society that were raised directly by 'the Rushdie affair' are revisited 'on the other side of the looking glass'/'the other side of terror/the War on Terror', they re-appear in connection with issues identified as being to do with 'social cohesion'; 'integration' (now used in a way more closely aligned in meaning to 'assimilation' than when both were clearly distinguished); and 'religious extremism'.

But before engaging with these issues as later reprised, it is important also to consider questions of unity and fragmentation in connection with the question of the extent to which shared values might be held or not, and which can be explored in particular through the relationships between religion and art, art as religion, and religion as art. It is possible that, in the process of this, the classical social scientific and modern distinction between the 'public' and 'private' domains will have at least to be modified, while the possibility or otherwise of 'shared values' will need to be engaged with. There might then be implications for all in any approach that might be taken to matters of artistic production and dissemination in a society that is religiously and culturally plural. It is therefore to a broader discussion of these matters, but as they arise directly from 'the Rushdie affair', that the following section of this chapter now turns.

In European history, secularization signifies that process by which religious beliefs have been relativized in relation to the elevation of individual subjectivity and the emancipation of social structures from religious control. Writing in *The Independent*, Matthew Hoffman (1989) speculated that the Rushdie affair:

> may prove to be just a chapter in a Muslim recapitulation of the history of Christianity, in which it will eventually adopt the values of the west. . . . Ironically, it may find that it has taken on the principles of the same spirit of individualism that defeated a once triumphalist Christianity. Despite great setbacks, the values crystallised in the Enlightenment continue, in the modern phrase, to set the agenda.

Religions and the Secular

The Secular and the Rise of Toleration

It is often argued that it has been the rise of the secular spirit, and its adoption by states and societies, that has enabled some degree of religious coexistence and has overcome the inheritance of religious absolutism. In the judgement of post-Enlightenment secular liberals, religions have been responsible for an enormous amount of bloodshed and human suffering and the *Satanic Verses* controversy is only the latest episode to confirm that religions should be marginalized from public life. As Professor Meghnad Desai of the London School of

Economics commented in a brief letter to the editor of *The Independent* (22.2.89), referring to Marx's famous 'opium of the people' dictum on religion, it can be argued that religion is in fact even more dangerous than opium, while in another letter to the editor (*The Independent*, 17.2.89) Arnold Wesker pointed out how much evil had been carried out in the name of religion.

There is undoubtedly considerable truth in the argument that the rise of the secular spirit in philosophy and art coincided with the rise of religious toleration, and the argument that a secular state can better deal with the plural nature of modern societies than the inheritance of establishment is a powerful one which needs to be considered. However, the precise definition of a 'secular state' is not uncontested (see Weller, 2006a) and how far a secular state can actually allow the full participation and contribution of religions depends upon the question of what is meant by secular in the context of a particular society and state.

According to context this may, for example, imply the exclusion of religions from the public sphere; the creation of an arena in which religious participation is not ruled out, but in which religious communalisms are to be challenged; or may be the product of religious motivations leading to the constitutional entrenchment of disestablishment and religious freedom. A 'secular state' may, therefore, not necessarily entail non-religious or anti-religious presuppositions.

Secularization and Contested Meanings

What is signified by the concept of secularization has clearly brought something distinctively and significantly challenging to all religions. However, an enormous amount has been written about the nature and meaning of the process identified as 'secularization', and the meanings associated with this are neither unified nor uncontested (Martin, 1978; Dobbelaere, 1981, 1984, 1988b; Bruce, 1992; Barker, Beckford and Dobbelaere, eds., 1993). The sociologist of religion, Bryan Wilson (1966: 14), characterized secularization as 'the process whereby religious thinking, practice and institutions lose social significance'.

Another definition, also from within the sociology of religion, came from Peter Berger, who defines secularization as 'the process by which sectors of society and culture are removed from the domination of religious institutions and symbols' (1967: 107). Both of these definitions have in common a position concerning the role of religion in the public sphere rather than an argument, as often popularly presented from the 1960s onwards, concerning an overall decline in religious belief and practice.

Christian orthodoxy has certainly declined (Abrams, Gerard and Timms, eds., 1985; Ashford and Timms, 1992; Barker, Halman and Vloet, n.d.). However, a large proportion of the population still share many 'folk beliefs' related to Christianity and the significance of this should not be underestimated. The arrival of the relatively new migrant and minority ethnic communities and the religious traditions associated with them have brought new configurations to the previous social and religious equations. As Parsons points out, 'the factors involved in the interaction between these traditions and the predominant religious and cultural traditions of recent and contemporary Britain are immensely complex' (1994b: 10). As a consequence, in their interaction with both Christianity and secularity, Parsons argued that:

> The responses may be in the direction of adaptation, adjustment, assimilation or accommodation; or they may be in the direction of reassertion, renewed vigour, restated distinctiveness or resistance. But whichever the direction of the response, there will have been change; for even the fiercest reassertions of distinctive and traditional identity will have been given new dimensions precisely by virtue of the new context and challenge which has produced the 'return' to tradition. (Parsons (1994b: 11)

For the time being, the religious traditions of minority ethnic communities have proved to have a considerable resilience to the secular challenge while playing a critical social role in terms of the reinforcement of identity in a minority context. But these traditions are also increasingly being used as a resource not only in the definition and protection of self-identity, but also as critiques of the dominant social patterns of the wider society. For example, in the context of 'the Rushdie affair' and the challenges that he perceived it posed to western societies, in an interview with Hugo Young, Kalim Siddiqui (in *The Guardian*, 24.11.89) talked of 'the filth of western culture'. He claimed that 'Rampant secularism is going to destroy mankind' and alleged that 'Christians have surrendered to the onrush of secular civilisation'.

Identity Politics

'The Rushdie affair' reinforced the arguments of those such as Vincent Cable (1994) who, in his Demos pamphlet, *The World's New Fissures: Identities in Crisis*, identified the religious and the cultural as key variants of the new identity politics through which contemporary global and social fissures are given expression. As a consequence, with the end of the ideological Cold War between capitalism and communism (Dickstein, 1993), political analysts such as Samuel Huntington (1993, 1996) saw the next global conflict as being along the fault lines of civilizations defined in terms of culture and religion rather than political ideology and Huntington suggested that the Christendom/Islamic fault line is one of the most critical of these.

One of the implications of the rise of this 'identity politics' is that religion, previously consigned by secular post-Enlightenment liberalism and Marxism to the sphere of the private, the marginal and the superstructural, once again makes its appearance in the public sphere in the guise of chosen corporate and personal identities (Beyer, 1990). The space for its resurgence has, ironically, in many ways been created by the postmodernist elevation of identity, even though the forms in which such identities are sometimes expressed can run counter to postmodernist relativist philosophical presuppositions (Inayatullah, 1990).

In the statements of political and philosophical liberals and postmodernists who do not wish to take account of religious identity, is there perhaps more than just a hint of the kind of position which fails to see its own tendency to absolutize its assumptions and which therefore cannot acknowledge its own weaknesses? Are the secular reactions to the controversy perhaps secularized versions of the kind of crusading Christian anti-Islam sentiment which Richard Webster (1990) warned against in his study of blasphemy within the historical triangle of relationships between Islam, Christianity and Judaism? As Bishop Jim Thompson (1989) pointed out:

> It is a sober fact that Muslims in east London have been made homeless, harassed, discriminated against, even murdered, and their voice was not heard, but when their religion took the stage, everyone reacted. Their faith threatened the secular consensus which, whilst allowing religion to potter on, does not want it to interfere with life.

At the same time, as Badawi (in *The Guardian*, 27.2.89c) observed of what appeared to be the general Muslim position in the controversy: 'Even our friends are reacting with despair and disgust, fearing a narrow-minded return to the Middle Ages. Race relations have been set back 20 years – and I shudder to think what would happen if Rushdie were killed.'

Dealing With What Is

Whatever one's judgement on the precise relationship between religion, ethnicity, secularity and other significant factors in identity such as social class, 'the Rushdie affair' made it clear that, in the context of a growing assertion of Islamic and other religious identities, unless the 'powers that be' learned to deal with people as they were defining themselves, including in religious terms, then what has since that time come to be identified as 'social cohesion' could be in danger. At the same time, the secular inheritance is a central and significant feature of British, European and North American societies and Muslims need more thoroughly to address a range of questions about the role of the secular in a non-Islamic society.

As Lewis (1990: 34) pointed out, it is not without significance that, in the Urdu language, there is no exact equivalent for the word 'secular'. In addition, the terms that are used to translate the English language concept into Urdu connote 'irreligious' in a sense of the word that conveys overtones of immorality. Around the time of the controversy, one of its key public figures, Shabbir Akhtar, undertook a serious Muslim engagement with the secular in his *A Faith For All Seasons* (1990a) and other Muslims have also been engaged in a similar task. But it is clear that if the construction and sustenance of a multicultural society containing a plurality of values and beliefs is to remain a viable project, then a commitment to creative dialogue rather than a fundamental antagonism between religious and secular people is an essential component of this and the question of what socio-religious structural arrangements might retard or facilitate this dialogue is one of the 'entails' of the controversy.

As a part of this dialogue, religious people – and in the present context, Muslims – will need to learn not to be so ready to equate secular with irreligious in the moral sense, and secular people to learn not to make a simplistic equation between Islam and fundamentalism. Fuentes (1989) argued that, if *The Satanic Verses* were understood properly, then 'Salman Rushdie has done the true religious spirit a service by brilliantly imagining the tensions and complements that it establishes with the secular spirit.' Here Fuentes is arguing for a dialogue with religious perspectives to which the secular artistic spirit can positively contribute. The difficulty is that often the methodology of the novel – of exploratory tentativeness, of 'unfinishedness', of fragmentary and contradictory truths – all too easily becomes an epistemology that liberal intellectuals demand dialogue partners must sign up to as a precondition of dialogue.

To many outside of the Muslim community, 'the Rushdie affair' appeared to be a replay of the conflicts of earlier European centuries between the secular Enlightenment and what is perceived to be religious obscurantism or extremism, while from within the Muslim community, the challenge of the secular was often perceived as threatening to the wider public role of religion. The integrity of religions demands that they do not betray their inheritance of making truth-claims that relate to the public sphere. While a religion will often be personal, to attempt to make it only applicable in a 'private' sphere is to undermine its integrity, certainly with regard to Islam and fundamentally for Christianity, too, despite the influence of secularization.

Religion, Art and Values in Contention
Religion and Art and Art as Religion

In relation to the question of whether a paperback edition of *The Satanic Verses* should have been published, John Berger (1989) argued that, if Rushdie 'is not caught in a chain of events of which he has completely lost control' then he might ask his publishers to prevent the publication of further editions for the sake of the innocent in the controversy; otherwise, he warned, in words that, with the benefit of hindsight, seem uncannily to prefigure many later developments, that: 'a unique 20th century Holy War, with its terrifying righteousness on both sides, may be on the point of breaking out sporadically but repeatedly in airports, shopping streets, suburbia, city centres, wherever the unprotected live'.

The historian of religion Gerald Parsons pointed out that, even where religiosity has no socially sanctioned means of influence, 'the Rushdie affair' has underlined its continuing significance. Thus:

It was the Rushdie affair . . . that stood as the most compelling and potent symbol of the resurgence and continuing relevance of questions about the claims and status of religion in late twentieth-century Britain. This was not only because it raised so many complex and demanding questions about the relationships between race, ethnicity and religion, but also because of the particular concept and issue that lay at the heart of the matter. The allegation against Rushdie was one of blasphemy: a quintessentially and fundamentally religious accusation. (Parsons 1994b: 17)

In connection with the tension between the religious and secular perspectives focused by 'the Rushdie affair', Tariq Modood made what the sociologist of religion Grace Davie describes as a 'hard-hitting, indeed almost shocking statement' (1994: 65) to the effect that:

> 'the Rushdie affair' is not about the life of Salman Rushdie nor freedom of expression, let alone about Islamic fundamentalism or book-burning or Iranian interference in British affairs. The issue is one of the rights of non-European religious and cultural minorities in the context of a secular hegemony. Is the Enlightenment big enough to legitimize the existence of pre-Enlightenment religious enthusiasm or can it only exist by suffocating all who fail to be overawed by its intellectual brilliance and vision of man? (Modood, 1990d: 160)

At popular street level it was the perceived diminution of the Prophet, the sexual language, and issues of communal honour that were among the strongest motivating factors for protest. But for those who could read it in an intellectualized way, *The Satanic Verses* was also troubling at a philosophical and theological level. This was because of the way in which Rushdie associated claims to revelation with the postmodern condition of general doubt and moral relativism. As Malise Ruthven put it, '*The Satanic Verses* . . . is a kind of "anti-Qur'an", which challenges the original by substituting for the latter's certainties a theology of doubt' (1991: 17). In connection with this, Shabbir Akhtar (1989a) commented that 'Rushdie's attack on the authoritative integrity of a fallible Koran is part of a larger indictment of Islam as a faith which routinely confuses good with evil, divine with diabolical imperative.'

Traditional Islamic epistemologies had often been critiqued before, including from within the Muslim cultural tradition itself. So, although these concerns did form part of the response articulated to the controversy by Muslim intellectuals and community leaders, it was the other – emotional outrage – aspects of the response to the book that were the more visible and extensive among ordinary Muslims. But it was also the case that, even in its philosophical dimensions, as Akhtar put it in conversation with Hugh Hebert, in *The Guardian* (9.5.89): 'The book does actually revive the medieval idea that nothing can explain the phenomenal success of Islam in the world other than the work of the Devil.'

For example, Rushdie describes Mahound as a 'businessman' doing 'deals' with the archangel in which the archangel was 'obliging' by reducing the original forty prayers a day to five obligatory prayers in what was summarized as being a 'revelation of convenience'. Mahound's revelations are described as 'spouting rules about every damn thing. If a man farts let him turn his face to the wind . . . which sexual positions had received divine sanction, so that they learned that sodomy and the missionary position were approved' (Rushdie, 1988: 363).

Values and Stability

In an article on the Muslim community written in the early days of the controversy, Sarah Helm (in *The Independent*, 28.1.89) points out that 'Muslims are in a state of hiatus, with little consensus about how far to integrate, how far to withstand the dilution of their faith and codes of conduct by British culture.' This is despite the fact that many of the Muslim organizations reflect subcontinental forms of Islam that were evolved specifically on the basis of differing responses to a non-Islamic environment of minority Muslim communities under the British colonial rule of India (Hardy, 1972). Helm observed that up until now 'The debate over how far Muslims should compromise their values has been fiercest in education' but that 'The Rushdie affair shows it spreading to broader cultural and legal questions' and that 'The issue is being watched by Home Office race relations advisors who see it as a potential source for increasing conflict' (*The Independent*, 28.1.89).

The controversy has therefore opened up to debate the possibilities for, and limits to, negotiation between radically different cultural understandings and values. In some ways all of the questions with which the controversy was concerned relate to the area of the unwritten assumptions that hold a society in balance or cause it to collapse. These are not the publicly explicit codes of law enshrined in legal systems, but are to do with the area of values and presuppositions which inform both the broader cultures and the particular ethical, political and legal stances taken by individuals, groups and societies. For Muslims, and for some other observers of the controversy at the time, it was critical that these values are fundamentally religious; while for others, cohesion in a plural society requires a strongly secular social framework to enable it to work.

Thus the Christian theologian, Lesslie Newbigin pointed out that the blasphemy laws were not originally designed to protect the Christian religion but were 'an acknowledgement of the fact that since God is the author and sustainer of our being, to blaspheme him is to inject poison into public life, a poison with more deadly long-term effects than anything offered by the drug merchants' (1990). In connection with this, in his book *The Persistence of Faith*, the Chief Rabbi, Jonathan Sacks argued that:

> as well as a physical ecology, we also inhabit a moral ecology, that network of beliefs, relationships and virtue within which we think, act and discover meaning. For the greater part of human history it has had a religious foundation. But for the past two centuries, in societies like Britain, that basis of belief has been profoundly eroded. And we know too much about ecological systems to suppose that you can remove an element and leave the rest unchanged. There is, if you like, a God-shaped hole in our ozone layer. And it is time that we thought about moral ecology too. (Sacks, 1991: 26–7)

The idea of a 'moral ecology' is a suggestive one which argues that the values and structures of social life, like the elements of the physical ecology, are either being maintained in balance or are being eroded. The elements of such an ecology exist even if we have not been aware of them and only gradually become so through the symptoms of an ecology which has been thrown out of balance. In contrast to a relatively homogeneous society, within a plural society the elements of this ecology and the balances between them are also contested.

Novel Text and Sacred Text

Rushdie, in his piece 'In Good Faith' (1990d), argued for the literary characteristics of the novel as being the form par excellence that expresses and allows people to experience the competing values of the modern and postmodern worlds. This is also very much in line with

Carlos Fuentes' (1989) view that, 'In the novel, realities that are normally separated can meet, establishing a dialogic encounter, a meeting with the other' and that the novel is therefore a 'privileged arena' which can be instrumental in 'bringing together, in tension and dialogue, not only opposing characters, but also different historical ages, social levels, civilisation and other, dawning realities of human life.'

Fuentes (1989) furthermore argued that these very characteristics of the novel are 'born of the very fact that we do not understand one another any longer, because unitary, orthodox language has broken down.' In the light of this he argued that if you 'Impose a unitary language: you kill the novel, but you also kill the society. . . . Fiction is but the expression of the cultural, personal and spiritual diversity of mankind.' This is a view of the novel form which, of course, has epistemological implications and connects with the fact that we are currently in an era in which the old certainties of modernism are also giving way, at least among the philosophical and cultural elites, to a postmodernism of shifting identities, values and approaches, in which the temporary and the provisional are celebrated over and against the traditional objective certainties of both religion and of the modernist, scientific world-view.

Mikhail Bakhtin (1981) has described the contemporary age as being one of 'competitive languages'. Writing in *The Guardian* (31.3.89), and speaking of what he characterized as the 'two tracks of Islamic fundamentalism, and existential, post-Christian modernism', W.L. Webb (1989a) reflected that 'The wonder is . . . that their collision didn't occur before now.' In his piece entitled 'Two books and two notions of the sacred', John Berger (1989) tried to unpack this version of the religious–secular clash in terms of both religious and secular people having a sense of the sacred, but locating it in different ways. Concerning the Qur'an and *The Satanic Verses*, Berger argued that:

> The two books at this moment represent two notions of the sacred. The Koran is a sacred book in the most traditional and profound sense of the term, a text dictated to the Prophet by the Archangel Gabriel, an emissary of the One and Only God. Rushdie's book has become a sacred cause to the European world because it represents the artist's right to freedom of expression. In Europe, as has been pointed out before, art has replaced religion.

Newbigin (1990: 17) argued that, for most of human history, religion has provided the integrative symbols of ultimate meaning within which the diversities of life were enabled to find their coherence, and that 'To acknowledge that ultimate symbol, to reverence the sacred, was the precondition for knowledge and understanding. If that is destroyed, things fall apart.' The phrase 'things fall apart' evokes the early twentieth-century poetry of W.B. Yeats. In 'the Rushdie affair' there is a perception on both sides of the debate, albeit in radically different ways, of 'things falling apart'.

At a number of levels – political, moral and economic – the perception of 'things falling apart' is precisely how many Muslims (and also many people of other religious traditions) perceive a Europe in which knowledge, religion, morality and social organization have become fragmented and are not understood to be part of an organic whole, nor are they related to an objective and externally existing truth. In this perspective, postmodernist relativism is precisely both a symptom and a cause of 'things falling apart'. By contrast, Islam posits a world of objective truths rooted in the perfect revelation of the Qur'an which is concerned for the whole of life, including corporate as well as personal existence. For Muslims, God's revelation provides a context and a foundation for all human knowledge, religion, morality and social organization.

As a critique of this approach from within a Muslim culture and civilization, the Egyptian playwright Kalim Alrawi (in *The Guardian*, 3.3.89) pointed out that 'Islam, in its practice once a tolerant faith, is now the culture of the Book that bears no rivals' and that, within this, the Qur'an is 'the ultimate text'. Alrawi therefore argues, by implication, that 'all other texts are, in one way or another, either commentaries on it, making its mysteries more accessible and promoting its values, or else they are hubristic' and concludes by lamenting that if this trend within Islam continues, then 'Our minds will then be neatly gift wrapped in the pages of the one true text, whose duplication and recitation will be our sole creative outlet.'

What Integrates and How Things Fall Apart

For many western secular people, the originally religious 'centre' of Christendom was replaced by one or another ideology, with Marxism as a particularly powerful force in the earlier part of the twentieth century. In the last decade of that century this ideology also lost its hold as centripetal forces destroyed it in the wake of the collapse of the communist regimes in the former Soviet Union and Eastern and

Central Europe, while China appears to have taken a capitalist pathway in all but name. For many, the postmodernist celebration of noncentredness (Jameson, 1991) and relativism was all that was left. It was this relativism that has been celebrated in the novels of Rushdie, where figures in stories metamorphose and the categories of 'good' and 'evil' appear ambiguous.

A number of those who might understand themselves as 'secular liberals' have also been concerned about 'things falling apart', although their perceptions of the constituents of the moral ozone layer are profoundly different. They are focused upon a sense of threat, which they saw as being embodied in the Bradford book-burning and the Ayatollah Khomeini's fatwa, which absolutist religious understandings of Muslim values appear to pose to the social projects of liberalism and multiculturalism. But in western liberal thought, individual subjectivity has sometimes been elevated so far that, as Martin Hoffman points (1989) out:

> The idea of the free individual whose moral worth is tampered with if he is not allowed to express himself freely, to exercise freedom of conscience, and to learn from others' criticism is, in fact, a quasi-religious construction. It is a religion without god: it puts man at the centre of the moral universe.

For Hoffman, the idea of truth winning out in the marketplace of ideas is one of 'the great postulates of secular humanism'. In contrast, Shabbir Akhtar, in his provocative piece entitled 'The Liberal Inquisition', argued that:

> Both Muslims and their liberal opponents should now shun the dramatic dogmatism of former days and ask themselves: is freedom of speech a negotiable value? Is it a contestable concept? Does the secular clergy have the right to canonise freedom of speech as an absolute value overriding all others? (Akhtar 1989b)

Philip Roth once famously distinguished between reactions to literature in the communist and the capitalist countries on the basis that in totalitarianism 'everything matters and nothing goes', whereas in liberal democracy, 'nothing matters and everything goes'. W.L. Webb argued that it would be a mistake to reduce the affair 'to a simple neo-Victorian opposition between our light and their darkness'. Instead of this, he suggested:

Try seeing the Rushdie affair, pre-Khomeini, for example, as a test case between a culture which knows the price of everything and the value of nothing, where the best lack all conviction, and the passionate intensity of people who do believe no price is too high to pay for obedience to the will of Allah as interpreted by his Imam. (Webb, 1989a)

In the light of 'the Rushdie affair', Fuentes (1989) commented that, '*The Satanic Verses* have pushed the "nothing goes" of intolerance right out into the public squares of indifference. Suddenly, we all realise that everything matters, whether it goes or not.'

'Public' and 'Private'

Modern societies have tried to build themselves on the basis of separating the technical from the moral, the public from the personal, and this has been classically analysed in the sociological distinction between the public and private spheres. With regard to its application to understanding a society with a plurality of cultures, John Rex's seminal essay, 'The Concept of a Multi-Cultural Society'(Rex, 1985), argued for a way forward based upon this classical distinction. But the controversy challenges this separation and, in a conference paper presented on 'Research on Muslims and the Rushdie affair' (Rex, 1990) as well as in his paper on 'The political sociology of a multi-cultural society' (Rex, 1991), Rex himself recognized such a challenge as one of the major entails of 'the Rushdie affair'.

It is the recognition that religion has a concern with the public sphere that has led to the initiation of a search for common values in a plural society. However, the wish to have a set of 'common values' is much more easily expressed than such values are actually identified. In fact, it is arguable that 'the Rushdie affair' has made clear that such a consensus does not exist. Indeed, in the light of the values clashes between autonomy and heteronomy, sacred and secular, objective and absolute, and subjective and provisional epistemologies revealed by 'the Rushdie affair' the question has to be asked as to whether the quest for common values is too idealistic and does not take sufficient account of the distinctive nature of traditions. In the light of the difficulties revealed by 'the Rushdie affair'; there are those within pluralist societies who, instead of seeking for commonalities, advocate a more 'separatist' or 'parallelist' solution to the challenges posed by social and religious plurality. For example, in the light of the controversy Shabbir Akhtar (1989b) commented that:

Those Muslims who find it intolerable to live in a United Kingdom contaminated with the Rushdie virus need to seriously consider the Islamic alternatives of emigration (hijrah) to the House of Islam or a declaration of holy war (jihad) on the House of Rejection.

While cooperation does not require consensus, but rather agreement on some 'commonly accepted practices and procedures,' it neverthe-less has to be recognized that to shift the emphasis from common values to 'commonly accepted practices and procedures' is not to avoid difficulties. Some within religious traditions might fear that such a process would inevitably involve an attempt to water down their non-negotiable values. How does negotiation, with its implicit assumption of the possibility of compromise, relate to the absolute claims that are often made by people within the religious traditions? Are not values, by definition, non-negotiable? Does not the very idea of 'negotiation' prevent the participation of those who make absolute claims, because it presupposes that there are no absolutes?

In response to such concerns, it can be argued that what are viewed as being negotiable are what might be termed 'values outcomes' rather than the values themselves. In such an understanding the focus of the negotiation is shifted from the values themselves, which for many may indeed be the non-negotiable presuppositions of the particular and distinctive position that they bring to the wider, common forum. Instead, the focus of negotiation moves to debate about 'values out-comes' among people with varied convictions and perspectives who must live together in a very diverse society.

Therefore, rather than speaking of 'values negotiation' it might be better to use the rather more clumsy, but perhaps more accurate term of 'values outcomes negotiation'. Here the focus of what is to be nego-tiated is not centred on the diverse and yet underlying values which individuals and communities hold as non-negotiable, but shifts to a process in which people with diverse convictions and perspectives commit themselves to 'holding the ring' for finding what are the most generally acceptable negotiated outcomes of their values for discerning ways of living together in a plural society.

Power and 'Commonly Accepted Values'

When possibilities for contribution to the common debate are denied, then it is inevitable that such figures as Kalim Siddiqui will make the argument that 'A sustained, well-thought-out and controlled campaign, that might also include symbolic breaking of the law and manipulation of the political process, may well be required if the British Muslim community is to secure its proper place in British society' (quoted in *The Guardian*, 3.4.89). But this in turn poses questions back to the wider society. This is because it is through the wider political process that the 'commonly accepted rules' are evolved into law, and it is therefore in relation to these further two clusters of issues concerned with law and with politics that this chapter concludes. But in reflecting on how things work in the 'common sphere' it is important to recognize that, as Webb (1989a) points out:

> . . . the thing about reality is that it's largely a construct of power. In the past we used to send out gunboats to readjust the view in parts of the world where other notions of reality had started to obtrude on ours. But in the precarious democracy of today's melting-pot world that's not such a straightforward operation. We have a rough theory of co-existence, of course, whose rules are followed when more dangerous games can't be got away with, but it's tended to depend fairly heavily on other political constructs like the Berlin Wall. No one quite knows how it works when the protagonists, close neighbours in fact, turn to look at each other with a wild surmise and discover their dismaying proximity and incompatibility.

Against such a background and reflecting carefully upon the issues which 'the Rushdie affair' raises for the negotiation between pluralities of cultures and values, Parekh (1989a) suggested that just as 'We have taken centuries to learn how to explore sexuality in literature without becoming either puritanical or pornographic' so 'religion calls for extremely delicate and sensitive handling.' In fact, he argues that it 'requires a greater degree of sensitivity'. In this connection, Parekh suggested (1989a) an understanding of what religious people mean by the sacred which might also be accessible to secular people:

> By sacred, I mean that which is beyond utilitarian consideration and has an intrinsic or non-instrumental significance, which transcends

and links up individuals with something greater than themselves and gives their lives depth and meaning. The holy represents sacredness anchored in, and defined in, terms of divine principle. Religion is the realm of the holy par excellence, but it does not exhaust sacredness. Even the atheist regards certain relationships, activities, experiences, life and fellow-human beings as sacred. Broadly speaking, holiness is a religious category, sacredness a spiritual category; and respect a moral category.

Mechanisms for Change

Only if these shifts of understanding occur on the part of both secular and religious people will the negotiated development of social structures that enable creative partnerships between Muslims, other religious people and secular people become a real possibility. Initially, however, what the controversy did was to embody the clash of these world-views. Perhaps significantly, while the subsequent Danish 'Cartoons Controversy' convulsed large parts of the media and public opinion across a number of European countries, this did not occur in the UK. Thus one consequence of 'the Rushdie affair' could arguably have been that writers and publishers in the UK did indeed become much more cautious, especially when dealing with stories or images which relate to Islam.

This later history might be seen as a 'deferred victory' for the opponents of *The Satanic Verses*. On the other hand, the supporters of *The Satanic Verses* could claim 'victory' in arguing that the book was never withdrawn from circulation and, indeed, was translated and distributed in many parts of the world, thus vindicating the commitment to freedom of expression and publication. But beyond claimed victories on either side of the debate, the continuing underlying tensions and the outbreaks of occasional specific hostilities mean that the need for dialogue remains. In the words of Jonathan Sacks:

> In a society of plurality and change, there may be no detailed moral consensus that can be inscribed on tablets of stone. But there can and must be a continuing conversation, joined by as many voices as possible, on what makes our society a collective enterprise: a community that embraces many communities. (Sacks 1991: 68)

This was a notion which later came to the fore in the (Parekh) report of the Commission on the Future of Multi-Ethnic Britain (2000), which characterized the UK as a 'community of communities'. But when the issues raised directly by 'the Rushdie affair' in connection with religion and art in a society characterized by religious and cultural plurality are revisited 'on the other side of the looking glass'/'the other side of terror/the War on Terror', they were reprised in debates around *Jerry Springer: The Opera*, the *Behzti* controversy, and the 'Cartoons' controversy. And when the issues of religion and secularity, the 'public' and the 'private' and matters of 'values' re-appeared, they did so in a context where any notion of a 'community of communities' has been largely displaced by language from the 'powers that be' that, instead, has highlighted notions of 'social cohesion' in which 'shared values' and 'Britishness' were being promoted and embodied into public policy.

However, in a democratic society, it is not naked power, but the evolution and exercise of the law that provides basic social frameworks and sanctions. These emerge and are eventually agreed (while being subject in due course to later change) out of a debate between the identified aims of government policy (which may itself to a greater or lesser extent reflect popular concerns and issues); representations made to Government and Parliament by professional and other special interest groups, as well as the general public; and the input of judges and lawyers in relation to matters of legal tradition, precedent, interpretation and application. It is therefore to the area of the law that the next section of this chapter turns.

Law in Contention: Rights and Restraints

The Challenge of Living in Diaspora

Referring to a July 1989 meeting of the Union of Muslim Organisations with Douglas Hurd and John Patten, *The Sunday Times* (9.7.89) reported that:

> The official government line is that ministers are anxious to maintain a 'constructive dialogue' with Muslim leaders and listen to grievances. But privately, they are known to be worried about the breadth of the issues now being thrown up by the Rushdie affair.

The column argued that 'The Rushdie affair has acted as a catalyst and a rallying point for an increasingly militant community that is demanding the right to a separate lifestyle governed by its own laws.' In Muslim understanding, of course, fundamentally religion and law are not separate entities concerned with separate spheres. This is because the sharia is the unified and holistic path in which Muslims should live. Thus Muslims aspire to live in a society in which individual and corporate existence are fully integrated as a seamless Islamic whole (Ferdinand and Mozaffari, eds., 1988; Khuri, 1990).

At the same time, when living outside of the sphere where Islam is predominant, Muslims are likely to seek for as much community autonomy as possible to enable as full an actualization of all the dimensions of faith (Speelman, 1995). Indeed, the idea of spheres of limited community autonomy within a wider whole is precisely the classical way (Breiner, 1995a, 1995b) in which predominantly Muslim societies have sought to accommodate the existence of non-Muslim minorities in their midst, as will be explored in a little more detail in the closing section of this chapter.

Law, Religion and Morality in Evolution

In the European and English situation in which 'the Rushdie affair' arose, the relationship between religion and the law has always been problematic (Mitchell, 1967; Berman, 1974; Blom-Cooper and Drewry, 1976). In the context of the Constantinian religion-state settlement there were originally both secular and ecclesiastical courts and, as English law evolved into a unified system, it did so on the basis of integrating aspects of ecclesiastical law into the developing common and statute law. This inheritance manifested itself particularly in respect of laws governing matters of personal and sexual morality. Consequently, in the 1960s, with the impact of secularization upon prevailing patterns of belief and morality, there was much debate about the relationship between religious belief and public law as, for example, in the debates on sexuality following the 1957 Wolfenden Report which recommended the decriminalization of private homosexual activity between consenting adults (Davies, 1989).

These debates led to a string of legislative changes at the interface between personal, religious and public moralities. In 1967, the Abortion Act legalized abortion if two doctors agreed that the operation was justifiable on grounds of psychological or medical health. Also in 1967, the Sexual Offences Act decriminalized homosexual activity in private between consenting adults (with some exceptions including, for example, serving members of the armed forces). In 1969, the Divorce Reform Act removed the idea of 'matrimonial offence' as the only ground for divorce, offering the alternative concept of 'irretrievable breakdown'.

The locus of conflict over the relationship between religion and the law has very often been at the interface of religion, state and sexuality, with debates between positions advocating moral and social arguments in favour of some degree of censorship and artistic claims to complete creative freedom. For example, in 1960, Penguin Books were prosecuted under the Obscene Publications Act for publishing a full version of D.H. Lawrence's book, *Lady Chatterley's Lover*. Following Penguin Books' acquittal the boundaries of censorship began to roll back. In 1968, theatre censorship was abolished and cinema censorship was liberalized with local authorities managing the licensing system in their areas. This, however, resulted in some varied decisions in different local authority areas as, for example, in 1979 when the film *The Life of Brian*, which contained jokes about the crucifixion, was banned in some local areas and screened in others.

In the context of 'the Rushdie affair' it has already been noted that, on 24 October 1988, the Islamic Society for the Promotion of Religious Tolerance held a conference to discuss *The Satanic Verses* in conjunction with Martin Scorsese's film of Nikos Kazantzakis' 1951 novel, *The Last Temptation of Christ* (Kazantzakis, 1985), the publication and distribution of which had already been opposed in North America by an alliance of Conservative Protestants and Roman Catholics who saw it as blasphemous in its portrayal of Jesus fantasizing about a sexual relationship with Mary Magdalene.

In the UK, it was reported in *New Life* (16.9.88) that a number of Muslim groups supported those Christians who called for the film of the book to be banned. As has already been noted, the Leicester MP Keith Vaz, later also to play a prominent part in the campaign against *The Satanic Verses*, had opposed screening of the film. It was also arising from this conference that the Islamic Society for the Promotion of Tolerance originally aimed to get an historical note of correction inserted in *The Satanic Verses*, distinguishing it from historical fact, but failure to achieve this or other similar measures proposed by other Muslim organizations eventually led to the emergence of calls for the prosecution of the novel's author and publishers under the terms of the blasphemy laws.

Blasphemy Laws in British History

In 1949, Lord Denning had said of the blasphemy law that:

> The reason for this law was because it was thought that a denial of
> Christianity was liable to shake the fabric of society, which was itself
> founded on the Christian religion. There is no such danger to society
> now and the offence of blasphemy is a dead letter. (1949: 46)

This perception at the time was confirmed by the disbandment, in
1959, of the Society for the Abolition of the Blasphemy Laws. In
England and Wales, the laws of blasphemy and blasphemous libel that
were current at the time of 'the Rushdie affair' were not part of statute
law enacted by Parliament, but arose from the history in which, before
the restoration of the monarchy, offences against morality and religion
were in the jurisdiction of ecclesiastical courts and the Court of Star
Chamber. It was following a 1676 case against one Taylor who
declared that 'Jesus Christ was a bastard, an imposter and a cheat' that
common law was used against blasphemy.

As part of the common law inheritance, interpreted in its application
by custom and case law, blasphemy in books became, broadly speaking, defined as something concerned with the publication of scurrilous,
offensive or abusive matter concerning God, Christ, the Christian
religion, the Bible or a sacred subject while the offence of blasphemous
libel appears to have related specifically to attacks upon the tenets of
the Church of England (see Nokes, 1928). The Blasphemy Act of 1697
disqualified from 'Ecclesiastical, Civil or Military' office anyone who
had been brought up in or professed faith in Christianity and who then
denied its truth, the inspiration of the Bible or Trinitarian doctrine,
or who advocated polytheism. The provision relating to Trinitarian
belief was abolished in the eighteenth century, but the rest of the Act
actually remained on the statute book until, on the advice of the Law
Commission, the 1967 Criminal Law Act removed it.

Publication of Tom Paine's book *The Age of Reason* was continually
subject to prosecution, but in the nineteenth century case against
one Richard Carlisle, St John Robilliard (1984: 26) pointed out that it
was decided that 'it was possible to discuss religious topics provided
that this was done with respect and moderation – it must not be
mere scoffing at the subject', thus beginning the distinction which
increasingly came to be made between blasphemy and the temperate
questioning of orthodoxy.

The likelihood of inducing shock, plus the undermining of the foundations of morality, were usually adduced as grounds for prosecution. For example, the journal *The Freethinker* was prosecuted three times for its attacks on Christianity, but Lord Coleridge held that, provided 'the decencies of controversy are observed', the fundamentals of Christianity could be attacked, adducing as evidence the recent changes in the law relating to Jews and other religious minorities. At this time, this was a considerably debated viewpoint, but eventually it became the accepted interpretation.

After the 1911 conviction of Smith, the then Attorney General, Sir John Simon, argued for ending the special protection accorded to the Church of England and also that opinions on religious topics should only be prosecuted if they were put forward in an indecent or obscene way (see Robilliard, 1984: 30). Concern for civil disorder resulting from blasphemy therefore became linked to the manner of expression of ideas rather than to ideas themselves.

The offences had evolved over the years with respect to their meaning and the burden of proof required for conviction. The debates around the definition of what constitutes the offences of blasphemy and blasphemous libel underline the fact that the history of these common-law offences has been very varied. Originally, objective statements and actions were considered sufficient for conviction, but as time went on, the presence of subjective elements had increasingly been thought to be necessary in order to secure a conviction.

At the beginning of the twentieth century there was a series of cases concerning one J.W. Gott who, in 1911, was given a four months' prison sentence for blasphemy; in 1916, fourteen days' hard labour for profanity; in 1917, six weeks for blasphemy; and in 1918, two months for a breach of a Defence of the Realm Order and the persistent sale and distribution of anti-Christian leaflets. At this trial, Judge Avory (in Robilliard, 1984: 31) guided the jury to ask the question: 'if a person of strong religious feelings had stopped to read this pamphlet whether his instinct might not have been to go up to the man who was selling it and give him a thrashing.'

Gott was sentenced to nine months' hard labour, with the Court of Appeal determining that the test for blasphemy should be that 'it must be offensive to any one in sympathy with the Christian religion, whether he be a strong Christian, or a lukewarm Christian, or merely a person sympathising with their ideals'. After this case, however, while arguments around its existence continued (for example, Cohen, 1922), the blasphemy laws themselves fell into disuse, leading to Lord

Denning's conclusion that they had, by the late 1940s, become a dead letter.

The Gay News *Trial and the Modern Revival of the Blasphemy Laws*

However, in the 1970s an attempt was made to revive the laws, beginning with Mary Whitehouse's 1972 complaint to the Director of Public Prosecutions about an episode of *Till Death Do Us Part* in which irreverent remarks were made about the Virgin Birth. The Director of Public Prosecutions thought a blasphemy prosecution unlikely to succeed, but the National Viewers and Listeners Association had received legal advice that it would be possible to bring a common-law prosecution for blasphemy, although the provocation of extreme anger would need to be proved. Then, in 1976, Jens Jorgen Thorsen proposed making a film in Britain that would have shown Jesus in explicit sexual activity with John the Baptist, Mary Magdalene and a Palestinian girl of today. The Archbishop of Canterbury said he would consider invoking the blasphemy law, but in the end the film was never made.

It was, however, the cases of *R v. Lemon* and *R v. Gay News*, brought as successful test case private prosecutions by Mrs Mary Whitehouse (see *All England Law Reports* [1979] 1 All ER, pp. 898–928), that finally revived the use of these laws. The cases concerned the publication of a poem by Professor James Kirkup entitled, 'The love that dares to speak its name'. This portrayed the centurion in attendance at the crucifixion of Jesus as having had homosexual fantasies about him. As in the later controversy over *The Satanic Verses*, this was an instance in which religious and sexual themes were interwoven. Significantly, the issue of subjective intention was not allowed as a defence and, unlike in the case of Gott, it no longer appeared to be necessary to prove a likely breach of the peace. The jury convicted the editor and the paper of blasphemy, with a fine being imposed upon the paper and a suspended sentence on the editor. There was an appeal to the Court of Appeal but this was rejected. A further appeal to the House of Lords was rejected by three votes to two.

Blasphemy Laws, Established Christianity and Other Religious Traditions

Historically, the laws established provided for the prosecution of blasphemy and of blasphemous libel in relation to Christian religion in general and, in particular, to the rites and formularies of the Church of England. The 1838 Gathercole case clarified that attacks on Judaism, Islam or other Christian denominations outside of Established Christianity were not covered by the law although, later in the nineteenth century, the Lords Macauley and Campbell had argued that blasphemy could apply to other religious traditions as well as to Christianity (see Robilliard, 1984: 36).

As noted in the previous section of this chapter that explored the issues of values within a plural society, the approach taken by law is critical in an evolving multicultural and multi-religious society (see Poulter, 1986, 1990a, 1990b) and there are a number of fundamental options here. It is possible to have traditions of law applying rigorously to all, and devolved or partially devolved systems of law applicable to particular communities (Allott, 1990). It is also possible to have more codified and logically consistent codes of law, or those that proceed in a way that is more informed by establishing general rules but also recognizing legitimate exceptions to those rules, as in the general approach of English law (see Bradney, 1993). Examples of this latter tradition in English law include the Slaughterhouses Act and the Slaughter of Poultry Act in which *schechita* and *dbah* slaughter were recognized as permissible for Jews and Muslims, respectively.

While these kinds of wider issues in the relationship between religion, values, law, society and the individual have been debated for many years, they were given particular impetus through 'the Rushdie affair' and its highlighting of the specific issue of the blasphemy laws. It was 'the Rushdie affair' that, as Wolffe put it, 'threw the issues into stark relief' (1994: 101). Of course, even had the blasphemy laws been explicitly extended to include other than Christian religious traditions, it is by no means certain that, in the case of *The Satanic Verses*, there would have been a successful prosecution. To prove that the book had caused outrage might have been done relatively easily. But, in the light of how blasphemy and blasphemous libel had increasingly become interpreted, it would have been more difficult to prove that such outrage was intentionally caused.

When, through 'the Rushdie affair', it became clear that the current terms of reference for the blasphemy laws did not include Islam, the extension of these laws to include Islam and other religions became one of the central demands of the Muslim campaigns, and Muslim leaders called for a change to the current position. Through the controversy the inequity was highlighted that, in England, Christians (and especially those of the established Church of England) had a legal right to seek redress in the courts when they felt that their faith was being maligned, but Muslims were denied that recourse to law while simultaneously they were being criticized for having resorted to symbolic book-burnings and street demonstrations because other possibilities seemed closed to them.

At the height of 'the Rushdie affair', the Home Office made it clear that the Government was not intending to extend the scope of the blasphemy laws. A *Church Times* editorial (24.2.89) argued that the Home Office's decision was, in this respect, 'well judged' on the basis that 'Defining blasphemy for legal purposes would be as difficult as defining religion itself; and if a Bill were ever drawn up and passed, the writs would be endless.' A number of commentators argued that the simple abolition of existing legislation without replacement would give the message that society held nothing to be sacred other than what writers might choose to write. Thus, following a 1989 religious leaders' meeting in Bradford convened by the Bishop of Bradford, it was reported in *The Baptist Times* (2.3.89) that Revd John Nicholson, the then North-East Area Baptist Superintendent, had said, 'We concurred in asking whether there are to be no constraints on freedom of expression. If the answer is no, then should there not be legal redress for non-Christians when material is published they consider blasphemous?'

Abolition or Reform?

In contrast, critics of blasphemy legislation, such as Paul O'Higgins, then Professor of Law at King's College London, argued in a piece entitled 'Relic that has no role' (1989) that 'Today, the crime of blasphemy is an historical accident consisting of the residue of a crime which in its original form should have no place in the 20th century.' In the tradition of such opposition to the blasphemy laws there have long been attempts to abolish them.

In 1886, Professor Courtney Kenny introduced a bill to abolish the law of blasphemy, following the conviction for blasphemy of Foote,

the editor of *The Freethinker*, although his proposals would, nevertheless, still have retained some measure of protection against unwar-
ranted attack upon religions. On 12 April 1898, Charles Bradlaugh,
MP for Northampton, introduced a bill seeking the end of the blasphemy laws. Other bills were introduced in 1890, 1894, 1914, 1922,
1930 and 1936 but all such attempts were unsuccessful including
when, just prior to the *Gay News* case, there was a further attempt on
23 February 1978 to abolish the law without replacement on the
grounds that it was outdated; that particular groups should not be
privileged in law; and that if material was offensive it could be dealt
with under obscenity laws.

This latter attempt at abolition was rejected on the basis that
England, its institutions and monarchy were still basically Christian
and that the law needed to give expression to this because repeal could
give a signal that would unlock the floodgates of attacks upon religion.
But in 1981, in the context of renewed public debate (Blom-Cooper,
1981) on the laws following the *Gay News* case, and as part of
its ongoing review of common law and statutory law, the Law Commission published its Working Paper No. 79 on *Offences Against
Religion and Public Worship*, in which the history of the common-law
offences were outlined and issues surrounding the desirability and
practicability of creating new statutory offences were examined.

After examining a range of arguments, the Commission (1981: paragraph 7.15) concluded that, in the context of 'overwhelming social
pressures, . . . the general presumption in favour of freedom of speech
both as to matter and manner may require modification either for the
benefit of particular members of society or for the benefit of society as
a whole.' It identified incitement to racial hatred as such an issue but,
at that time, seven years prior to the outbreak of 'the Rushdie affair', it
judged that the likely social dangers to result from attacks upon
religion were not so great.

As alternatives to the blasphemy laws, the Law Commission considered the possibility of introducing offences of 'publishing insulting
matter likely to provoke a breach of the peace by outraging the religious
convictions of others' (1981: paragraph 8.3–4); 'incitement to religious
hatred' (1981: paragraph 8.5); and 'publicly insulting the feelings of
religious believers.' On balance, if it were thought expedient to have a
law at all, then the Commissioners (1981: paragraph 8.15) favoured
the first of these options, qualified by the necessity to prove intent and
allowing a valid defence in the instance of attacks upon 'particular
religious sects.'

In 1985, after receiving submissions on this Working Paper from many different organizations, the Commission published its Report No. 145 entitled *Criminal Law Offences Against Religion and Public Worship*. By a majority of three commissioners to two the report recommended abolition of the common-law offences of blasphemy and blasphemous libel without replacement by statute law, on the grounds that 'where members of society have a multiplicity of faiths or none at all it is invidious to single out that religion [the Church of England], albeit in England the established religion, for protection'. However, the two outvoted commissioners felt so strongly that a new statutory offence should be enacted and extended to other religions that they produced a minority Note of Dissent that also appears in the report. In this, they advocated the enactment of a new offence that 'would penalise anyone who published grossly abusive or insulting material relating to religion with the purpose of outraging religious feelings'.

The Issues Refocused

The matter then lay there without action from the government or significant attention from others until the outbreak of 'the Rushdie affair'. During the controversy, however, on 12 April 1989, the centenary of Charles Bradlaugh's bill for the repeal of statutory blasphemy laws, Tony Benn, MP presented to the House of Commons the first formal reading of a Private Member's Bill entitled The Religious Prosecutions (Abolition) Bill (*Church Times*, 21.4.89), which was again unsuccessful although supported by MPs of all parties including Sir David Steel and Sir Ian Gilmour.

The Committee Against the Blasphemy Law, including supporters such as Bernard Crick, David Edgar, Glenda Jackson, Dennis Potter, Jill Tweedie and others, wrote a letter to the editor of *The Guardian* (30.5.89) opposing the Muslim campaign to extend the law on the grounds that it would restrict freedom and encourage fanaticism. Among the general public, a survey of 1,792 people over the age of 15 questioned by the Public Attitude Survey (see *The Independent*, 10.10.89a) suggested that one in three people would like the blasphemy law scrapped altogether, with an equal proportion wanting it extended to cover other religious traditions, whilst 7 per cent believed it should remain solely related to Christianity. Perhaps not surprisingly, most atheists were in favour of abolishing the laws while nearly all Muslims wanted it extended to cover Islam.

As Wolffe summarized the issues as they were thrown up by 'the Rushdie affair' around these matters: 'The problem, in a nutshell, was whether the law should treat England as a secular society in which religion had no special protection; or as a multi-religious one in which all faiths were accorded some legal recognition' (1994: 101). Debates about the blasphemy laws therefore link intimately with the debates about secularization, secularity and secularism as well as with issues of religious, cultural and values plurality that have been explored earlier in this chapter. As explained in a piece in *The Times*, John Vincent – then Professor of History at Bristol University – agued that protection should be given to Islam under blasphemy legislation. With regard to the Law Commission's arguments for and against extension of these laws, he concluded that 'The balance is still a fine one. The arguments have not changed, but the sociology has' (Vincent, 1989), citing the significantly changed composition of English society.

As previously noted, following a 31 July 1989 meeting between the Archbishop of Canterbury, the Archbishop of York, the Bishop of Bradford, Phillip Lewis (the Bishop of Bradford's Adviser on Inter-Faith Relations) and Revd Graham James, the Archbishop's chaplain, together with eight leading Muslims, a joint six-person working group was set up with Muslim representatives to explore the law in relation to the protection of religious sensibilities. A *Church Times* editorial (11.8.89) on 'Talking to Islam' commented that 'the law is a weapon of doubtful usefulness against blasphemy; yet, if the group were to say so, the disappointment of a failure at the outset would be intense and damaging.'

From within the minority religious communities, in *The Jewish Chronicle* (10.3.89b) Philip Kleinman argued against the Chief Rabbi's proposals for the extension of blasphemy legislation on the grounds that 'For the one-time Christian monopoly of published opinion, the Chief Rabbi apparently wants to substitute an ecumenical cartel in which purveyors of all brands of religious nonsense will be protected from criticism.'

While the issues around these laws were pointed up sharply during the opening years of 'the Rushdie affair', for many years afterwards the common-law provisions remained, being neither abolished nor reformed. As such, they were a continuing reminder of the enshrined privilege in the structures of the state and of society for one section of one religious community as well as being a reminder of the exclusion of others. Having failed to make progress by means of the blasphemy laws, Muslim attention shifted to the use to which other legal instruments might be put with respect to the matters at stake in 'the Rushdie affair', including, for example, the possibilities relating to defamation, group libel or incitement to religious hatred.

In doing so, they found resonance with the position adopted by a number of other religious, social and legal commentators, who did not favour extending the blasphemy laws, but who did feel that there should be some legal provisions in place for the protection of religious sensibilities. In considering both the issues and the other potential legal instruments, writing in *The Guardian* (3.3.89c), Melanie Phillips (1989) argued that:

> There is a significant difference between curtailing free expression so as not to give offence and doing so to protect the civil rights or physical safety of minority communities. That's why the blasphemy law is wrong but the Race Relations Act or Public Order Act are right.

This broad approach was also supported by Professor Simon Lee (1990, 1993), now Vice Chancellor of Leeds Metropolitan University, but then a legal academic with a special interest in religion and law. Often seen to be of relevance at the time, too, was an appeal to international law that was followed by debates around the possibility of incorporating the European Convention of Human Rights and Fundamental Freedoms into UK law. This was seen as particularly important since, in the absence of a written constitution in the UK, there were no written constitutional guarantees in English law with respect to religion, but the UK Government is a signatory to the European Convention on Human Rights, which provided a channel of appeal beyond UK law and could affect the interpretation and application of national law. With regard to religion, the Convention includes Article 9, stating that:

1. Everyone has the right to freedom of thought, conscience and religion; this right includes freedom to change his religion or belief and freedom, either alone or in community with others and in public or private, to manifest his religion or belief, in worship, teaching, practice and observance.
2. Freedom to manifest one's religion or beliefs shall be subject only to such limitations as are prescribed by law and are necessary in a democratic society in the interests of public order, health or morals, or for the protection of the rights and freedoms of others.

The debates connected with all of these issues raised directly by 'the Rushdie affair' have rumbled on (see Simpson, 1993) over the past two decades – and especially those concerned with legal protection for religious sensibilities. But when revisited 'on the other side of the looking glass'/'the other side of terror/the War on Terror', these particular issues were reprised in contexts in which some relatively settled new legal outcomes had been brought about that significantly changed the legal territory with regard to matters of religious discrimination and equity, blasphemy and incitement to religious hatred.

Together with these changes also came new challenges arising from the contested relationship between the different 'equalities strands', and the impact of legislation designed to tackle terrorism. At the same time, new challenges connected with the interface between law and religion emerged – not least in relation to the balance and tension between the different equalities 'strands' (gender, ethnicity, disability, age, sexual orientation, and religion and belief) in equality and human rights law, policy and strategy. And also, new and highly sensitive issues have emerged with regard to the relationship between freedom of thought and expression (including that related to religion) and what might be considered to constitute the promotion or support of terrorism.

Some of these new challenges will be explored in the final chapter of the book, together with an outline of the new developments that have occurred since 'the Rushdie affair'. However, since law is both made and changed through elected representatives, the final section of this chapter will explore the way in which, at the height of 'the Rushdie affair' itself, the relative powerlessness of Muslims within the political structures and processes of British society was exposed.

Political Representation and Participation in a Plural Society

Muslims and Politics in the UK

Mohammed Ajeeb who, in 1985, had been appointed as Bradford's first Asian and Muslim Lord Mayor, pointed out (in *The Sydney Morning Herald*, 20.2.89) that there had been years of political frustration and oppression for Bradford Muslims and that 'Muslims feel totally ignored by this society. They cannot attack this book in the courts because the blasphemy law only covers Christianity. They talk and write letters and are ignored – and so their frustrations erupt.' The 'entails' of 'the Rushdie affair', when brought into conjunction with wider relevant social, religious, cultural, legal and political trends and developments, both signalled and contributed to a critical moment in relation to then current arrangements in the relationships between religion(s), state and society in England within the UK state.

At the operational level of politics, the majority of the Muslim population in the UK traditionally looked to the Labour Party to represent their interests and aspirations as members of minority ethnic communities suffering from racism and discrimination on the basis of skin pigmentation and ethnicity. But among Muslims who were being radicalized on the basis of Islam, there was increasing debate about the role of electoral politics (Andrews, 1996), while among the broad swathe of Muslims there was an increasing sense that the Labour Party was failing to support their specific interests as Muslims (see also McLoughlin, 1996) as, for example, in the widespread Labour reluctance to support public funding for Muslim voluntary-aided schools.

Muslims and the Labour Party

In the context of 'the Rushdie affair', this perception of Labour indifference to Muslim concerns was heightened when the then Labour Party Leader, Neil Kinnock (reported in *New Life*, 21.7.89b), met with Salman Rushdie socially at a mutual friend's house, and defended his right to publish. Outside of the Bradford epicentre of the controversy where, due to electoral demographics, the local Labour MPs had little choice but to try and accommodate Muslim concerns, it was left to Labour's then only Asian Member of Parliament, Keith Vaz, to come out firmly in support of the Muslim community's case. In *New Life* (14.4.89b), Vaz argued that the issue would be a turning point in community perceptions of the Labour Party. Dr Michael Le Lohe (quoted in *The Sunday Times*, 9.7.89), a politics lecturer at Bradford University and a Labour Party member, corroborated this view of the controversy when he concluded that 'It could cause the Labour Party terrible problems. I think this will become a long-term constitutional problem for the Labour Party.'

In July of 1989 *The Islamic Charter* was issued and distributed through the mosques. In this charter, Muslims were urged not to vote for any candidate who did not support them in the Rushdie issue. In *The Sunday Times* of 9.7.89, Sher Azam was quoted as explaining that

'In the past large numbers of Muslims have supported the Labour
Party; we are now saying we shall not support any political party that
does not support us.' Michael Le Lohe calculated (see *The Guardian*,
22.7.89b) that ten or more Parliamentary seats were at risk from
such a tactic and it is increasingly clear that Muslims have significant
influence and power in some local politics and at the level of some
Parliamentary constituencies. *The Independent* editorial (18.2.89)
entitled 'Limits to mutual tolerance' pointed out that:

> Already Labour councillors and members of parliament in places
> with a high proportion of Muslims find it expedient to express an
> understanding of practices and values which they would be tempted
> to denounce as reactionary if embraced by the Anglican church.

The Emergence of Muslim Political Platforms

The increasing dissatisfaction with Labour and frustration at lack
of progress on 'the Rushdie affair' resulted in independent Muslim
candidates standing in local elections in May 1989. However, no
independent Muslim candidate managed to unseat a Labour councillor and, despite the general dissatisfaction with the Labour Party
nationally, the divided evaluations of this approach can be illustrated
by what happened in local elections in the Leicester area (*New Life*,
14.4.89d) where two Muslim independent candidates – Mr Ibrahim
Bayat and Mr Ismail Mullah – ran, respectively, for a city council
by-election and the 4 May 1989 County Council election. Jacob Khan,
chair of the Leicestershire Pakistani Association, supported these
moves, while Mohammed Butt, chair of the Pakistan Welfare Association, argued that the issue should be pursued within existing parties,
thus representing the bifurcation of Muslim approaches to politics that
was highlighted by the controversy.

The Independent reported (14.9.89) that, on 13 September 1989,
with the publication of its manifesto *The Way Ahead*, the Islamic Party
of Great Britain had been launched at the Regent's Park Mosque in
London. The manifesto stated that the party's aim was to provide
'effective, adequate representation of Islamic principles in the UK' and
to 'present a viable political, economic and social alternative to the
British people' (quoted in *The Independent*, 14.9.89). The party was
led by an English convert to Islam, Daud Musa Pidcock, and its secretary was Mustaqim Bleher, a German convert. At the party's launch,

six of the twelve speakers were white converts to Islam or, as Muslims would prefer it to be expressed, 'reverts'.

The party's launch underlined the extent of the challenge which religious plurality was beginning to pose to existing political parties in terms of the adequacy of the representation they had been providing for the concerns of cultural and religious minorities. The *Muslim News* (22.9.89) argued that the launch of the Islamic Party of Great Britain 'is the result of dissatisfaction amongst Muslims with the traditional parties', although an editorial (15.9.89) in *New Life* had expressed doubt that the party would secure the support of even a small number of Muslims.

Maulana Abdur Rahim, director of the Sparkbrook Islamic Centre in Birmingham, stated that 'I don't think an Islamic party is appropriate' and that 'It's not in the best interests of the Muslim community to have a segregated political party', while Zaki Badawi commented on the party's leaders that 'Few have any roots in the community; a Muslim in Birmingham told me that it would be the screaming Lord Sutch party number 2' (*The Independent*, 14.9.89). However, the *Muslim News* editorial (22.9.89) claimed that, while 'as expected there has been some opposition by some leaders of Muslim organizations and councillors', nevertheless the party 'has been cautiously welcomed by the majority of the Muslim community as an alternative to the existing political parties.' The editorial pointed out that in a Huddersfield local by-election in the Paddock ward in May, an independent Muslim candidate had taken 5.3 per cent of the total vote and 60 per cent of the Muslim votes.

Therefore, while Muslims were beginning to exert some influence upon local political representation, at the national level they (and perhaps even more so, Hindus, Sikhs and Jains) were clearly marginal to the political mainstream. Wolffe writes of the more recently established non-Christian groups that, 'Although they did not face any constitutional obstacles to election to parliament, unlike Roman Catholics and Jews in the early nineteenth century, they remained under-represented or even un-represented' (1994: 96). At the time of 'the Rushdie affair' – and in contrast with the position today – there was no Muslim Member of Parliament and thus no directly sympathetic channel of direct representation for Muslim concerns.

Furthermore, despite a number of attempts to create a generally acceptable umbrella body to provide a unified focus for Muslim political lobbying and mobilization at a national level there had up to that time been no real success, the controversy having pre-dated the emergence of the Muslim Council of Britain. However, an early attempt to organize a representative Muslim body along the lines of the Board of Deputies of British Jews was The Muslim Parliament, sponsored by the London-based Muslim Institute, founded by Dr Kalim Siddiqui, with The Muslim Institute (1990) launching *The Muslim Manifesto: A Strategy for Survival*. However, the adequacy of its representation of the Muslim community as a whole was keenly contested within the community. In particular a number of critics raised the question of how far it represented the ordinary working-class Muslims who formed the majority of the community in such centres of British Islam as Bradford.

Muslim Access to Influence: Comparisons and Contrasts

In contrast to the marginalized position of Muslims within the national political arena, the Church of England continued to have at least 'access' to the corridors of power through the role of its bishops in the House of Lords. And as Wolffe noted, 'the continued presence of the bishops in the Lords, and a sense that the Church of England remained at least on the fringes of mainstream power structures, distinguished it from other religious organisations which were prone to see themselves more as outsiders, seeking to influence the political process through a pressure-group kind of activity' (1994: 94).

With regard to Christian attempts to influence the political process, Wolffe also noted that this kind of activity could be quite effective due to a 'tendency for Christian commitment, or at least sympathy, to be proportionately more widespread among MPs than in society at large' (1994: 94–5). Finally, with regard to the other than Christian traditions, Wolffe noted that 'the Jews, who had acquired the right to sit in Parliament in 1858, had formed institutions and connections that gave them effective political influence' and that 'Indeed, the proportion of Jewish MPs in the later twentieth century was substantially greater than their proportion in the population as a whole' (1994: 96). Geoffrey Alderman, however, has contended that 'most Jewish MPs consider themselves as politicians who happen to be Jewish rather than as Jewish politicians' (1983: 153, 174–5).

In summary, Wolffe commented that, 'around the core of formal ties between the Church of England and the state was a wider circle of Christian and Jewish influence, not recognised constitutionally, but politically quite significant' (1994: 96). As evidence of this, at the height of 'the Rushdie affair' a number of Muslim critics emphasized the contrast between their own experience of campaigning against *The Satanic Verses* and the success that Jewish opposition had in relation to the staging, at the Royal Court Theatre, of Jim Allen's play, *Perdition*.

The Jewish commentator Chaim Bermant (1989) argued that the cases were different on the basis that 'Allen's work was not a novel, but purported to be a reconstruction of recent events which touched on the personal experience of countless people still living, and which was a blatant piece of anti-Zionist propaganda.' However, in a letter to the editor of *The Jewish Chronicle* (10.2.89), Ibrahim Hewitt of the Islamic Organisation for Media Monitoring argued that Bermant had failed to see the parallels with the play *Perdition* and that without the benefit of any sympathetic newspapers, Muslims could really only express their concerns through demonstrations.

It was therefore precisely the lack of formal legal protection through the blasphemy laws, together with the lack of Muslim informal networks of political influence comparable to the Jewish and wider Christian circles of influence noted by Wolffe, that underlined Muslim political impotence. Thus, Muslims protesting against *The Satanic Verses* found it impossible effectively to pursue their case through legal and political means.

When revisited on 'the other side of terror/the War on Terror', the debates connected with all of these issues as raised directly by 'the Rushdie affair' have a new context in the sense that Muslims now have a relatively well-established representational body in the shape of the Muslim Council of Britain, and there are now a number of Muslims both in the House of Lords and as elected Members of Parliament. However, through a number of key events Muslims now also find themselves in a substantially changed global context, in which the association of Islam and Muslims with terror in the name of religion is now a significant part of the social and political environment with which they have to deal.

Through the Looking Glass to the 'Other Side of Terror/The War on Terror'

What Has Been Done So Far?

This chapter has therefore taken some of the key incidents, actions and reactions in 'the Rushdie affair' that were set out in chapters 1 and 2 of the book, and has begun to explore some of the wider issues arising from them. At the same time, the discussion of these issues has remained largely contextualized in relation to matters arising directly from 'the Rushdie affair' itself.

What Next?

In looking into and through the other side of 'the mirror' provided by 'the Rushdie affair', the next and final chapter of the book will explore a range of subsequent 'echoes and reverberations' that have reprised aspects of the original controversy over the past two decades. These echoes and reverberations, when examined together with 'entails' of 'the Rushdie affair' itself, lead finally into a consideration of the future of multiculturalism in the context of current social policy concerns about 'integration', 'social cohesion', terror and security.

Chapter 4

Echoes, Reverberations and 'Social Policy Shock'

On the Other Side of Terror/The War on Terror

Has 'Everything Changed?'

It is perhaps not without significance for a study on 'the Rushdie affair' as a 'mirror for our times' and its implications for the future of multiculturalism that 2008 was not only the twentieth anniversary of the publication of *The Satanic Verses*. It was also the twentieth anniversary of a meeting held on 11 August 1988 in Peshawar, Pakistan, that led on 20 August 1988 to the founding of a new group called 'al-Qaeda al-Askariya', meaning 'the military base', and which, according to the secretary of the meeting, was 'an organised Islamic faction, its goal is to lift the word of God, to make His religion victorious' (in Wright, 2006: 133).

In many ways *The Satanic Verses* controversy prefigured the kind of issues that emerged more fully and in more extreme forms in the closing years of the first decade of the twenty-first century. From this perspective, even if one is critical of the more 'apocalyptic' evaluations of 9/11 as having 'changed everything', the issues of religion, public life and multiculturalism look considerably different than they did prior to the destruction of the Twin Towers, the invasions of Afghanistan and Iraq, and the attacks on the Madrid railway and London transport systems (see MacCabe *et al.*, 2006).

One major difference is that during 'the Rushdie affair' any sense of threat for Europe and North America was mainly associated with the (potentially containable) actions of one theocratic state, albeit linked with a degree of passive support among significant numbers of

Muslims throughout the world and the possibility of an unpredictable individual or group acting to implement the fatwa. On the 'other side of terror/the War on Terror', the sense of threat in the wider society became much more widespread.

Multiculturalism, Segregation, Social Cohesion and 'Social Policy Shock'

Twenty years ago, 'the Rushdie affair' had already given rise to a number of social policy concerns that impinged on the future of multiculturalism (see Asad, 1990). The content of such 'multiculturalism' was classically articulated by the former Labour Government Home Secretary, Roy (now Lord) Jenkins, who was the architect of the UK's 1968 Race Relations Act. Jenkins' argument was that, 'I do not think that we need in this country a melting-pot, which will turn everybody out in a common mould, as one of a series of someone's misplaced vision of the stereotyped Englishman' (1967: 269). Rather, he clarified that the aim of the Government's policy was for 'integration' (understood in those days as the *opposite* of 'assimilation'), defined as 'equal opportunity, coupled with cultural diversity, in an atmosphere of mutual tolerance.'

Already, in the light of *The Satanic Verses* controversy, an editorial (18.2.89) in the generally liberal UK newspaper, *The Independent*, under the title 'Limits to mutual tolerance' had noted with regard to the multicultural policy approach originally espoused by Roy Jenkins that:

> Roy Jenkins' philosophy was predicated on the expectation that the minorities would also demonstrate tolerance, and the implicit belief that all manifestations of cultural diversity would be benign. It is becoming disturbingly apparent that this is not the case. The time has therefore come for an examination of how a tolerant, multicultural society should handle the intolerant behaviour on the part of a minority.

In fact, it should be noted that in response to *The Satanic Verses* controversy even Roy Jenkins himself had been recorded as saying, 'In retrospect, we might have been more cautious about allowing the creation in the 1950s of substantial Muslim communities here' (1989). And as we have already seen, the writer Fay Weldon had put it even more starkly, claiming that, 'Our attempt at multiculturalism has failed. The Rushdie Affair demonstrates it' (1989: 31).

The aftermath of summer 2001 disturbances in the northern towns (which themselves were followed by the global impact of 9/11 in the USA) led to a political 'gear shift' in relation to how questions of cultural and religious plurality, community and shared belonging were being approached. The publication of the 'Parekh report' from the Runnymede Trust's Commission on the Future of Multi-Ethnic Britain (2000) represented the latest point at which an approach based on a development of previous understandings of multiculturalism had made a major public impact, with its vision of Britain as a 'community of communities'. From 2001 onwards, the political focus of both local and national government was both signalled and given substantial policy impetus by the Denham report on *Building Cohesive Communities* (2001) and the Cantle report on *Community Cohesion* (2001), which were commissioned in the light of the 2001 disturbances involving Muslim youth across a number of northern English mill towns.

But it is especially in the context of the atmosphere of heightened tension following the 7/7 bombings in London that developments have taken place in British society that led to what appears to have been an official retreat from the previous bipartisan approach to multiculturalism. That approach had, since the mid-1960s, shaped the social policy and political consensus in the UK. It had informed the equality and diversity policies of central and local government and other significant social institutions, and had shaped the development of law in this field. But in the light of what I have elsewhere called 'the social policy shock' (Weller, 2008: 195) of 9/11 in the USA, of 11/3 in Madrid, Spain, and 7/7 in London, UK, a new social policy language developed around 'social cohesion', 'shared values' and 'Britishness'. The overall change of approach that accompanied this was illustrated in a statement released by the Chair of the former Commission for Racial Equality, Trevor Phillips. In this, Phillips argued:

> the aftermath of 7/7 forces us to assess where we are. And here is where I think we are: we are sleepwalking our way to segregation. We are becoming strangers to each other, and we are leaving communities to be marooned outside the mainstream. (Phillips, 2005)

At a government level, following a 2006 cabinet reshuffle, the emphasis on 'cohesion' led to the establishment of a Race, Cohesion and Faiths

Directorate in what was then the newly created Department for Communities and Local Government (DCLG). The new Directorate continues the work initiated by the former Faith Communities Unit in the Home Office, but it linked this to the wider agendas of race and cohesion, and in 2006 it set up a Commission on Integration and Cohesion that reported in the following year (Commission on Integration and Cohesion, 2007).

Significantly, the Directorate is now also responsible for tackling racism, extremism and hate, as well as for promoting interfaith activity in England and Wales. Thus, earlier concerns around 'social cohesion' have, on the other side of 7/7, in many ways coalesced with concerns around countering 'religious radicalism' and/or 'religious extremism', leading to a very close relationship being established between the policy aims, objectives and instruments of 'social cohesion' and 'security' (see McRoy, 2006).

During 'the Rushdie affair', as well as the threat to Salman Rushdie's own life arising from the Ayatollah Khomeini's fatwa, there were also firebombings of some bookshops that stocked *The Satanic Verses*. In addition, there were threats against those supporting Salman Rushdie; there was the killing of a translator in Japan and in Norway; there was the killing of an imam and his aide in Belgium; and there were threats to a number of Muslim organizations and places of worship, as well as acts of violence against other individual Muslims. While not in any way wishing to diminish the seriousness of these matters, in their original UK and European contexts, the debates that ensued were played out primarily in the cultural, social and political domains rather than in the register of terrorism and/or warfare.

Since that time, however, echoes and reverberations of the controversy have intensified in both their nature and their impact. Many of the issues involved in 'the Rushdie affair' were reprised in the so-called 'Cartoons Controversy' (see Lægard, 2007 and Ammitzboll and Vidino, 2007) that developed around the images published in the 30 September 2005 edition of the Danish daily newspaper, *Jyllands-Posten*, and which gave rise to widespread media, public and street-level debate of a type that was quite similar to the kind of incidents and debates that took place around *The Satanic Verses*. But the 'Cartoons Controversy' took place in a European context that, in between, had more generally come to associate Islam and Muslims with religious extremism and violence.

What had happened in between was, of course, the seismic and global impact of the events of 9/11 (11 September 2001) in the USA, followed in Europe by the 11/3 (11 March 2004) Madrid train bombings; the 2 November 2004 murder of the Dutch artist, Theo van Gogh; and the 7/7 (7 July 2005) London transport bombings. In other words, in between 'the Rushdie affair' and the 'Cartoons Controversy' the violence involved had become very explicit and extreme, and had also taken place in the heart of Europe (Guelke, 2006; Abbas, 2007b). Because of these events, and others like them that would have taken place had they not been foiled by the security services, debates arising about the possibilities or otherwise for peaceful coexistence between Muslims and non-Muslims in a secular and European context have taken on both a new sharpness and also a new poignancy (Abbas, 2007a).

Bombings and 'Hard' Wars

9/11, Afghanistan and Iraq

In many ways, the 9/11 al-Qaeda attack on the World Trade Center and the Pentagon brought about a seismic shift in the social, cultural and political climate in the UK, Europe, and indeed globally (Griffith, 2002; and Jewett and Lawrence, 2003). As a consequence, social and political commentators, politicians and policy-makers began increasingly to focus on the role of religion. The seismic shift also informed the US and UK invasion of Afghanistan, which commenced on 7 October 2001, the stated purpose of which was to capture Osama bin Laden, to destroy al-Qaeda, and to remove the Taliban from power because of the support and safe haven they had provided to bin Laden and al-Qaeda. Although the invasion succeeded in its third main aim, it has not to date resulted in the capture of Bin Laden, or destroyed al-Qaeda. At the time of writing it has also still not resulted in peace, stability and security in the country, and is unlikely to do so in the foreseeable future. In fact, and especially in the south of Afghanistan, the Taliban have regrouped as a guerrilla fighting force, leading to the necessity of the so-called 'Operation Enduring Freedom' continuing as a long-term military campaign.

There was then the 20 March 2003 invasion of Iraq, the rationale for which was articulated on the basis of the alleged threat posed by supposed weapons of mass destruction held by the secular Baathist regime of Saddam Hussein. The aim of that invasion was to remove Saddam Hussein from power and to replace him with a democratic government. Once again, an apparently quick initial military victory gave way to a violent insurgency in which al-Qaeda militants, Iraqi Sunnis, and Iraqi Shi'a militia have all been involved.

There has also been the ongoing use by the USA of the Guantanamo Bay base in Cuba for the detention of terror suspects and enemy combatants, many of whom have been held for many months and years without trial, and whose trials will not be held according to civilian judicial norms. This has also been in a context that has included authorization of methods of interrogation which, in Abu Ghraib prison in Iraq, as well as in other places, have led to the abuse of prisoners. This has also included the so-called 'rendition' of prisoners to countries where legal norms and interrogation methods are less constrained. In plain language, actions have both been directly carried out, and also indirectly condoned, that most reasonable people would be likely to see as torture or, at the very least, as degrading treatment.

11/3 (Madrid) and 7/7 (London)

It is possible, of course, that in a European setting, the implications of all the events outlined in the previous section could have been largely confined to foreign policy. But this changed with the 11/3 (known in Spanish as the '11-M') bomb attacks in Madrid. Of course, terror bombings are far from new in Europe. On the grounds of Marxist, nationalist or fascist political ideologies, terror bombings formed a significant part of late twentieth-century European history from the activities of the Baader–Meinhof Group in Germany; to the PIRA (Provisional Irish Republican Army) and ETA (Euzkadi ta Askatasuna) in Spain; and the NAR (Nuclei Amati Rivoluzionari) in Italy. Also, coming from outside of Europe, groups have perpetrated bombings and other terror actions in connection with the Palestinian struggle and the conflict in Algeria, among others. But until the Madrid train bombings of 2004, substantial bombings in the name of Islam had not taken place in Europe.

Such bombings had, of course, previously and frequently been carried out in other parts of the world, such as the 12 October 2002 nightclub bombings in Bali (in which over 200 people died). But on 11 March 2004, the reality of this threat was brought directly into the heart of Europe by a coordinated series of ten bomb explosions that struck four commuter trains between the Alcalá de Henares and Atocha train stations in Madrid, killing 191 people and wounding 1,755.

The attack took place three days before the Spanish General Election was due to take place, in which the ruling PP party (Partido Popular) of José María Aznar – who had been strongly in support of the war in Iraq – was defeated and replaced by the PSOE (Partido Socialisto Obrero Español). In the initial aftermath of the bombings, the government of the ruling party had cited the Basque group ETA as likely to be responsible. But it soon became apparent that there was a different source for this violence and, after a full judicial investigation, a group of Moroccan, Syrian and Algerian Muslims, together with some Spanish nationals, were prosecuted.

While it appeared that the bombers had been inspired by al-Qaeda, there was no evidence found of the attack specifically being an al-Qaeda one. However, for some, the ensuing change of government was an outcome that seemed to confirm that terror actions can bring about change, although in Spain it was always the case that the majority of the Spanish population was deeply unhappy about their government's position in relation to Iraq.

The 7/7 (2005) attacks on London transport, which resulted in the deaths of 52 people and the injury of 700 others, deeply shocked the UK Government, many Muslims, and the wider civil society. 'Mainland' Britain, and especially London, had previously experienced high levels of violence designed to inculcate terror and to advance a political cause – namely that pursued by the Provisional IRA in pursuit of British withdrawal from the North of Ireland. But there was a widespread sense that these most recent atrocities were different in nature.

First of all, in contrast with the PIRA bombings that took place in Belfast, London, Birmingham, Manchester and other cities during the 1970s and 1980s – and also, in contrast with the 11/3 (2004) Madrid train bombing – the bombers acted without regard for their own personal safety and security. Indeed, from videos later seen and made by those who took part in the 7/7 bombings, it was evident that the fact that the bombings brought death to their perpetrators was something not to be avoided but rather to be embraced, being understood by them as an act of martyrdom. Indeed, these attacks were the first instance of such 'suicide bombings' to occur in Europe.

Secondly, while bombings of this kind had been carried out in the name of Islam in other parts of the world, another dimension of 7/7 that particularly shocked and concerned many in the UK was that the bombings were perpetrated not by people coming from outside the country and whose experience might have been directly shaped by the horrors of war and destruction experienced by people living in

Chechnya, Bosnia–Herzogovina, Afghanistan, Iraq, Gaza, the West Bank and the Occupied Territories. Rather, what was shocking to the government and to many members of British society, including Muslims, was that these bombings had been carried out by young men brought up in the UK who were, to all outward appearances, integrated members of British society.

The bombers who died were: Mohammad Sidique Khan, aged 30, who lived in Dewsbury, Yorkshire, with his pregnant wife and child; Shehzad Tanweer, aged 22, who lived in Leeds, Yorkshire, with his mother and father and worked in a fish and chip shop; Germaine Lindsay (19), who lived in Aylesbury, Buckinghamshire, with his pregnant wife; and Hasib Hussain (18), who also lived in Leeds with his brother and sister-in-law. On 1 September 2005, a tape featuring one of the bombers, Mohammad Sidique Khan, was broadcast on the Arab satellite TV station, Al Jazeera. In this tape, Khan explained that he saw himself as being a soldier and at war. He stated that what motivated him and others like him was not something that could be measured in terms of material things, but was rooted in his understanding of obedience to God. He cited atrocities being perpetrated against Muslims and he argued that the general public shared responsibility for this and would therefore be targets until Muslims felt secure.

This message, and one from Shehzad Tanweer, later broadcast on the eve of the first anniversary of the bomb attacks, was edited and accompanied by statements from Ayman al-Zawahri, often described as second in command to Osama bin Laden, who sought to associate the bombers with al-Qaeda. On the second tape, Zawahri claimed that Khan and Tanweer had attended an al-Qaeda training camp – although this claim has not been independently verified.

Culture and 'Soft' Wars (continued)

Introduction

In the new context created by the eruption of the 'hard' wars highlighted in the previous section, continued cultural conflicts, or what might be called 'soft wars', have both reprised and echoed aspects of the paradigmatic instance of the *Satanic Verses* controversy. In the UK these were focused on controversies that did not directly have to do with Muslims. They were around the musical *Jerry Springer: The*

Opera and the play *Behzti*, and therefore had, respectively, to do with Christians and Sikhs.

While both resulted in conflict that included the threat of violence, in the Netherlands, the murder of the Dutch artist, Theo van Gogh began to change the terms of the debate in a sharper way. While the *Jerry Springer: The Opera* and *Behzti* issues did not significantly move the terms of the debate on in the UK from those that had pertained during 'the Rushdie affair', the murder of Theo van Gogh sent shock-waves through a Dutch polity and approach to multiculturalism that, in mainland Europe, had previously had the most similarity to that developed in the UK.

All of this took place against a background in which the threat of terror violence had more generally escalated. And the contextual change of the 'hard wars' of terror/War on Terror and the continued reprising of the 'soft wars' of cultural conflict eventually came together in the so-called 'Cartoons Controversy' that initially broke out in Denmark in 2005, and briefly seemed as if it would become almost a replay of the *Satanic Verses* controversy.

The Play Behzti *and Sikh Protest*

Behzti was a play written by a British-born woman of Sikh background, Gurpreet Kaur Bhatti. It opened at the Birmingham Repertory Theatre on 9 December 2004 and it was originally planned for it to run until 30 December. The title of the play means, in English, 'dishonour' and it was the writer's intention to use the play to uncover the kinds of hypocrisy that can be found among Sikhs and, by extension, all religious people. The play was billed as a 'black comedy'. It featured three lead characters, of whom one was male and two were female.

The mix of issues that the play sought to explore was wide-ranging, including those to do with social status, mixed-race relationships, corruption, drug-taking, domestic violence, rape, paedophilia and murder, with the play set in the context of the precincts of a Sikh gurdwara. Because the management of the theatre realized that this might represent a controversial and potentially explosive cocktail of topics, in contrast to the publication of *The Satanic Verses* (where there was no dialogue ahead of publication and precious little in the early days of the controversy), the theatre decided to undertake proactive consultations with the local Sikh community.

Significantly, these consultations broke down before the play opened.

The immediate reason for this was not in relation to the content of the play itself but related to the request of the community representatives that the play should be staged as being set in a community centre rather than in a gurdwara. This was because such a staging would violate their sense of Sikh sacred space. However, the theatre management did not feel able to accede to this on the ground that such a change would be tantamount to accepting censorship.

As an echo of what some Muslim groups had asked for, but had not received from Viking Penguin as the publishers of *The Satanic Verses* – but which Bradford City Council had done in relation to copies of the book in their libraries – the theatre offered the possibility for Sikh community representatives to compose a written statement concerning their views. In this instance, not only was the offer made for this to be handed out in printed form to all those attending the play, but the theatre also offered that it could be read out publicly at the beginning of each performance.

But following the breakdown of the talks the play faced daily protests by Sikhs. These were at first peaceful, but on 19 December around four hundred Sikhs attempted to storm the theatre. A foyer door was destroyed, windows were broken in the restaurant, and theatre security guards were attacked. Police were called and arrived in force, including some in riot gear. Five police were injured and two protestors were arrested. In due course, it became clear that many of those taking violent action on 19 December had come from well outside the local area. Following this, the play was cancelled for an indefinite period. The theatre stressed that this cancellation was not in deference to Sikh concerns or actions, but was based on the theatre's 'duty of care' to its audiences, staff and performers.

As with the *Satanic Verses* controversy, what might otherwise have been a local issue in one city in the UK reached the global media and many Sikhs in other parts of the world expressed outrage, while the local Sikhs who had been involved in negotiations with the theatre expressed their concern that there was no legal protection for their religious sensibilities. In an echo of what happened during 'the Rushdie affair', a group of leading artists, both white and South Asian, pulled together an 'Open Letter' in support of Gurpreet Kaur Bhatti's freedom of artistic expression (see *The Guardian*, 23.12.94). Following receipt of hate mail, including death threats, like Rushdie, Bhatti found herself forced to go into hiding. And, as was the case for many years with Salman Rushdie, she has since not appeared in public.

The Case of Jerry Springer: The Opera

Jerry Springer: The Opera is a musical, written by the British writers Stewart Lee and Richard Thomas. It picks up on *The Jerry Springer Show*, a famous US television talk show that established a reputation for loud and controversial interactions with its interviewees and audiences. As a live musical, the play ran for two years (2003 to 2005) in London before starting to tour the UK more widely in 2006.

But it was catapulted into national and international controversy at the start of 2005 when, despite receiving many thousands of complaints, the BBC2 television channel planned to broadcast it on 8 January 2006. Public protests were organized at a number of BBC offices and were coordinated by the campaigning organization, Christian Voice, which also announced its intention to initiate blasphemy charges against the musical as a result, particularly, of its depiction of characters in the Jewish and Christian traditions.

As in case of *The Satanic Verses*, so also in relation to *Jerry Springer: The Opera*, the way in which the play constructed the intersection between revered and loved figures of religion and lewd sexuality proved particularly controversial, with a character of Jesus being introduced who bears similarity with a previously introduced character who had a nappy fetish. Furthermore, in other echoes of *The Satanic Verses*' confusion or reversal of good and evil, so also in *Jerry Springer: the Opera*, the figures of Jesus and of Satan are made to indulge in a battle of wits in which Eve is called as a witness and ends up attacking Jesus. Finally, a character of Mary the mother of Jesus is introduced, although in this version of the story, she leads a general condemnation of him.

The Christian Institute tried to initiate charges against the BBC but these were rejected by the High Court. Many Christians, however, were left feeling that the play's depiction of what they held sacred had been gratuitously attacked. At the same time, the tactics of some of the Christian campaigning groups caused concern to other Christians who felt that, through their actions, the show had received far more publicity than it would otherwise have done.

The Murder of Theo van Gogh

The tensions and challenges to peaceful coexistence that have emerged between Muslims and others in a secular context were particularly sharply and poignantly expressed in the Netherlands following the 2 November 2004 murder of the artist Theo van Gogh. Van Gogh was a descendent of the brother of the famous Dutch artist, Vincent van Gogh. He was a friend and supporter of Pim Fortuyn, the controversial Dutch politician who was assassinated in 2002.

In 2003, van Gogh had strongly supported the invasion of Iraq, although he later modified that support. He also supported the nomination of the Moroccan-born Ayaan Hirsi Ali to the Dutch Parliament who, in 2002, had renounced Islam and declared herself to be an atheist. Van Gogh worked as a columnist in newspapers, often expressing controversial opinions. In 2003, his last book was published, called in Dutch, *Allah Weet Het Beter* (in English, *Allah Knows Best*), which presented Islam in a very mocking and cynical way. But it was his association with Ayaan Hirsi Ali in the making of the film *Submission* that appears to have led to his murder. Ali wrote the script for this film, which criticizes the mistreatment of women in Muslim societies. It does so, among other things, by juxtaposing Qur'anic verses with pictures of Muslim women in scanty clothing and suffering abuse. Most controversially of all, naked actresses, appearing behind semi-transparent shrouds, had texts from the Qur'an that are often used in justification of the abuse of women projected onto their bodies.

Following the broadcast of the film on Dutch television, both Ali and van Gogh received death threats, although van Gogh refused police protection, arguing that he was not really at risk. He was killed by Mohammed Bouyeri, a 26-year-old Dutch citizen who shot him eight times with a handgun, and then proceeded to cut his throat, nearly decapitating him, and finally stabbed him in the chest. Indeed, two knives were left impaled in van Gogh, to one of which was appended a note that contained threats to western governments, to Jews, and to Ayaan Hirsi Ali, who subsequently went into hiding.

This murder sent shock waves through a society that, on the basis of its historical roots as a seventeenth-century refuge for Christian religious minorities, as well as its more recent history, had held to an image of itself as being, on the whole, politically liberal, and of its religious minorities as being generally well integrated with the wider society. But in the remainder of November following the murder, the Dutch Monitoring Centre on Racism and Xenophobia recorded 106 violent incidents against Muslim targets.

The Cartoons Controversy

What initially looked as if it might become a global reprise of *The Satanic Verses* affair emerged after the Danish newspaper, the *Jyllands-Posten*, published a series of twelve cartoons under the headline of 'The Face of Muhammad' on 30 September 2005. A number of the cartoons already contravened the strict Islamic tradition which does not allow any images of the Prophet to be portrayed.

Other cartoons linked the Prophet Muhammad with suicide bombers and terrorist violence. One of these portrayed the Prophet refusing suicide bombers entrance into heaven, not because of what they had done, but on the grounds that heaven had run out of virgins. The most controversial of all the images was one drawn by the artist Kurt Westergaard. This showed Muhammad as a terrorist, and instead of wearing a turban, he wore a bomb with a lit fuse that was inscribed with the words of the Muslim *shahada* (or confession of faith).

Initial protests were, as with 'the Rushdie affair', peaceful. Thus a fortnight after publication there was a peaceful protest in Copenhagen. However, very quickly this originally local controversy became 'glocal' (see next section) and, as had happened with protests against *The Satanic Verses*, as the demonstrations spread throughout Europe and beyond, violence became an increasing feature of them. Thus, in Pakistan and in a number of other countries with majority Muslim populations, Danish flags were burned; Danes were officially advised to leave Indonesia and to avoid travelling to the Middle East; and a Muslim boycott against Danish goods was called for.

In an attempted show of solidarity with the *Jyllands-Posten*, many newspapers in Europe and beyond decided also to publish the cartoons. Each newspaper in which the cartoons appeared further inflamed the controversy. In the UK, which had been the epicentre of *The Satanic Verses* controversy, the responses were, in general, altogether more muted and it is noteworthy that, in contrast with the situation in continental Europe, not a single British national newspaper republished the cartoons. This included those newspapers not generally known for 'pulling punches' in terms of their sensationalist style of reporting and commenting.

But in Bradford, where the Council of Mosques had been among the leading groups protesting against *The Satanic Verses*, and the city had been the location for the public burning of a copy of *The Satanic Verses*, there appeared (as reported in *The Times Online*, 4.2.2006) to be little appetite for stoking the fires of another major cultural and religious conflict by taking to the streets. While Bradford Muslims spoke of their hurt and anger, and of being insulted, they were wary of initiating any street demonstrations because of a concern about provoking a backlash against Muslims.

'Glocalism', Globalization and the Media Age

The 'Annihilation of Distance'

'The Rushdie affair' and the echoes and reverberations that followed it gave new impetus to the issues in longer-standing debates surrounding the contested relationship between religious and other kinds of personal and social identity, including questions of national identity. There has been some continuity with issues that were addressed in nineteenth- and early to mid-twentieth-century debates, but the contemporary version of these debates has been transformed by the new context of contemporary global societies in which fundamental changes have taken place and, in so doing, have reopened questions concerning the basis upon which individuals find a corporate identity.

These questions have especially focused upon tensions between national identities and universal religious belonging. They also connect with wider contemporary questions concerning the viability of the nation state in the context of contemporary globalization (Balibar and Wallerstein, 1992). The creation of a kind of 'global village', or what might be called 'glocalism', has come about because of the impact of what the historian Arnold Toynbee characterized as the 'annihilation of distance' (1958: 87) effected by technology and the modern means of transportation. According to Toynbee, it was this 'annihilation of distance' that led to 'all local problems' being converted into 'world-wide problems'.

Asymmetry and the Media

As well as the physical 'annihilation of distance' the modern news media have also massively contributed to globalization and to 'glocalism' through almost instantaneously connecting local occurrences in one part of the world with global audiences throughout the world. At the same time, the ownership and value base of the global media mean that they are shot through with an asymmetry of power (see Brown, 2006) in relation to how concerns and events are depicted and, indeed, 'created' as media events.

Therefore, although hurt and outrage were key constitutive features of many Muslim responses to *The Satanic Verses*, it is important not to fall into what might be called an 'Orientalism of explanation' in which emotional Muslims are pitted against the rational secularists. The reaction of some artists and writers to the burning of *The Satanic Verses* shows that this is too simplistic. In fact, some of the reactions expressed by secular critics were not too far removed from the rhetoric of the British National Party in their eagerness – albeit ever so much more politely – to tell a group of British citizens with whom one is in conflict that they might like to consider emigration.

Any such Manichaean division between obscurantist Muslims and enlightened secularists, besides being a travesty of cultural history, fails to take account of the degree to which, in protesting against *The Satanic Verses*, Muslims were keying into the asymmetry of cultural and economic power from which they and their societies have suffered since the victory of colonialism. It is because of this that Carlos Fuentes' view of the novel as a 'privileged arena' that can be instrumental in 'bringing together, in tension and dialogue, not only opposing characters, but also different historical ages, social levels, civilization and other, dawning realities of human life' can only be a partial view of how writing and other works of art function in an asymmetrical world.

In a domestic and a global context where Islam and the inheritance of Muslim culture and tradition is routinely, and often wilfully, misrepresented and denigrated, this somewhat ahistorical approach to the novel as that in which 'realities that are normally separated can meet, establishing a dialogic encounter, a meeting with the other' cannot be fully adequate. This is because such a view is based upon the personal and social privilege of 'space' that the global leisured classes enjoy, but which is not accessible to very large numbers of the world's population.

In fact, the asymmetrical nature of Muslims' position in the contemporary world is itself a critically important factor for understanding the background to Khomeini's fatwa. Khomeini was, of course, a leader within the minority Shi'a branch of Islam. He had come to power in the Iranian revolution against the Shah of Iran's western-backed regime, transforming it into an Islamic revolution that, in its attempt to establish a theocratic form of government, offered a role model for Muslims struggling against corrupt leaderships in predominantly Muslim societies.

But it is one of the ironies of history that it is only because of the instruments of modernity in the mass media that what would otherwise have been a judgement issued by a religious leader in another continent became something that, connected with an issue that originated in the UK, became a global event. It was therefore not Muslim outrage and powerlessness alone, or even the events of the 'book-burning' that 'framed' the controversy, but also its *packaging* as a *media event*.

As Edward Said (1981) has previously shown, how the media 'frame' Islam is extremely powerful. Thus, as noted earlier, when Sayyid Abdul Quddus burned a copy of *The Satanic Verses* in Bradford during a demonstration on 14 January 1989, it was not the first occasion on which a copy of the book had been burned. But the 2 December 1988 burning of a copy in Bolton had been ignored, while in Bradford the media had been pre-alerted and thus at least 'co-created' the incident, tapping into a cocktail of imagery and history of which the protestors who used the tactic may not have been fully aware.

Thus the first major event that led to a vehement reaction against Muslim concerns was itself an explicitly arranged media event. Because of this, Muslims – and also Rushdie in a different way – both found themselves at the centre of a cultural storm, reaping the consequences of having transgressed cultural and symbolic codes. The title of one of the chapters of Richard Webster's 1990 book on the controversy and its roots – *A Brief History of Blasphemy* – underlined the ambiguous and contextual nature of the symbolism involved: the chapter was called, evocatively: 'On Not Burning Your Enemy's Flag'.

When associated with a radical critique undertaken from *within* societies – as in American opposition to the war in Vietnam – flag-burning has a long and honourable history. However burning the symbols of *'the other'* can (either literally or figuratively) often inflame. Thus it could be said that by dealing with the figures and sanctities of Muslim history in the way that he did within a phantasmagoric novel, Rushdie had been engaged in burning 'Muslim flags'. Equally, in burning a copy of *The Satanic Verses*, those Muslims who did so (whether they realized it or not) were also engaged in 'flag-burning' in relation to European cultural values.

This action in many ways became paradigmatic of the controversy – indeed, so much so that it is used by the publishers on the cover of this book as the 'natural' image for a book that deals with the controversy, although it is hoped that the contents of the book make clear that the issues involved are, in reality, much more complex than that. However, at one level the 'book-burning' succeeded. Among Muslims, it effected a mobilization of Muslim sentiment (Samad, 1992), while among the wider public, it at least brought into public view concerns that had hitherto largely been unknown or ignored. But it did so at the price that, in the minds of many secular artists and the general public, Muslims became linked with cultural and historical resonances that, in the living memory of European history, were associated with Nazism. In this context, writers and other artists took up strongly expressed positions on the barricades of public debate, characterizing the Muslim campaign and concerns as a threat to freedom of expression and recalling Heinrich Heine's comment with reference to the Nazis that, if one burns books, one will soon end up burning men and women. For others, the action of book-burning was linked with older cultural memories of religious intolerance linked with the Inquisition's activities in also banning and burning books.

Of course, in reality things cannot be so simply contrasted. Secularism, as an ideology at least, is far from being always associated with humanitarian principles as only a glance the twentieth-century history of Marxist Leninism in power or the impact of global capitalism upon the 'Two-thirds World' will show. It is also the case that book-burning is not entirely alien to British history. Burgess (1989), for example, had to acknowledge the fact that the law had ordered the burning of D.H. Lawrence's *The Rainbow* in 1916 and that the British customs authorities had burnt James Joyce's *Ulysses* in 1922. But it is precisely because these episodes are, for Europeans, framed in the ongoing tension between forms of collective authority and individual freedom that any such event does become perceived as a kind of 'flag-burning' that is likely to produce a reaction of a kind that is not always characterized by a measured response.

What was so with regard to the book-burning and its media 'framing' was also the case in relation to the fatwa. This needs to be seen in a global context, and it is this global sense of struggle and of conflict that forms a significant part of the context of the debate. After 9/11 this can perhaps be seen more clearly than many could understand it the time, when the ideological fault lines of the world were still concerned with capitalism and communism.

While Samuel Huntington had not yet penned his thesis on the coming clash of civilizations (Huntington, 1993, 1996), Muslim activists and many thinkers were increasingly coming to see the world in polarized terms based on the history of western imperialism and colonialism, and their experience of corruption at the hands of the rulers and secular parties of many of their post-colonial societies. Coupled with this, as we have seen, were also currents of conspiracy theory that have a strong plausibility structure when anchored in the material basis of the history of colonialism and were clearly revealed in the contours of the coming 'War on Terror'. But they can also assume fantastical forms in ways that historical facticity finds it difficult to challenge and deconstruct.

Religious Radicalism, 'Otherness', Freedom, Terror and Public Policy

Plus ça Change?

Returning by way of the previous discussion on the asymmetry of the global media from the (relatively) 'soft wars' of culture to the impact of the 'hard wars' in the reprisal of issues and themes from the original 'Rushdie affair', among politicians today one hears the often-repeated notion that, after 9/11, 11/3 and 7/7, 'the rules of the game have changed'. However, such an analysis is open to serious question as a matter of historical record, and therefore perhaps should also be questioned as a rationale for contemporary politics and policy.

For example, in an 'Opinion' column in *The Observer* (9.12.07), under the headline of 'There is really nothing new about terrorism', the author recounted taking his children on a visit to the London Transport Museum, where he revealed that he learned about a terrorist bomb that exploded in a London underground train, in which a carriage was completely destroyed and 62 people were injured. The year in question was 1883, and the attack, which took place at Praed Street, London, was the start of a campaign by the Fenians, who were waging a violent struggle for Irish independence. The campaign went on to explode a bomb at Scotland Yard, and led to numerous arrests of Irish people in London.

The column had begun with the observation that 'Rather than stuffing their private offices with spin doctors, ministers have been urged to employ those with doctorates in history' and it concluded that this story suggested that 'all that is fundamentally new about terrorism is the hysterical response of ministers'. Of course, *fears* that are very *real* are elicited by the actions of those who are identified as terrorists. And there is also *some* degree of *real danger* to life, limb and property that can result from terror actions. In this context, the public places an expectation upon government to do all that it can to protect populations against such attacks, the security of its population being one of the first responsibilities of government. So the description of ministerial response to the 7/7 bombing of the London transport system and of other subsequent threats of terror attack as 'hysterical' may be somewhat uncharitable in relation to the very real sense of outrage that politicians can feel in the face of such events, as well as with regard to the considerable public pressures under which political representatives can come to 'do something'.

However, what the *Observer* piece referred to above did achieve was to highlight the importance of having some historical perspective on these matters. And as the columnist put it, reflecting on his visit to the London Transport Museum, although 'the assumption that spotting an ancient cowpat makes you less likely to stumble into one is a little simplistic', nevertheless, 'historians might at least teach ministers a little humility; that many of the challenges they face, far from being "unprecedented" are entirely precedented.'

In other words, in examining the relationship between 'terror', 'religious radicalism', 'religious freedom' and 'public policy' in the UK, it is important to try to get behind the 24-hours news culture 'chatter' and 'comment' about these matters in order to critique what often passes for interpretation. In the first instance, this means that it is important to attempt some scoping of terms in relation to 'terror' and/ or 'terrorism' because, in doing so, what at first sight might seem a fairly self-explanatory description of the kind of violence upon which moral judgement can be passed in the name of the wider community, turns out not to be so simple after all.

The Terminologies and Referents of 'Terrorism'

In the introduction to his book *Invitation to Terror: The Expanding Empire of the Unknown*, the sociologist Frank Furedi notes that, according to his estimate, 'since 9/11 nearly 8,000 books have been published in the English language' on the subject of terrorism (2007: xix). Furedi goes on to say that: 'When I consulted the International Bibliography of the Social Sciences I found 1,413 academic monographs published since 2001 that had the word "terrorism" in their title.' This in itself is indicative of the very real popular, political and academic concern with the subject. However, the subject is one in relation to which meanings are contested.

Thus Alex Schmid's survey *Political Terrorism: A Research Guide* (1984) included over a hundred pages examining different definitions of terrorism, but without arriving at even one that he felt was satisfactory. In his book *Inside Terrorism*, after reviewing various discussions of 'terrorism' and its characteristics, Bruce Hoffman concludes with a definition of 'terrorism' as the 'deliberate creation and exploitation of fear through violence or the threat of violence in pursuit of political change' (2006: 40), going on to argue that:

> terrorism is specifically designed to have far-reaching psychological effects beyond the immediate victim(s) or object of the terrorist attack. It is meant to instil fear within, and thereby intimidate, a wider 'target audience' that might include a rival ethnic or religious group, an entire country, a national government or political party, or public opinion in general. (Hoffman, 2006: 40–1)

Such an approach contrasts with the emotional and moral reaction to terror that often – perhaps understandably – seems to characterize public and political response to terror more than such sober reflection. Such emotional and moral responses tend to emphasize the incomprehensibility of the use of terror, which can encourage a strong sense of individual and political powerlessness in the face of terror. This can, in turn, give rise to perceptions of the risk of terror that assume a very nearly omnipresent sense of almost apocalyptic proportions and that threaten to rupture the fabric, stability and normality of daily life, while at the same time being out of proportion with the more casually accepted but deadly toll of death as a consequence of motor vehicle accidents on the roads.

Even more worryingly, if such out of proportion perceptions become what primarily informs policy responses to 'terror', then they are likely to lead to the adoption of measures that are themselves both disproportionate to the risks involved and which may indeed, in themselves, precisely feed what those who use terror as means to achieve their ends seek to achieve through it. This is because, far from being irrational, those who use terror in relation to the achievement of social, political and/or religious goals usually turn out to be not crazy incarnations of evil. As the Preface to the first (1998) edition of Hoffman's *Inside Terrorism* disconcertingly begins:

I have been studying terrorists and terrorism for more than twenty years. Yet I am still always struck by how disturbingly 'normal' most terrorists seem when one actually sits down and talks to them. Rather than the wild-eyed fanatics or crazed killers that we have been conditioned to expect, many are in fact highly articulate and extremely thoughtful individuals for whom terrorism is (or was) an entirely rational choice, often reluctantly embraced and then only after considerable reflection and debate. It is precisely this paradox, whereby otherwise apparently 'normal' people have nonetheless deliberately chosen a path of bloodshed that has long intrigued me . . . (quoted in Hoffman, 2006: 15).

Muslims and Terror

Approaching the contemporary phenomenon of terror in the name of Islam within such a frame of reference rather than through the lens of an apocalyptic view of Islam and its role in the contemporary world, it might become more possible to seek rationally to understand what informs the approach of those who commit terror actions. In a *Guardian* article under the title of 'Denial of the link with Iraq is delusional and dangerous', Seamus Milne (2007) challenged the loose kind of thinking which has sought to explain terror in the name of Islam in terms of a perceived contest that presupposes an almost Manichaean dichotomy between an Islamist vision of the world and the values of 'western society' – in other words, as a kind of 'Hot War' expression of a new ideological Cold War struggle between Islam and the West (as in Huntington's 'Clash of Civilizations' thesis) that has replaced the previous one between capitalism and communism.

While totalizing Islamist visions of a kind that advocate and reinforce such a way of looking at the world do exist, Milne pointed out that, if the real focus of the bombers had, for example, been on sexually permissive lifestyles, then Stockholm and Amsterdam would have been just as much targets as London, if not more so. But the UK did not become a target of such terror bombings until it participated in attacking the Muslim world through its military actions in Afghanistan and Iraq.

It might, of course, be argued that the 2004 murder of Theo van Gogh is an example that gainsays Milne's general assessment. However, while profound in its impact on Dutch society, that killing does, in the European context, appear to have been very much a one-off action, while the 'terror' with which states and societies are much more concerned are the larger-scale, more 'theatrical' events, with greater loss of life than that of an individual, such as those that were seen in the Madrid and London transport bombings. But while the British Government persists in its attempts to decouple terror actions visited upon western societies from the military actions in Afghanistan and Iraq, Milne argued that, in the light of Britain's role in the Muslim world, what was surprising was that there had so far not been more attacks than there have been.

Thus the actions of the group that bombed the London transport network on 7/7 were not, in fact, as is so often rhetorically claimed, 'incomprehensible'. Rather, for those who had 'ears to hear', they were sadly predictable. For example, in 2001, while clearly condemning the 9/11 attacks on the USA, the Turkish Muslim scholar and activist Fethullah Gülen had warned about the kind of response that the USA might make to 9/11, and had presciently highlighted the likely consequences from the kind of responses against which he had cautioned. And he did so in words the force and resonance of which, not only for the USA, but also for the UK, are only underlined by what has occurred since then:

> Before America's leaders and people respond to this heinous assault out of their justified anger and pain, please let me express that they must understand why such a terrible event occurred and let us look to how similar tragedies can be avoided in the future. They must also be aware of the fact that injuring innocent masses in order to punish a few guilty people is to no one's benefit; rather, such actions will only strengthen the terrorists by feeding any existing resentment and by giving birth to more terrorists and more violence. (Gülen, 2004: 462)

Sadly, the prescience of Gülen's warning can be seen all too clearly in the quagmire of death and destruction that Iraq became; the continuing war in Afghanistan; the tangled metal and bloody aftermath of the train bomb in Madrid on 11 March 2004; and the London Transport bombings of 7 July 2005. In his statement about the bombing, Shehzad Tanweer, one of the 7/7 bombers, said that he had realized that the general public were likely to ask what they had done to deserve such an action. Like Mohammad Sidique Khan, Tanweer pointed out that people had elected a government which oppressed people in Palestine, Afghanistan, Iraq and Chechnya. He spoke of the absolute commitment to Islam of himself and others like him as well as of their love of death in the same way that others loved life.

In the face of such deep-seated rage, articulated in a way that clearly undermines the Government's oft-repeated mantra that these actions are nothing to do with foreign policy, how should the wider society understand this and how should public policy proceed? The events of 7/7 led to the introduction of new anti-terrorism legislation. Among other things, despite substantial concern among lawyers and misgivings among a large number of Members of Parliament, the government introduced one of the longest periods of possible detention without charge (up to 28 days) in any jurisdiction.

But matters did not rest there. In the Counter-Terrorism Bill, 2008, the government of Tony Blair's successor, Gordon Brown, sought to extend that period still further, if necessary, for up to 42 days. The proposed legislation led to a Parliamentary rebellion from a significant number of Labour Party Members of Parliament. It also resulted in the resignation of the Conservative Party Shadow Home Secretary, David Davies, MP, in order to fight an election in relation to a cluster of issues around the erosion of civil liberties in modern Britain. In October 2008, the Bill was defeated in the House of Lords, where there were considerable concerns about the proposals, including those expressed by the former head of the British internal security service, MI5, Baroness Eliza Manningham-Buller, who used her maiden speech to criticize the proposals on grounds of both practicality and principle (see *Independent.co.uk*, 9.7.2008).

The original anti-terror legislation also introduced legal concepts relating to the support and promotion of terrorism. One of those later to be tried and convicted under the original legislation for possession of items 'likely to be useful to a person committing or preparing an act of terrorism' was 23-year-old Samina Malik, the so-called 'Lyrical Terrorist'. Malik was the first Muslim woman to have been imprisoned in Britain after having been found guilty of terrorism offences.

Malik was a Heathrow Airport shop assistant, working for W.H. Smith, and she posted a series of poems on websites, about martyrdom, raising children to fight, and killing non-believers. In internet messages she called herself 'Stranger Awaiting Martyrdom'. She also wrote a poem called 'The Living Martyrs' that expressed a view of the world which not only terrorists, but also many young Muslims had come to share. It is one that is bleak and, in many ways, shocking. But one should not forget that it reflects some of the horror that was in Europe itself, during the break-up of the former Yugoslavia, in the camps and mass murder sites of Bosnia–Herzogovina. Perhaps even more shocking was her poem 'How to Behead', which encourages the executioner using this method of killing to be bold in what they are doing in language that has a capacity to shock.

From 2003, while at school, Malik had written poetry using rapping style under the name 'Lyrical Babe'. But in 2004, she had changed this pen-name to 'Lyrical Terrorist' and she started wearing the hijab. She joined Jihad Way, a group that was oriented towards support for al-Qaeda, and police found a copy of bin Laden's *Declaration of War* at her house. Although such a view of the world is certainly unattractive and may, if not challenged, eventually lead to real danger, Malik did not – so far as is known – either directly commit or indirectly support any specific acts of violent terror. She claimed that she had written the material to 'show off' to eligible bachelors, while her defence counsel said her poetry was, in principle, no different to that of Wilfred Owen's First World War poetry in its shocking depiction of violence and anger.

'Moderation', 'Radicalism', 'Extremism' and 'Terrorism'

Against this background, one of the intriguing aspects of recent developments is that political leaders around the world, when talking of the 'war on terror', have nevertheless sought to distinguish between the terror actions of those of Muslim background, and what is described as a 'real Islam'. Thus, in his 1 August 2006 Middle East policy speech to the Los Angeles World Affairs Council, the former British Prime Minister Tony Blair (2006) argued that 'we will not win the battle against this global extremism unless we win at the level of values as much as force'. In this context, Blair referred to 'an elemental struggle about the values that will shape our future'.

While it is in many ways both commendable and helpful for politicians to make these distinctions when popular pressures might have led them to a looser language that would have condemned Islam and Muslims in general, in practice it can compound a range of other confusions that then become quite important for the way in which the 'powers that be' seek to combat terror. For example, when Blair's speech went one step further to argue that 'It is in part a struggle between what I will call Reactionary Islam and Moderate, Mainstream

Islam', he was straying into rather more confused and therefore potentially dangerous territory for public policy.

Through seeking to isolate a stream of Muslim thought and action that can be identified as 'radicalized' or 'extremist', there has been an attempt on the part of government and other public bodies to promote what is identified by them as a 'moderate Islam' and 'moderate Muslims' and thereby to marginalize by association with terrorism what can be seen as 'radical', 'fundamentalist' or 'extremist' Islam or Muslims. However, it is the argument of this chapter that such an approach is ultimately not helpful in tackling the real threat of terror and that, in addition, it compounds its ineffectiveness by catching within its sweep a whole range of ordinary Muslim people. These would include those whose standpoints are certainly (from some perspectives) 'radical', and who may even have views that might be thought 'extremist', but who would never dream of perpetrating an act of terror in the name of religion.

In seeking to differentiate in this way, the 'powers that be' are, in effect, starting to arrogate to themselves the possibility of adjudicating between a 'good Islam' and a 'bad Islam'. Reflecting on some of the possible implications of this in a *Baptist Times* editorial (7.6.2007) entitled 'The problem with a little moderation', the editor took as his starting point the Government's pledge of one million pounds to promote the study of Islam in British Universities, the rationale for which was in order that 'the voice of moderation can be heard', and argued that 'it's a pity, to say the least, that "extremist" and "moderate" have been pitched against each other like that'.

A good example of what can occur when there is a conceptual confusion that equates a range of apparently related terms into an overall model of 'terror' instead of seeking carefully to distinguish between that to which they refer, can be found in the kind of public discourse that followed the most recent, 30 June 2007, attack on Glasgow Airport. That attack came as Gordon Brown took over the office of Prime Minister from Tony Blair, and among Brown's new appointments was Admiral Sir Alan West, appointed as Security Minister.

Admiral West's 2007 interview on ITN (Independent Television News) of 8 July was reported in the online media service, *itn.co.uk* (8.7.2007) under the headline of 'Tackling *terror* "will take 15 years"' (my italics added for emphasis). Having, in its headline, introduced the theme of 'terror', the report then went on (with my italics again added for emphasis) to say the following, in which it will be seen that while key words are switched, an assumed continuity of reference is maintained:

'Tackling *radicalisation* could take 15 years, Gordon Brown's new Security Minister has warned'. The report then went on to say that: 'Admiral Sir Alan West conceded the Government was failing to get its anti-terror message across, but stressed that preventing people from being recruited to *extremism* was central to beating *terrorism*.'

From the above it will be noted how easily the editorial voice slides from 'tackling terror' to 'radicalisation' to 'extremism'. While it is certainly the case that, through personal, organizational and ideological means there can be some linkage between these phenomena, both in general and with regard to particular instances, it is very important that they should be clearly distinguished. Failing to do so will, in fact, result in additional difficulty in trying to isolate those who are prepared to use indiscriminate and criminal terror in pursuit of their goals from those who may share some aspects of their understanding of the world, but who would not resort to criminal violence.

In other words, it is very important to be clear that – even taking the popular and general usage of such words at their face value – 'radicalized' Muslims are not necessarily 'extremists', and that 'extremist' Muslims are not necessarily going to undertake terrorist actions. 'Extremism' is frequently a weasel word that pits an assumed (and often unexamined) 'centre ground' seen as 'natural' and 'right' over and against those who are perceived to take a position that is 'beyond the pale' of the prevailing consensus. Thus, depending on one's starting point, the designation of others as 'extremists' can simply be a way of marginalizing people from engagement, but without recognizing or seeking to understand the content of their views and positions.

With regard to 'radicalism', the matter is even worse since, from the perspective of religious seriousness, it could be argued that 'radicalism' is an entirely appropriate way of being religious, in which one goes back to the roots in terms of quality of commitment and critiques traditionalist religion when it is upheld for its own sake. Therefore the issue at stake is not 'radicalization' per se among Muslims or other religious people, but rather the *forms* taken by such radicalization and in what such radicalization *results* (see Abbas, 2007b). In a world in which naked power and military violence do seem to be stacked against predominantly Muslim countries and people, it is perhaps not surprising that the prevailing economic, cultural and military 'powers that be' will be questioned by Muslims. And this would indeed be likely to be the case among young Muslims in the UK who have experienced religious discrimination and disadvantage (see Weller, 2006b; and Weller, Feldman and Purdam, 2004).

It is therefore important not to legitimate simplistic distinctions between 'good' (understood as 'liberal' or 'modernist') and 'bad' or 'suspect' (understood as 'traditionalist', 'radical' or 'fundamentalist') Muslims and forms of Islam. Such reactions run the risk of eliding the condemnation of terrorist crimes against humanity conducted on religious grounds into the criminalization, or at least social marginalization, of religious conservatism and/or radicalism.

Defining the issues in simplistic ways could, in fact, even undermine the development of inclusive approaches to the common good. This is because, especially in the context of the high levels of distrust that exist among Muslims in the context of British foreign policy and the military actions in Afghanistan and Iraq, it can be counterproductive for government overtly to try and define (and, even more so, to try to create) a 'good moderate British Islam' over against a 'bad radical Islam'.

Diversity and Struggle among Muslims

One of the dangers of the current approach of the 'powers that be' towards promoting 'moderate' Islam and attempting to marginalize other forms is that of eliding different groups together when what is really needed is a more sophisticated and grounded understanding of the tendencies present among Muslims and in Islam that goes beyond the ephemera of political rhetoric and media reportage. In this connection, Tariq Ramadan in his book *Western Muslims and the Future of Islam* identified what he calls 'six major tendencies among those for whom Islam is the reference point for their thinking, their discourse and their engagement' (2004: 24–30) – thus excluding 'sociological' or 'cultural' Muslims for whom, in their own self-understanding, Islam is not a major point of reference.

The trends that Ramadan identifies include what he calls: 'Scholastic Traditionalism'; 'Salafi Literalism'; 'Salafi Reformism'; 'Political Literalist Salafism'; ' "Liberal" or "Rationalist" Reformism'; and 'Sufism'. These categorizations can, of course, be questioned. Others could be put forward (see Andrews, 1994b), and especially for the diversities among Muslims of South Asian origins (see Robinson, 1988) who comprise the majority of Muslims in the UK. Those suggested by Ramadan are noted here, not because they have to be agreed with, but for the illustrative purpose of underlining that there is diversity as well as unity in Islam and among Muslims, and this is one way of attempting to describe that diversity. But they are also included because Ramadan is a Muslim intellectual who has worked on issues concerning the acculturation of Islam in the European context and whose approach has been referred to in a number of debates in Britain post-7/7, and also because Ramadan himself is a victim of the kind of ignorant and undifferentiated approach to the movements that can be found within Islam, with the US authorities having denied him entry to the USA to take up an academic post there.

Ramadan argues that what he calls 'Scholastic Traditionalists' have a distinct way of referring to the Qur'an and Sunna by strict and sometimes exclusive reference to one of the classical schools of jurisprudence, relying on scholastic opinions that were codified between the eighth and eleventh centuries. He says: 'There is no room here for *ijtihad* or for a rereading, which are taken to be baseless and unacceptable liberties and modernizations' and that 'They are concerned mostly with religious practice and in the West do not envisage social, civil or political involvement' (Ramadan, 2004: 25).

Of 'Salafi Literalism', Ramadan explains that, although those from this tendency are often confused with 'Scholastic Traditionalists', in fact they reject the mediation of the texts by the interpretation of traditional schools and scholars: 'The Qur'an and the Sunna are therefore interpreted in an immediate way, without scholarly enclaves.' Ramadan points out with regard to this tendency that it 'refuses any kind of involvement in a space that is considered non-Islamic' (2004: 25).

What Ramadan calls 'Salafi Reformists' have significant differences among them. However, what unites them is 'a very dynamic relation to the scriptural sources and a constant desire to use reason in the treatment of the Texts in order to deal with the new challenges of their age and the social, economic, and political evolution of societies' (Ramadan, 2004: 26). In terms of social engagement, Ramadan observes that 'The aim is to protect the Muslim identity and religious practice, to recognize the western constitutional structure, to become involved as a citizen at the social level, and to live with true loyalty to the country to which one belongs.' (2004: 27).

'Political Literalist Salafists' are 'Salafi Literalists' of a kind that Ramadan (2004: 27) says is 'essentially born of the repression that has ravaged the Muslim world.' Their approach is 'a complex blend that tends towards radical revolutionary action . . . the discourse is trenchant, politicised, radical and opposed to any idea of involvement or collaboration with Western societies, which is seen as akin to open treason.'

'Liberal' or 'Rationalist' Reformism is born from the influence of Western thought in the colonial period which, 'presenting itself as *liberal* or *rationalist*, has supported the application in the Muslim world of the social and political system that resulted from the process of secularisation in Europe' (Ramadan, 2004: 27). Of this approach in relation to the wider society, Ramadan says, 'In the West, supporters of liberal reformism preach the integration/assimilation of Muslims from whom they expect a complete adaptation to a Western way of life' (2004: 27).

In relation to 'Sufism', Ramadan says that 'Sufis are essentially oriented toward the spiritual life and mystical experience' and that 'There is a call to the inner life, away from disturbance and disharmony.' However, and importantly, Ramadan notes that 'This is not to say that Sufi disciples . . . have no community or social involvement; the contrary is often the case' (2004: 28).

Thus it is very important clearly to distinguish between various visions of Islam, including 'Islamist' ones. Just because there are Muslims whose vision of Islam is to establish Islamic rule in the context of various polities around the world does not mean that they would either use or support means of terror to effect this change. Rather, 'Islamist' projects can be concerned with a nation-state-based initiative (as, for example, Iran under the mullahs, or Afghanistan under the Taliban) or else they can be projects to bring about more global forms of theocratic system (of the kind that Hizb ut-Tahrir and others are seeking to establish).

In recent years there has been considerable debate among both Muslims and others around the relationship between Islam and democracy. Radical secular liberals, traditional 'Islamists' such as the Muslim Brotherhood or the Jamaat-i-Islami, and modern 'Islamists' have all shared agreement that there is a fundamental incompatibility between the two. However, beyond that basic point of agreement, these three groups diverge. Secular liberals, for example, insist that Muslims have to 'reform' and to 'modernize' Islam in order for Islam and democracy to be compatible in a way that, from the perspective of the 'Islamists', would be tantamount to a 'selling-out' of authentic Islam.

Traditional 'Islamists' – while seeking to introduce a polity based on the application of the sharia throughout society – have generally been prepared to use electoral politics and the modern instruments of the state as a means towards this end. Others, such the Wahhabis of Saudi Arabia, assert their traditions as the authentic form of Islam, while the dominant clerical groupings among the Shi'a in Iran claim that the revolution that was ushered in by the Ayatollah Khomeini has created a real Islamic state.

In contrast to the regimes in majority Muslim countries that claim to adopt the mantle of Islam, modern 'Islamists' seek to bring about an Islamic polity that is not national in scope, but global, under what is understood to be a recreated global Muslim Khalifate. As set out in his autobiographical book, *The Islamist: Why I Joined Radical Islam in Britain, What I Saw Inside and Why I Left*, Ed Husain explains that, in such a vision, existing majority Muslim countries are 'imperial creations and deserved no recognition' (Husain, 2007: 142), while the duty of Muslims living in any historical state is 'to prepare the *ummah* for the caliph, to swear allegiance to the future Islamic state' (Husain, 2007: 135).

Such an approach is based upon the conviction that '*al-Islam huwa as-hall*' or 'Islam is the solution'. This is a phrase that was originally coined by the Egyptian Muslim Brotherhood. It also has widespread resonance among ordinary Muslims. But in the thinking and action of 'Islamists' of both the more traditional and more modern kinds, this is reinterpreted to refer to the establishment of an Islamic state as the answer to the fragmentation, tensions and conflicts of the contemporary world.

The more global 'Islamist' visions are, in some ways, analogous to aspects of the history of the political and organizational forms taken by communism. By analogy with what used to be the internal perspective of Soviet Communism and its fellow-travelling supporters, there is an 'Islamism' that takes the form of an idealization that is blind to the failings of the communities of 'really existing Islam'. At the same time, that is to be distinguished from the (ironically) modernist and political 'Islamism' which (also by analogy with the history of communism) could be seen as a kind of 'Trotskyite Islam'. That form of Islam is dedicated to what might be called a 'permanent revolution' against not only 'secular', but also all existing forms of governance developed among 'really existing' Muslims. Instead it seeks the future establishment of an ideal global Muslim Khalifate which is not yet here.

As a defensive mechanism in societies in which there is clear evidence of at least some degree of hostility towards Muslims and Islam (see Allen and Nielsen, 2002), a significant section of the 'really existing' Muslim community with migrant origins tends towards a defensive cultural and intellectual insularity over against their perceptions of the secular. Such Muslim reactions and groups are concerned primarily with trying to preserve Islam in the midst of what can be perceived as a sea of alien cultural, religious, intellectual and legal influences.

Other Muslims – also often identified by the term 'Islamists' – have a more ideological project in relation to the secular. This is concerned with what, for example, Hizb ut-Tahrir calls the 'carrying' or 'passing on' of 'the concepts' (see Husain, 2007) which they seek to inculcate among Muslims in contradiction to what is seen as a *kafir* (infidel) secular system. Thus they campaign against this system using the slogan 'democracy is hypocrisy', on the basis that it is *haram* or forbidden to participate in something that is rooted in secular principles that are, by them, deemed to be contrary to the fundamental principles of Islam.

With regard to 'Islamism', the contradictions that can emerge among the adherents to its principal groupings are well illustrated in Ed Husain's writing. Of his personal experience, Husain says, 'My life was consumed by fury, inner confusion, a desire to dominate everything, and my abject failure to be a good Muslim. I had started out on this journey "wanting more Islam" and ended up losing its essence' (2007: 148). Within Islam, people like the Turkish Muslim scholar, Fethullah Gülen, stress that only those who are self-critical can make an effective contribution. Instead of the spiritually bankrupt 'Islamism' vividly portrayed by Husain, Gülen (in Ünal and Williams, eds., 2000: 9) argues that 'Those who want to reform the world must first reform themselves. In order to bring others to the path of traveling to a better world, they must purify their inner worlds of hatred, rancor, and jealousy, and adorn their outer worlds with all kinds of virtues.'

How what Husain says of himself could come about relates to a debate that is now raging among Muslims. In a *Guardian* newspaper piece entitled 'Hearts and minds of young Muslims will be won or lost in the mosques', the journalist Madeleine Bunting (2007) wrote of the reaction of Muslim leaders gathered in London immediately following the 7/7 bombings. Of these leaders, Bunting said that many 'refused to accept that it might have been Muslims'. This was reminiscent of the refusal of many Muslims to believe that 9/11 had been carried out by Muslims, blaming it instead on a Zionist global conspiracy. Bunting said that because of the initial reaction:

> The discussion had the younger generation of professional British-born Muslims grinding their teeth with frustration at the stubborn naivety of an older generation of leadership. Their elders had completely failed to grasp how the community had been swept up in a

global political conflict that was interacting with a local crisis of identity and a generational conflict.

By contrast, after the attempted central London and Glasgow airport bombings of June 2007, on 7 July imams and activists from across the country gathered to challenge terror in the name of Islam. Full-page adverts were taken out in national newspapers by the Islam is Peace organisation. The adverts of its 'Not in Our Name' campaign (see http://www.islamispeace.org.uk, accessed 23 October 2008) stated clearly that 'The Muslim communities across Britain are united in condemning the attempted bombings in London and Glasgow'; that 'Islam forbids the killing of innocent people' and that 'We reject any heinous attempts to link such abhorrent acts to the teachings of Islam.' This development is evidence for what Bunting had earlier noted, which is that 'Britain's Muslims have launched their most concerted attempt yet to win the hearts and minds of the public and distance themselves from the activities of violent extremists who claim to act in the name of their faith.' Bunting's (2007) conclusion was:

> What's remarkable is that these subjects are being aired in public and even discussed with non-Muslims; for years the charge of washing dirty linen in public ensured silence. But Britain is now the arena for one of the most public, impassioned and wide-ranging debates about Islam anywhere in the world.

Incitement to Hatred, Conspiracy Theories and Islamophobia

'Hate Literature' and Religions

As noted previously, the early reaction of some Muslims to 9/11 was that it was part of a global anti-Islamic conspiracy and that it had possibly been carried out either by, or at the behest of, Mossad, the Israeli secret service. It has been known for some time that conspiracy theory material has had a significant circulation among Muslims in the UK as elsewhere in the world, with much of it having been available in mosques and other Islamic centres, including the notorious anti-Semitic forgery, *The Protocols of the Learned Elders of Zion* (see Feinberg, Samuels and Weitzman, eds., 2007).

Because of this, research has recently been conducted in relation to the role of such literature and which resulted in the Policy Exchange report (MacEoin, ed., 2007) entitled *The Hijacking of British Islam: How Extremist Literature is Subverting Mosques in the UK*. But the fraught nature of this territory is underlined by the controversy that erupted around the conduct of the research itself, which was conducted by the think tank Policy Exchange, the political complexion of which can be seen from a description of its aim to 'develop and promote new policy ideas which will foster a free society based on strong communities, personal freedom, limited government, national self-confidence and an enterprise culture'.

During 2006 to 2007 four Muslim researchers visited 100 sites, including mosques and Islamic bookshops, to research how far literature that inculcated 'Muslim separatism and hatred of nonbelievers' was available, either openly or 'under the counter'. However, the report itself became news when, on 12 December 2007, BBC2's *Newsnight* television programme reported on an investigation into the Policy Exchange report, having identified material (see *BBC.co.uk*, 14.12.2007) that seemed to suggest that at least some of the evidence cited in the report may have been fabricated. The Policy Exchange's Director of Research stated that the organization stood completely by the report and also that Muslim researchers had helped to compile it, claiming that the research had been thoroughly checked and that the allegations made by *Newsnight* did not affect the substance of the report.

That there is an issue in Britain's mosques is not to be doubted, but as with the Government's tendency to equate 'radical Islam' with terror, the Policy Exchange report tended, problematically, to link together 'separatism' and 'hatred of nonbelievers'. While these two attitudes may significantly overlap in any one group, to associate them too closely is arguably unhelpful since, while 'separatism' may or may not be seen as desirable by the wider society, it is not necessarily at all the same as 'hatred of nonbelievers'.

For example, in a Christian context in the USA, would it be appropriate to associate literature from the separatist Amish with that from 'Christian survivalists'? It would also be interesting to see what the results and the reaction to them might be if a similar survey were undertaken of the kind of apocalyptic literature that can commonly be found among Evangelical Christian congregations and bookshops, and what the influence of that might be in Christian circles. For example, there is the phenomenon – at its strongest in the USA, as compared with the UK or the rest of Europe, but none the less also present here – of what Grace Halsell, in her book entitled *Forcing God's Hand: Why Millions Pray for a Quick Rapture – and Destruction of Planet Earth* (1999), calls 'Armageddon Theology', the influence of which can be seen in the enduring publication of Hal Lindsey's book, *The Late, Great Planet Earth* (1971) and that was followed by other similar works including his *The 1980s: Countdown to Armageddon* (Lindsey, 1980). Lindsey's work has sold around twenty-five million copies while LaHaye and Jenkins' (1995) post-Rapture book, *Left Behind*, sold three million. There is also a 'Christian Identity Movement' that links disparate right-wingers and 'survivalists'.

Noting any of this is not, of course, to excuse the issue of literature that might incite hatred circulating among Muslims or indeed any other religious or other group at all. But it is to set it in a wider context, as the failure to do so can result in Muslims being unfairly singled out. In terms of public policy, how such material might be tackled is perhaps best stated by Iqbal Sacranie, the former General Secretary of the Muslim Council of Great Britain, who argued (quoted in *telegraph-.co.uk*, 31.10.2007) that, 'If there is any material which falls foul of the law, then the law should take its course. We cannot accept messages of hate – there is zero tolerance of that. But it is irresponsible to target religious texts and take them out of context.'

Islamophobia: Historical Roots and Contemporary Manifestations

One of the lessons of 'the Rushdie affair' and of the echoes and reverberations of related events over the past two decades is the powerfully destructive role that enemy images and conspiracy theories can play in the creation of conflict and the incitement of hatred. Such hatred can, of course, be directed from any one group towards any other group and no groups are immune from this possibility (see Weller, 2007a). It can also emerge in systematic and/or arbitrary ways, as substantial components of social and political programmes, and/or as individual outbursts. It can both feed upon and feed the oxygen of individual prejudice, leading to direct and indirect discrimination against minorities, but can also poison minority views of majorities, leading eventually to actions based on hatred that can contribute to a dangerously unstable social and political cocktail of highly combustible ingredients.

The terminology of 'Islamophobia' is often currently used to describe the particularity of Muslim experience of these phenomena. In the context of the UK, a Runnymede Trust report on discrimination against Muslims that used this word in its title (Commission on British Muslims and Islamophobia, 1997: 1) brought the terminology into wider public use, with the authors of the report describing the use of this word as follows:

> The word is not ideal, but is recognisably similar to 'xenophobia' and 'europhobia', and is a useful shorthand way of referring to dread or hatred of Islam – and therefore to fear or dislike of all or most Muslims. Such dread and dislike have existed in western countries and cultures for centuries. In the last twenty years, however, the dislike has become more explicit, more extreme and more dangerous. It is an ingredient of all sections of our media, and it is prevalent in all sections of our society. Within Britain it means that Muslims are frequently excluded from the economic, social and public life of the nation . . . and are frequently victims of discrimination and harassment.

In 2002, the European Monitoring Centre on Racism and Xenophobia (EUMC) produced a *Summary Report on Islamophobia in the EU after 11 September 2001*. Based on an overview of country reports provided by EMUC's RAXEN network of National Focal Points in each of the then fifteen countries of the European Union, a rise was identified in what the report called 'ethnic xenophobia' which it saw as being 'distinctly separate from the xenophobia that exists within both Islamophobia and indeed . . . anti-asylum seeker sentiment'. Such 'ethnic xenophobia' was linked with a 'greater perceived threat of the enemy within, and an increased sense of fear and vulnerability both globally and locally' (Allen and Nielsen, 2002).

Within all this, what the report called 'expressions of Islamophobia' found justification in what was identified as a 'catalytic justification' with regard to 'both latent and active prejudices'. Such images are recycled in crude ways in the propaganda of organizations such as the British National Party which, in recent years in the UK, has particularly targeted Muslims. This has been done by separating out Muslims as a specific category of 'undesirable other' from among other religious and ethnic minority groups, such as the Hindus and the Chinese, who are portrayed as being more acceptable than Muslims.

Thus in Allen and Nielsen's 2002 report, instances were cited with special reference to the UK, where 'anti-Muslim alliances have been formed . . . between right-wing groups and immigrant and ethnic minority groups', and in which generally racist agendas appear to have been suspended in favour of a (presumably temporary) alliance with extremist groups of Sikh and Hindu backgrounds. However, Islamophobic incitement to hatred is not the preserve of neo-fascist or extreme right-wing populist politics because, despite its variety of form, such literature draws upon a common store of images. These images charge Muhammad with being a liar and a deceiver. They also suggest (due to the permissibility, under certain conditions, of polygamy in Islam) that Muhammad in particular, and Muslim men in general, have insatiable sexual appetites. Finally, these images associate Islam and Muslims per se with violence and intolerance.

Some of the negative images associated with Islam go very deep into European history (Daniels, 1960, 1967), and in this regard the legacy of the Crusades continues to have an impact in the contemporary world (Armstrong, 1988). In 1213 Pope Innocent III described Muhammad as 'the Beast of the Apocalpyse' and, as Richard Webster explains, 'In subsequent centuries, the view of Islam as a demonic force, and of Muhammad himself as Antichrist, became deeply established in the Christian imagination' (1990: 79). Today, and especially in the wake of the September 11 attacks on the World Trade Center and the Pentagon and the bombings in Madrid and London, many of these images appear in forms secularized by 'Orientalism' (see Said, 1978) in ways akin to those in which the store of classical anti-Semitic images also became secularized through the development of pseudo-scientific theories of racial eugenics.

Therefore Islamophobia can also be found among those who would characterize themselves as political liberals. As previously stated, at the height of the *Satanic Verses* controversy, the Muslim intellectual Shabbir Akhtar wrote an essay published in *The Independent* newspaper (Akhtar 1989b) entitled 'The Liberal Inquisition'. In its juxtaposition of two key words usually seen as incompatible, the title of this essay reflects how Muslims in Europe can often see their experience at the hands of a sneering, ignorant journalism, of a kind that can sometimes be found among those who would otherwise claim to be politically liberal but who nevertheless draw unselfcritically on the store of anti-Islamic imagery that many Muslims felt was also embodied in Rushdie's book.

Conspiracy, Incitement to Hatred and Communalism

Of course, this is not to say that there were no serious issues at stake in 'the Rushdie affair' as seen from perspectives other than those of Salman Rushdie's opponents. As noted in connection with the kinds of materials that can be found in mosques and Islamic centres – and in particular with *The Protocols of the Learned Elders of Zion*, which has long been a mainstay of European anti-Semitism – it is clear that some Muslims are themselves receptive to conspiracy theories and incitement against other groups; that there are also *some* who are active in their promotion; and also *others* who are complicit in not challenging this.

But with regard to the incitement of hatred directed *against* Muslims, arguably the most dangerous kind of incitement is not the kind of crude propaganda that is disseminated by a number of racist and neo-fascist groups, but rather, that which is based on a *plausibility structure* that mixes the historical *fact* of military conflict along the fault lines between the House of Islam and the territory historically identified with Christendom, together with the recent terror actions of al-Qaeda, leading to contemporary *fictions* about Islam as a whole and Muslims per se.

In the atmosphere of heightened tension consequent upon the impact of foreign and military policy abroad, terror attacks at home, and popular anxiety arising from this, for the future of a cohesive society it is important to try to find possible ways of transforming 'enemy images'. In trying to do this, one could do worse than to try to learn from analysis of other seemingly intractable conflicts. Thus, in their instructive book *Moving Beyond Sectarianism: Religion, Conflict and Reconciliation in Northern Ireland*, Joseph Liechty and Cecelia Clegg (2001) identify what they call a 'scale of sectarian danger' through which the conflictual 'temperature' and destructive potential of 'sectarianism' is escalated by words and by actions in the following kind of way:

1. We are different, we behave differently
2. We are right
3. We are right and you are wrong
4. You are a less adequate version of what we are
5. You are not what you say you are

6. We are in fact what you say you are
7. What you are doing is evil
8. You are so wrong that you forfeit ordinary rights
9. You are less then human
10. You are evil
11. You are demonic

(Liechty and Clegg, 2001: 245)

In considering Islamophobia, both in the UK and globally, one can see how this scale of sectarian or communal danger can operate. What is particularly dangerous about Islamophobia is that it does not remain only at the level of images, but all too easily translates into an ugly reality for the daily lives of Muslim minorities. Thus, in the UK, in the period immediately following September 11, many ordinary Muslims in western societies had reason to be living in fear. 'Enemy images' of Islam and of Muslims were beginning to develop and be reproduced, associating the entire religion of Islam and all Muslims with the actions of al-Qaeda. The atmosphere of the time is well evoked in the following extracts from Humayun Ansari's summary in a recent Minority Rights Group International Report on *Muslims in Britain*:

> Muslim adults and children were attacked, physically and verbally. They were punched, spat at, hit with umbrellas at bus stops, publicly doused with alcohol and pelted with fruit and vegetables. Dog excrement and fireworks were pushed through their letterboxes and bricks through their windows. They were called murderers and were excluded from social gatherings . . . Vandals attacked mosques and Asian-run businesses around the country. Nine pigs' heads were dumped outside a mosque in Exeter. Many mosques were said not to have reported attacks because of fear of reprisals. (Ansari, 2002: 4)

Of course, sometimes in Europe, but certainly also in other parts of the world, experiences of this kind can also be recognized by Jews, Sikhs, Hindus, Christians and others. But while attempting to keep a global perspective, each individual and group can only act personally in the specific contexts in which we find ourselves. In the 'western' world, when modern media images of contemporary terrorist violence mingle with powerful inherited imagery, such an atmosphere is focused primarily around Islam and Muslims and brings with it significant dangers that can affect religious communities as also the wider society. For further understanding of how this works in practice, there is much that could be learned from the history of anti-Catholicism in England – both for religious groups and for governments and the wider societies in which they are set.

Anti-Catholicism and Islamophobia, Past and Present

Religious Discrimination in British History and Today

Work such as that of the Runnymede Trust's Islamophobia Commission and research findings such as those in the 1999 to 2001 Home Office-sponsored Religious Discrimination in England and Wales Research Project have underlined the extent to which Muslims in our contemporary society experience a high degree and frequency of discrimination and unfair treatment on the basis of religion (see Weller, Feldman and Purdam, 2001, 2004).

In earlier phases of British history, Roman Catholic (and also Nonconformist, or Free Church) Christians experienced both active persecution and, later, more passive but nonetheless real discrimination and civil disabilities. In their main forms, these lasted until the nineteenth century. Such an inheritance still has some remnants even today in which the freedom of choice of marriage is limited for those in line to the Throne and who wish to remain so, albeit that, at the time of writing, proposals are being developed to end this exclusion. But in wider public and political culture, it is not without significance that Tony Blair waited until after leaving office before completing the process of his personal Christian journey by being received into full communion with the Roman Catholic Church.

Catholics as the Demonic 'Other'

This chapter began by referring to the Fenian bombings of Praed Street. It now looks at the possibility that the place of Roman Catholics and of anti-Catholicism in English social, political and religious history might be helpful for illuminating aspects of the current debates around 'terror', 'religious radicalism', 'religious freedom' and 'public policy' in the UK, as these are at present manifest in relation to Muslims and to Islam. Just as there *are* Muslims who today have actually chosen the path of terror, so also in English history there were indeed Catholic Christians who *were* a danger to the civil settlement in England. When Mary had been Queen, persecution of Protestants was unleashed. Others, like Guido Fawkes, plotted with foreign powers to overthrow Parliament and the government of the day. Similarly, there are those who understand themselves as Muslims who really do want to establish a global Khalifate, if necessary by force.

In both cases this leads to the challenging issue that was well expressed in Timothy Larsen's book, *Friends of Religious Equality: Nonconformist Politics in Mid-Victorian England*, albeit originally in connection with the issue of Roman Catholic emancipation in England. In other words, it is the issue of, 'the old, liberal dilemma of how to treat the illiberal; the recurring bugbear that they will exploit the opportunities afforded by a liberal society in order to destroy it' (Larsen 1999: 239). This aspect of the nineteenth-century debate is one that, especially following 'the Rushdie affair', and even more so after 9/11 and 7/7, has re-emerged in our contemporary religiously plural society in a particularly sharp way (see Hepple and Szyszczak, eds., 1992; Horton, ed., 1993). Writing *before* 9/11 or 7/7, Larsen went on, tellingly, to reflect on this in the following way:

> In today's world, liberals in various nations wonder uneasily if radical Islamic groups will mount a systematic attack on all they hold dear from the safe harbour of liberal rights, liberties and protections. In Victorian Britain, the Church of Rome was seen as a persecuting, illiberal body. The Inquisition was its heritage, and the treatment of Protestants in Catholic countries was still thought to be despicable. It was assumed that if Catholicism ever came to dominate Britain again, religious liberty would be swept away. There was a long tradition of viewing Catholicism as a threat to the established government of the nation, with the Gun Powder Plot as just one link in the chain. (Larsen, 1999: 239)

The ubiquity, depth and visceral nature of this historical concern about Catholics and Catholicism is perhaps difficult to appreciate today. But Arthur Marotti's book on *Religious Ideology and Cultural Fantasy: Catholic and Anti-Catholic Discourses in Early Modern England* brings it very much into focus. Marrotti specifies that, as a scholar of literature, he was not so much concerned with the historical 'facts' but rather the place of 'Catholics' and 'Catholicism' in what he calls the 'cultural imaginary'. As Marrotti summarizes it:

> The Gunpowder Plot produced England's first national day (Gunpowder Treason Day, later Guy Fawkes Day), and it established a firm association of Catholicism with terrorist ruthlessness, heightening the fears of Catholic murderousness and subversion that lasted not decades but centuries. (2005: 144)

Faced with the threat of destabilization from external political powers working with an internal religious minority, Catholics found themselves at the mercy of powerful forces of the state. Among religious people, very few Protestants were prepared to grant them any room for manoeuvre. In that situation, among Catholics at the beginning of the seventeenth century, a number of lay Catholics and secular priests tried to take a more accommodationist line with the Elizabethan government, seeking to distinguish themselves from the Jesuits who defended papal supremacy and the right to depose monarchs for establishing the wrong religion.

An example of this was the secular priest John Mush, one of the so-called Appellant Catholics who appealed against the Pope's decision to appoint a Jesuit-sponsored secular priest as 'Archpriest' for England. As Marrotti explains it: 'Like other Appellants, Mush defended his patriotism and loyalty by characterizing the Jesuits as dangerous aliens ...' (2005: 43). So also today, there are some accommodationist Muslims who feel the need to protest their loyalty more loudly than would people of other religions.

Dangerous Religion and Government Attempts at Control

Just as historically was the case in England with regard to Roman Catholics, so also in the current atmosphere surrounding Islam and Muslims in Britain and Europe, there is a tendency in political and government circles to want to 'control' the manifestations of religion by use of a variety of mechanisms. Similar issues were current in mid-1980s Europe in the context of widespread concerns about what are popularly called 'sects' and 'cults' following deaths in connection with the Ordo Solaris group in Switzerland, and the Aum Shinrikyo attack on the Tokyo underground by groups which were also motivated by a deeply apocalyptic view of the world. At that time, Richard Cottrell (1984), a UK Conservative Member of the European Parliament, argued for special legislation to govern the activities of these groups, which academics tend to call by the less pejorative terminology of 'New Religious Movements' (NRMs). Many politicians were attracted to such proposals on the basis that some NRMs were at least potentially dangerous forms of religion that the state needed to control. Indeed, a number of religious leaders also supported the proposals, believing that they could distinguish appropriately between 'reasonable' and 'moderate' religion and 'extremist' and 'cult' religion.

However, by contrast, the Executive Secretary of the then Committee for Relations with People of Other Faiths of the British Council of Churches, Kenneth Cracknell, argued against such legislation on the basis that there can be serious dangers involved in inviting the state to distinguish between 'good religion' and 'bad religion'. On the basis of this, Cracknell persuaded the then British ecumenical Church body – the British Council of Churches – to back a position that, instead of creating new laws, the existing criminal laws relating to deception, extortion, kidnap, and murder were sufficient and adequate. What was needed in instances where religious groups might be seen to transgress such norms was for these normal laws to be applied. Although the context and content of those issues are not the same in that the forces of violent terror in the name of Islam appear to be substantially stronger than were the relatively isolated new religious movements, it could be argued that many of the principles involved might be similar.

To argue this is neither to ignore the religious content of some terror threats nor is it to be naive about them. In order to combat such religiously informed terror there is a need precisely to understand its religiously related content. This is because it will not be defeated either by calls to liberalism and reasonableness, since that could too easily be dismissed as a betrayal of ultimate convictions. Nor will it be defeated by brute force and naked power, since that will only reinforce the self-righteousness of those who experience it. Before she was killed in 2007, the murdered Pakistan People's Party leader Benazir Bhutto, when asked about the kind of violence that it appears may have played a part in her own death, ventured the opinion that it could not be defeated, only contained, and that it might, in time, die out.

Religious Self-identity and Freedom within the Law

For those who are not Muslims, it would be a salutary lesson to try to imagine what it is like to have continuously to apologize for who you are and to explain that you do not support atrocities. To have some understanding of this, mainstream Christians might consider what it would be like to have to put themselves in the position of justifying to predominantly Muslim or secular media why they, as Christians, are not to be confused with the white supremacist 'Christian identity' movement in the USA.

Just as for Catholics, emerging out of the active persecution and passive exclusion of British history, it is important for members of the wider society to try to imagine how it must it feel, in the context of a society in which Islamophobia and discrimination on the basis of religion is real, for Muslim fellow citizens to have to keep on demonstrating one's loyalty to the country of which one may be a citizen. At the same time, just as Christianity had to struggle to emerge from the bloody legacy of the European Wars of Religion and the use of civil power to enforce religious conformity, what could ultimately defeat those visions of Islam that promote and deploy terror is likely to be a combination of weariness among the faithful combined with the influence of those co-religionists whose religious vision is one that affirms the dignity of the human in the theological freedom given to them by God to be who they are and to choose who they might be.

Lessons From Baptist Tradition on Religious Freedom and Civil Constraint

Within the European Christian heritage, the Baptist tradition of Christianity is one that, more or less consistently, has sought to uphold the principle of religious freedom for all and has stood against the use of 'the sword' to bring about personal religious or social change (see Weller, 2005). This was not just because of Baptists' own historical experience as a restricted minority, but also because of the theological conviction that, as one of the earliest advocates for religious freedom writing in the English language, Thomas Helwys, put it, because 'men's religion to God, is betwixt God and themselves: the King shall not answer for it, neither may the King be judge between God and man' (Helwys, 1612, in Groves, ed., 1998: 53).

However, religions do have social implications, and so it is not surprising that while religious liberty is the nearest thing to a 'Baptist universal' that exists, there were exceptions to this general stance. Therefore, for example, in his 1644 statement on religious liberty, *The Storming of the Antichrist, in His Two Last and Strongest Garrisons: Of Compulsion of Conscience and Infant Baptism*, the Baptist theologian Christopher Blackwood made an exception of religious liberty for Catholics, even going so far as to say that it could be appropriate for the earthly powers to remove them from the country if their numbers threatened – or, in modern parlance, to deport them – at the point of a sword, in other words with the use of force, at least backed up by the threat, if not actuality, of violence.

But T. George's survey article 'Between pacifism and coercion: the English Baptist doctrine of religious toleration' stressed in relation to such quotations and exceptions that 'They clearly are exceptions to the larger Baptist consensus that continued to advocate unrestricted religious liberty' (1984: 49). But also, in contrast to Mennonites, Baptists did not rule out the use of the sword by Christians since they allowed their church members to become magistrates. As George noted:

> This positive position on magistracy was reflected at three crucial points (1) a defence of the ethics of war (2) a recognition that coercion was the precondition of social order and religious toleration (3) a willingness to admit magistrates to church membership. (George, 1984: 37)

For example, Thomas Helwys had criticized the Dutch Mennonite Christians for attacking the office of magistrate while living under the protection afforded by the Dutch rule of law, pointing out that this protection was lacking for many of their co-religionists in other countries. Referring to the Anabaptists' deliverance from the threat to their religious liberty posed by the Duke of Alva, Helwys wrote *An Advertisement or Admonition Unto the Congregations, which men call the New Fryelers in the Lowe Countries*, in which he argued that:

> Of all the people on earth none hath more cause, to be thankful to God for this blessed ordinance of Magistracy than you, and this

whole country and nation, in that God hath by his power and authority given unto you magistrates who have so defended and delivered you from the hands of a cruel destroyer, and will you notwithstanding condemn this ordinance, and consider it a vile thing. (quoted in George, 1984: 38)

Thus, the Baptist Christian stance was one that, while advocating religious freedom as both a theological value and a social good, also acknowledged that there may be need for use of the coercive power of the state, acting through law, when the social conditions that upheld and made possible religious and other liberties were under threat. Clearly, though, there is a delicate balance involved in this, in which, if not continually corrected by a strong emphasis on the foundational value of freedom of thought, conscience and religion, the legitimacy of the use of civil coercion can all too easily slide over into an approach in which 'the end justifies the means'. In addition, in the Baptist Christian vision, advocacy of religious freedom does not mean indifference to religious beliefs, especially where those beliefs appear in themselves to contradict the values of freedom of thought, conscience and religion. But it does mean that such beliefs are to be opposed in a way consistent with the upholding of religious freedom.

The tensions involved in such issues were very much to the fore during the nineteenth-century debates in England on emancipation for Catholics. Baptists taking part in such debates generally upheld the right to civil liberties for Catholics, while also maintaining a position generally opposed to aspects of Catholic doctrine – and especially those aspects which might have undermined the foundational value of religious freedom. For example, in the Preface to his book, *Modern Popery: A Series of Letters on Some of its More Important Aspects*, the Baptist Benjamin Evans argued in the robust language of the times that he was 'second to none in his unmingled hatred of their doctrines', nevertheless, 'with regard to the civil rights of Romanists, he is still an unwavering friend' (Evans, 1855: v–vi).

In relation to the issues highlighted in 'the Rushdie affair' and their echoes and reverberations over the past two decades, by updating Evans' approach to a new context and translating it with regard to new referents, in relation to those of both Muslim and other back-grounds who would try to turn the world into a Manichaean battle ground and are prepared to use the violence of terror to achieve any kind of theocratic or, indeed, secular dictatorship, I would wish to be second to none in my 'unmingled hatred of their doctrines'.

At the same time, with regard to the civil rights of Muslims and other religious minorities I would wish, like Evans, still to be 'an unwavering friend'. This is because I am also opposed to those who, in an Orwellian way, seek to justify 'waterboarding' of suspects as something other than torture and launch military adventures on the basis of what turned out to be threadbare claims about the threat posed by weapons of mass destruction, the evidence for the existence of which has never subsequently come to light.

Maintaining a balance of this kind in a world of complex and specific personal and social policy choices is not easy. But in contrast to an approach that runs the risk of demonizing Muslims and others, I would suggest that to try to work out this tension in practice represents the best hope for positively encouraging those developments from within the integrity of religious traditions that can, in the end, most effectively overcome the ideological hold upon some religious believers of religiously-informed support for terror. I would also argue that, pragmatically, it is the kind of approach that is most likely to deliver the rights of the general public to live in safety and security.

Social Policy Challenges, Legal Developments and Religious Responsibilities

Some Key Questions

In an essay entitled 'Deciding how far you can go' that opened his edited volume on *The Growth of Religious Diversity: Britain From 1945: Volume II: Issues*, Gerald Parsons concluded with a series of the kind of questions that he argued had been opened up by 'the Rushdie affair' – in the first instance, for Salman Rushdie himself, and by extension for other authors and the wider society, but also for Muslims, and by extension for other religious believers:

> How far could Rushdie legitimately go in his literary critique of Islam? How far could the Muslim community go in legitimate protest against the book in question? How far could other religious believers, from other traditions, go in supporting them? How far could the state go in meeting religious grievances in this matter? How far could you go in maintaining that Britain was a genuinely plural society if these grievances were not met (or at least treated

with a similar seriousness and potential for redress as had applied in the *Gay News* case a decade or so earlier).

Conversely, just how far could Muslim action go? And how far could sympathisers with Muslim outrage go in their support of such protest, without causing equal – though opposite – effect to those in Britain who believed the issue of free speech, and the avoidance of censorship on religious grounds, to be the primary issues at stake? Or again, how far could critics of the Muslim reaction go in supporting Rushdie without themselves being guilty of offence to Islam? And if Rushdie were to be regarded as having gone too far, then how far could any writer – whether poet, novelist, academic, critic or journalist – go in criticising particular religious beliefs and traditions without being accused of 'blasphemy' or giving offence to the religious community in question? How far, indeed, were religious opinions and sensibilities entitled to claim protection from criticism or offence at all? How far could you go – supposing you wished to at all – in defining, legally, what constituted criticism or portrayal of religion in an offensive and unacceptable manner? (Parsons, 1994c: 18–19)

What Can Be Done and Who Can Do What?

Consideration of such questions alone, however important, is not enough. Practical issues in a multi-faith and multicultural society require policies to be developed, decisions to be made, and actions to be taken. In this context condemnation and critique of violence in the name of religion – or, indeed, within other social conditions, of secularism – while necessary and important, is not sufficient. The question is also what can be done to prevent such outrages.

In the face of the terror that is today being associated with Islam, there can be a tendency to believe that the only way to fulfil a strategy of 'preventing extremism' is to promote a 'liberal Islam' or a 'modernist Islam'. While understandable, such an approach is likely to be self-defeating. The issue of terror crimes should not be confused with religious conservatism or 'radicalism' as such. However, where there *are* such issues then, just as historically a number of Christian movements used theological resources to challenge the logic of the European Wars of Religion, so Muslims have a responsibility to address those matters related to Muslim interpretations of Islam that form part of the context for terror. Among others, the Turkish Muslim leader,

Fethullah Gülen, offers a way forward for Muslims that both recognizes issues that need tackling and also promotes a particular vision of how to do this. Thus Gülen argues:

> When those who have adopted Islam as a political ideology, rather than a religion in its true sense and function, review their self-proclaimed Islamic activities and attitudes, especially their political ones, they will discover that the driving force is usually personal or national anger, hostility or similar motives. If this is the case, we must accept Islam and adopt an Islamic attitude as the fundamental starting-point for action, rather than the existing oppressive situation. (in Ünal & Williams, 2000: 248)

What approaches such as Gülen's offer in the struggle against terror, and also injustice and unfair treatment, is not a wishy-washy modernist version of Islam, evacuated of its content merely to adapt to the prevailing social, political and economic norms. Such an approach cannot, even on pragmatic grounds, connect with Muslims of traditionalist orientation. Rather, what is needed is a robust *renewal* of Islam, based on deep knowledge of authentically Islamic sources that is recognizably rooted in the Qur'an and in the Sunnah of the Prophet. Only a resource of this kind can, at the level of values and world-view, find resonance with the broad sweep of traditional Muslims.

In so doing such approaches can also effectively challenge and marginalize the influence of those who have turned Islam into an instrumentalist political ideology and who see themselves as the revolutionary vanguard of a theocratic world order. What is important about such resources and approaches is also that they are not only reactive, but they are also *constructive*. As Sardar and Wyn Davies put it, arising from their reflections on the *Satanic Verses* controversy:

> For Muslims to persist in demands for the withdrawal of the book is an inadequate response to the needs of the time . . . They, too, have an active part to play in building a plural society which requires them to become articulate on the lack of plurality and the dearth of comprehension that is the status quo. Muslims must learn to articulate their vision of a dynamic Islamic civilization of the future, how they envisage their own tradition transforming itself by its own values and mores; they must make audible their own critique of extant tradition. The task for Muslims is to cease to be reactive and become proactive in mobilizing their own values to contribute to

remaking Western society for the betterment of all its people, as part of their inclusion in a plural society in a plural world. (Sardar and Wyn Davies, 1990: 262)

Such a reflection is, of course, not only a challenge for Muslims (though it is that too). Rather, given the asymmetry of cultural and economic power and the widespread existence of Islamophobia, it is also a challenge to the wider society in that it poses the question of whether the rest of us will recognize and encourage this when it takes place, or whether we are more in love (as the title of Sardar and Wyn Davies's book puts it) with our own 'distorted imaginations' than we are ready to deal with both Islam and secularity in a realistic way.

In order to move forward in a way that does not abandon multi-culturalism, it is important for society to find a more inclusive way of both understanding and talking about itself. The words 'we', 'us' and 'they' are small but very revealing words in terms of who is 'defined in' and who is 'defined out', in either conscious or (perhaps more often) unconscious ways. For a multicultural society, the aim should be what, in his book *Towards a World Theology* (where it was set out with reference to an inclusive approach to the study of religion), the histor-ian of religion, Wilfred Cantwell Smith called a process of engaging with the otherness of the other that culminates in a 'we all' who are talking with each other about an 'us':

> The traditional form of Western scholarship in the study of other men's religion was that of an impersonal presentation of an 'it'. The first great innovation in recent times has been the personalisation of the faiths observed, so that one finds a discussion of a 'they'. Presently the observer becomes personally involved, so that the situation is one of a 'we' talking about a 'they'. The next step is dialogue, where 'we' talk to 'you'. If there is listening and mutuality, this may become that 'we' talk *with* 'you'. The culmination of this process is when 'we all' are talking *with* each other about 'us'. (Smith, 1981: 101)

What Cantwell Smith describes in relation to a methodological approach in the academic study of religion, might also appropriately be read in ways that could be translated and applied to social policy.

The Role of Law

As has been noted earlier, the legal position of Muslim minorities was, at the height of 'the Rushdie affair', relatively weak and exposed. However, with the coming into power of the New Labour Government, European human rights law was incorporated into UK law by means of The Human Rights Act, 1998. Also, protection from discrimination on the grounds of religion or belief was introduced in the fields of employment and vocational training by the Employment Equality (Religion or Belief) Regulations, 2003, making discrimination in these fields illegal for the first time in England, Wales and Scotland (it having previously been illegal for many years in Northern Ireland). Such protection was then extended beyond employment and vocational training alone to the provision of goods and services through the passage of the Equality Act, 2006.

Also, in a coming together of the inheritance from 'the Rushdie affair' with the impact of 9/11, in the week beginning 11 September 2001, the British Government proposed an Anti-Terrorism, Crime and Security Bill, which included provisions to make 'incitement to religious hatred' an offence in England and Wales alongside the existing offence of 'incitement to racial hatred'. The proposals in that form gave rise to fairly widespread concern (including among a range of religious groups) that such a law might have the effect of constraining robust debate and criticism of religion (Cumper, 2007). In response, the Government emphasized that there is an important distinction to be made between robust verbal debate and the kind of incitement activity that the Bill was intended to address. However, in the end, at that time the 'incitement to religious hatred' clauses of the Bill did not pass into law. But the Bill, when passed as the Anti-Terrorism, Crime and Security Act (2001) did create a new category of religiously 'aggravated' offences. And public and political debate continued on the possibility and problems associated with such legislation.

It was partly because the original measures were rushed that they did not find a consensus of support, even among religious groups (Iganski, 2002). Further attempts to legislate followed with the Private Members' Religious Offences Bill, 2002, and then in the Government's Serious Organised Crime and Police Bill, 2004. Each of these attempts was based on modifications to the existing provisions for incitement to racial hatred found in the Public Order Act, 1986. The proposals remained controversial throughout, because of the inevitable difficulties involved in trying to balance the freedom of people within religions to live without fear of intimidation and hatred being stirred up against them, and the freedom of people to satirize religious topics and also advance either strong religious convictions or convictions critical of religion.

At the same time, according to the *Racist Incident Monitoring Annual Report* of the Crown Prosecution Service (which covered the period April 2004 to May 2005) for offences under the Anti-Terrorism, Crime, and Security Act in England and Wales, 27 of 34 defendants were prosecuted for religiously aggravated offences, and in 23 of these cases, the actual or perceived religion of the victim was Islam. The 2005 Labour Party Manifesto for England and Wales (though not for Scotland) contained a commitment to legislate balancing protection, tolerance and free speech, on the basis of which the Government introduced further measures into Parliament. Despite this being a manifesto commitment, in October 2005, the Racial and Religious Hatred Bill, 2005 was defeated in the House of Lords, with amendments from the Lords separating out racial and religious hatred; making the offence refer only to 'threatening' words and behaviour and not 'threatening, abusive or insulting'; and requiring the prosecution to prove an intention to stir up hatred.

In January 2006, the Government attempted to reinstate the reference to 'abusive and insulting behaviour' and the notion of being 'reckless' about stirring up hatred, but suffered its second defeat in the Commons, losing by one vote. The measure was finally passed in an amended form, as the Racial and Religious Hatred Act, 2006, referring only to England and Wales, and being concerned with 'acts intended to stir up hatred' where religious hatred is understood as being hatred against a group of persons defined by reference to religious belief or lack of religious belief.

Specific explanation was included to the effect that this law should not be read in a way that prohibits or restricts debate, antipathy, dislike or even ridicule or insult of religions, their belief and practices, nor to exclude proselytism. It was also made clear that prosecution of an offence under these provisions can only proceed with the permission of the Attorney General. At the time of writing many, but not yet all, of the provisions of this Act have been brought into force.

Finally, as this book was being written, in June 2008 the common law offences of blasphemy and blasphemous libel were abolished in the Criminal Justice and Immigration Act, 2008, which came into effect from 8 July 2008. Therefore, in many ways, the landscape of religion and law in relation to issues of incitement, blasphemy and free speech has been completely transformed as compared with what was the case during 'the Rushdie affair'.

Combating Enemy Images

Consideration of 'the Rushdie affair' as a 'mirror for our times' underlines that it is an important part of the responsibility of citizens to press for governments to develop and use law in ways that both contain and roll back the environments in which 'the future of multiculturalism' can have the possibility to survive and even to thrive. But at the same time, it is also important that members of the public, both *individually* and as members of any groups to which they might belong, accept the responsibilities and opportunities that we have in the places where we belong and in the groups in which we are active. And in this, there is a special responsibility that lies with religious groups themselves.

In an essay on 'Religious identities in a secular state', Stanley Samartha – an Indian Christian theologian and former Director of the Dialogue Sub-Unit of the World Council of Churches – argued for the importance of maintaining a distinctive vocation of religions over and against both the vacuous superficiality of a consumer secularism and the dangerous forms of limited belonging based upon blood and ethnicity:

> In an age dominated by science and secularism one of the tasks of genuinely religious people is to draw attention to the Mystery of transcendence, a centre of values, a source of meaning, an object of loyalty beyond the smaller loyalties to one's particular caste, language or religion. (Samartha, 1991: 57)

Since all religious traditions affirm the centrality of truthfulness and integrity, religious leaders in particular, but also ordinary religious believers, have a responsibility actively to intervene in relation to the production and circulation of ephemera and other literature that defames those of other religions – and especially so when it circulates among worshippers in churches, mosques, synagogues, gurdwaras and mandirs, and other places of worship. Academics also have an important vocation of bringing 'truthfulness' to bear where false enemy images and conspiracy theories are developed and disseminated and individual religious believers also have a responsibility. As an example of the issues involved and, as originally told elsewhere:

> . . . around the time of 9/11, I happened to have been asked to be responsible for leading a service of evening worship in the Baptist Christian congregation in Derby, and of which I am a member. The Baptist Christian tradition is a Christian tradition that has had an honourable tradition of upholding religious liberty and standing against intolerance and persecution on the grounds of religion. The Baptist founder, Thomas Helwys' 1612 pamphlet, *A Short Declaration of the Mystery of Iniquity* (see Groves, 1998) is one of the earliest English language justifications for religious liberty that specifically included Jews, Muslims and heretics within the scope of its arguments in favour of religious freedom.
>
> At the same time, historical positions are no guarantee of contemporary fidelity to such traditions. The members of the local Baptist congregation of which I am a member are good people. But, in truth, I wasn't sure how they would react to facing issues relating to relationships with Muslims post-9/11 in the context of worship. In the end, I decided that it was not good enough for me to be a Professor of Inter-Religious Relations, to write and publish on inter-faith relations, if I did not also try to address these issues in the place of worship of which I was also a member.
>
> Although uncertain of how this would be received, I resolved that I should seek the agreement of the church's minister for me to invite a Muslim both to be present, and to take an active part in that evening's worship. What I wanted people to do was to meet and hear a real Muslim and not the media images encountered on the TV screen. Agreement was given and I invited the Muslim faith advisor from the University of Derby to attend the evening worship of my church and, as part of the service itself, to be interviewed about what it means to be a Muslim in post-September 11 western societies. (Weller, 2007a: 196)

I tell this story not to claim any personal credit for such an initiative, the impact of which has probably not been particularly significant in the scale of things. But I recount it precisely to underline how easy it might have been *not* to do this. One of the characteristics of conspiracy theories, incitement to hatred and violence informed by religion is that they are very much to do with fear. They feed on popular fears. They stimulate popular fears by solidifying and ideologizing them. They create understandable and objectively grounded fear among those who are their targets. And there can also be fears – professional, personal, and religious – about taking the necessary steps to confront popular fears, including the fear of becoming targets by association with those who are the original objects of conspiracy theories and the incitement of hatred.

Twenty years on from the original *Satanic Verses* controversy, it remains 'a mirror for our times'. The diversities of religion and belief in the UK and the world, and the opportunities and issues that arise from them, are complex and challenging. Individuals and communities no longer live in a national vacuum. Rather, they live at the intersection between the global and the local in a world that is both increasingly globalizing and localizing. They are simultaneously part of transnational communities of information and solidarity, while also sharing in the civic society of the state of which they are citizens. The challenge facing those of diverse religion and belief and the wider states and societies in which they are set is that of encouraging the common visions and structures necessary for sustaining an integrated but richly diverse community, but avoiding both assimilation or fragmentation.

Today, more than was ever recognized for much of the twentieth century, there is a realization that societies and states need to respond in more inclusive ways to the challenges and opportunities presented by increasing religious diversity. At the same time, it is also more evident than ever that religious communities and groups will need to develop still further their own responsibilities within the civil societies of which they are a part and, at all levels of their organization and activity, intensify their commitment to the development of positive interfaith relations and to the furtherance of the common good.

Concluding Notes Towards a Common Future

Words Matter

As has previously been noted, Gerald Parsons concluded his essay on religion and politics in Britain since 1945 with a warning that, without an effort on the part of religious leaders and politicians, political parties and religious groups to 'understand the subtleties and complexities of the interactions to which their various commitments give rise' then 'the alternative is the reduction of increasingly complex issues to the convenient slogans of competing religious-cum-political pressure groups – a bleak and unhappy prospect indeed' (Parsons, 1994b: 154)

In offering a retrospective reflection on the 'Rushdie affair' that might also prospectively inform current debates on the future of multi-culturalism, it has been the aim of this book precisely to contribute to a context in which the inevitable and necessary ongoing debate about the future of our multicultural societies in an increasingly globalized world does not become the kind feared by Parsons. What is clear is that while, like all proverbs, the old saying 'sticks and stones may break my bones but words will never harm me' has some validity, when it comes down to it, and especially in social and political con-texts that are deeply contested, words *do* matter, and they can still be a matter of life and death.

Philip Roth once differentiated reactions to literature in the com-munist East and the capitalist West on the basis that, in totalitarianism, 'everything matters and nothing goes', whereas in liberal democracy, 'nothing matters and everything goes'. Commenting on this in relation to 'the Rushdie affair' in a *Guardian* (24.2.89) essay on 'Words apart', the South American writer Carlos Fuentes commented that *'The Satanic Verses* have pushed the "nothing goes" of intolerance right out into the public squares of indifference. Suddenly, we all realise that everything matters, whether it goes or not.'

It is precisely because words 'matter' that, in ending this book, it remains a responsibility to try not only to offer a descriptive summary of the key events and debates of the controversy and how aspects of it have subsequently been reprised in the succeeding twenty years; nor even only to provide an analysis of the 'entails' of the controversy and the issues involved in what has subsequently transpired. Rather, there remains a responsibility on the author to try clearly to articulate his own positions, if only so that readers, by using these as a foil for their own consideration, agreement and disagreement, can then be encour-aged to undertake their own reflections and arrive at their own conclusions.

In truth, even twenty years on from the original 'Rushdie affair', many (including this author) experience at least a slight sense of anx-iety about declaring a position. This is both because the taking of positions may easily be misunderstood by one party to the controversy or another, but also because the pressure to summarize may lead to an unhelpful oversimplification in the context of undoubted complexity and layerings of the issues involved. However, in closing this book it seems important to try to overcome these difficulties in order to make as clear a set of statements in conclusion as it is possible for me to make, both about the *Satanic Verses* controversy and about its later 'entails' in relation to issues around the future of multiculturalism.

Ten 'Learning Points' from 'the Rushdie Affair'

What follows is therefore presented as ten 'learning points' that arise from reflection directly on 'the Rushdie affair' as a 'mirror for our times', but also in the light of the way in which the issues originally heralded in 1998 and 1989 have been reprised in subsequent two decades. They are this author's attempt to make at least a small contribution to overcoming the atmosphere of social fear engendered both by the discourse and actions of those of Muslim background who are prepared to utilize or support the use of terror violence in pursuit of their aims; as well as to break out of the wider society's straitjacket of expectation of the sufficiency of moral outrage about terrorism; and finally to challenge a governmental approach that by failing to locate the phenomena in a social and historical context, and by seeking to create a 'liberal' Islam may, tragically, only be exacerbating the phenomena that it is seeking to address:

1. The threat of death against Salman Rushdie, his publishers and translators was not and is not acceptable in British society.
2. The expression of Muslim concern, including robust opposition to the book and calling for it to be withdrawn from circulation, using all democratic and legal means, was and is acceptable.
3. The ability of Muslims to express such concern and opposition without being cast as outside of, or disloyal to, civic society and the state is necessary for the evolution of a properly inclusive pluralistic society.
4. Many of the reactions of secularists to Muslim concerns gave expression to a deep-seated ignorance of Islam and stimulated Islamophobia among the general other than Muslim population.
5. No states and societies are without legal constraints upon freedom of expression, and in a pluralistic society it is probably necessary to have some constraints upon at least the style, if not the content of what is expressed, but drawing such lines is never easy or final.
6. In the totality of a global historical perspective it should be

remembered that it is the 'secular' that must be considered to be a new experiment in social organization and integration.

7. The origins of the 'secular' in politics can be found in the reactive responses of economic liberalism, revolutionary Republicanism, socialism and Marxism to the seventeenth-century Wars of Religion.

8. The European roots of the 'secular' can, of themselves, make it problematic for people, cultures, religions and societies whose other experience of imports from Europe has been one of colonialism and imperial conquest.

9. There is an important and as yet not sufficiently attempted task, for both Muslims and others, to reflect on how the 'secular' tradition and Muslim civilizational heritage might positively engage with each other.

10. Acknowledgement of the need explicitly to consider the nature of the 'secular' as well as of the religious, can lead to formerly 'common sense' formulations of issues being turned on their head, making it possible to see them from previously unrecognized perspectives.

Seven 'Working Principles' for Religion(s), State and Society Relationships

In addition to these ten 'learning points' derived from reflection directly on 'the Rushdie affair', during the period following the outbreak of the controversy, and relating to social policy development and religious issues between then and the impact of the 'social policy shock' of 9/11, I previously identified (see Weller, 2002a, 2002b, 2002c and 2005b) seven 'working principles' on religion and public life in the UK and in Europe. The developmental history of these can be found in Weller, 2005a: xiii). They are set out again here for further consideration in the light both of 'the Rushdie affair' and the issues highlighted by it as they have been reprised over the following two decades.

As with the ten 'learning points' arising directly from 'the Rushdie affair', these do not claim to be either a detailed survey or a last word. But they are intended to focus attention and to provoke reaction, debate, discussion and, ultimately, action in terms of a direction for change of a kind that could sustain a current and future public and political engagement with, and commitment to multiculturalism.

Principle 1: The Importance of Not Marginalizing Religions from Public Life

States which assign religions to the private sphere will impoverish themselves by marginalizing important social resources and might unwittingly be encouraging of those reactive, backward- and inward-looking expressions of religious life that are popularly characterized as 'fundamentalisms'.

Principle 2: The Need to Recognize the Specificity of Religions

Religious traditions and communities offer important alternative perspectives to the predominant values and power structures of states and societies. Religions are a reminder of the importance of the things that cannot be seen, touched, smelled, tasted and heard, for a more balanced perspective on those things that can be experienced in these ways.

Principle 3: The Imperative for Religious Engagement with the Wider Community

Religious communities and traditions should beware of what can be seductive calls from within their traditions to form 'religious unity fronts' against what is characterized as 'the secular state' and what is perceived as the amorality and fragmentation of modern and post-modern society.

Principle 4: The Need for a Reality Check

National and political self-understandings that exclude people of other than the majority religious traditions, either by design or by default, are, historically speaking, fundamentally distorted. Politically and religiously such self-understandings are dangerous and need to be challenged.

Principle 5: The Need to Recognize the Transnational Dimensions of Religions

Religious communities and traditions need to pre-empt the dangers involved in becoming proxy sites for imported conflicts involving their co-religionists in other parts of the world. But because they are themselves part of wider global communities of faith, religions have the potential for positively contributing to a better understanding of the role of the states and societies of their own countries within a globalizing world.

Principle 6: The Importance of Religious Inclusivity

Religious establishments as well as other traditions and social arrangements that provide particular forms of religion with privileged access to social and political institutions need to be re-evaluated. There is a growing need to imagine and to construct new structural forms for the relationship between religion(s), state(s) and society(ies) that can more adequately express an inclusive social and political self-understanding than those which currently privilege majority religious traditions.

Principle 7: The Imperative of Inter-religious Dialogue

Inter-religious dialogue is an imperative for the religious communities and for the states and societies of which they are a part. There is a need to continue the task of developing appropriate interfaith structures at all levels within states and societies and in appropriate transnational and international structures.

Six 'Points of Challenge' on 'The Other Side of Terror/The War on Terror'

And finally, in addition to those ten 'learning points' that arise directly from reflection on 'the Rushdie affair' and the seven 'working principles' set out above, a further six 'points of challenge' are identified. These also arise from reflection on the issues first highlighted in 'the

Rushdie affair', but have in particular been focused by the way in which these issues have been reprised after the 'social policy shock' of 9/11:

1. Governments must learn from history that to combat terror with methods that undermine human rights will only strengthen those forces that use terror as a means of advancing their cause.
2. To ignore or deny the reasons that those who use terror to advance their cause give for their actions is unlikely to lead to a resolution of the problems caused by terror.
3. Terror in the name of religion is particularly dangerous both to the wider body politic and to religions themselves, because it harnesses ultimate convictions and commitments in its destructive service.
4. Attempts by the 'powers that be' artificially and externally to create a 'liberal' or 'moderate' Islam (or indeed any other religion) are likely to prove ineffective and may also backfire.
5. Muslims (and indeed people of other religions) have to accept a greater responsibility for combating the dissemination and propagation of 'enemy images' among their faithful.
6. For multiculturalism to continue to have a future, governments and societies must acknowledge and tackle Islamophobia, and indeed all other forms of discrimination and hatred on the grounds of religion or belief.

In conclusion, to return to what in the Introduction to the book Bhikhu Parekh was quoted as saying, and which provided the overall image that inspired the writing of this book: 'A political crisis is like a magnifying mirror reflecting some of the deepest trends and tendencies developing in society. A wise nation meditates on it, and uses it as a means for self-knowledge. The Rushdie affair has raised issues likely to preoccupy us for a long time' (Parekh, 1989b).

Bibliography

The bibliography is organized in several parts:

Newspaper editorials: these are listed in alphabetical order of newspaper and, within that, by date of publication.

Letters to the editor: these are also listed in alphabetical order of newspaper and, within that, by date of publication. The names of the authors of the letters are given. Where there are two letters to the same publication on the same date, precedence is given by alphabetical order of surname.

Newspaper reports: these are also listed in alphabetical order of newspaper and, within that, by date of publication. Where there are named reporters or authors, these are given. Where a piece published in a newspaper is written more as an essay than a report, it is also listed by author surname in the bibliography section that lists authored and edited books and newspaper, magazine and journal articles.

Online newspapers and other online resources: these are also listed in alphabetical order of media source and, within that, by date of publication. Where there are named reporters or authors, these are given. Where appropriate, web addresses are given, together with the date at which the online source was accessed.

Authored and edited books and newspaper, magazine and journal articles: these are listed in alphabetical order of author surname and, within that, by date of publication. Where a piece in this section was published in a newspaper, it also appears in the bibliography section that lists newspaper reports.

Newspaper Editorials

Baptist Times, The
(7.6.2007), 'The problem with a little moderation'

Church Times, The
(24.2.89), 'Islam and modernity'
(11.8.89), 'Talking to Islam'

Financial Times, The
(16.2.89), 'A Satanic warrant'

Guardian, The
(25.2.89), 'Beyond the threat'
(4.3.89), 'Rude, as in rudimentary'

Independent, The
(18.2.89), 'Limits to mutual tolerance'
(21.2.89), 'Too tolerant for too long'
(22.2.89), 'British law for Britain's Muslims'
(27.2.89), 'Viking must stand firm'
(28.2.89), 'Lifting some earthly barriers'
(6.3.89), 'A false sympathy with Islam'
(20.5.89), 'Dangers of the Muslim Campaign'
(31.7.89), 'Dissent and fundamentalism'

Muslim News, The
(22.9.89), 'Can Islamic Party Britain do a Bhika?'

New Life
(3.2.89), 'Burning beyond reason'
(3.3.89), 'Mistified message'

Publishers Weekly, The
(13.10.89), 'A Rushdie paperback?'

Newspaper Letters to the Editor

Guardian, The
(23.1.89), Madden, M.
(23.1.89), El-Essawy, H.
(25.5.89), Voices for Salman Rushdie
(30.5.89), Committee Against the Blasphemy Law

Independent, The
(17.2.89), Wesker, A.

(21.2.89), Newbigin, L.
(22.2.89), Desai, M.
(25.2.89), McEwan, I.
(7.3.89), Lewis, N.
(16.3.89), World Conference on Religion and Peace
(2.6.89), Chapman, G., *et al.*
(24.7.89), Foot, M.
(25.10.89), Rushdie, S.

Jewish Chronicle, The
(10.2.89), Hewitt, I.

New Life
(11.8.89), Ali, A.

Sunday Times, The
(29.1.89), Islam, Y.
(9.7.89), Le Lohe, M.

Times, The
(4.2.89), Jakobovits, I.

Newspaper Reports

Baptist Times, The
(2.3.89), Hardy, B., 'Faiths forum could help keep the peace'

Bradford Telegraph and Argus, The
(20.6.89), Buck, P., 'Muslims reject plea to end Rushdie protests'

Church Times, The
(24.2.89), 'Violence in book row condemned'
(3.3.89), Brown, D., ' "God, the merciful, the compassionate" '
(31.3.89), 'Bishop calls for book's withdrawal'
(27.10.89), Johnson, D., 'British Islam draws together'

Daily Mail, The
(31.1.89), Burgess, A., 'The burning truth'
(19.7.89), Deans, J., 'Minister spells it out to ethnic groups: here is how to be a true
    blue Briton'

Guardian, The

(1.2.89), Schwarz, W., 'Shame is the spur'

(15.2.89a), Murtagh, P., 'Rushdie in hiding after Ayatollah's death threat'

(15.2.89b), Vulliamy, E., 'Authors angry and bewildered'

(15.2.89c), Murtagh, P., 'Rushdie "lies" which inflamed Muslims'

(15.2.89d), Ezard, J., 'Passages "put the needle into Islam" '

(15.2.89e), Morris, M. and Sharratt, T., 'Death threat wins support'

(15.2.89f), 'Bonfire of the certainties'

(16.2.89a), Ezard, J., 'Satanic accusers cite line and verse'

(16.2.89b), Pick, H., 'Relations with Iran in balance'

(16.2.89c), Cook, S., 'Radical minority feared most as likely assassins'

(16.2.89d), Murtagh, P., 'Writers rally to Rushdie as publishers rethink'

(16.2.89e), Barker, D., 'Wall between the factions'

(16.2.89f), Wainwright, M., 'Faith, hope and threats stir Muslim believers'

(17.2.89a), Webb, W.L., 'The Imam and the scribe'

(17.2.89b), Stern, J., 'By any other name'

(18.2.89), Ezard, J. and Pick, H., 'Tehran pulls back on threats to Rushdie'

(22.2.89), Goodwin, S., 'Commons unites behind Howe in Rushdie affair'

(23.2.89a), Murtagh, P., Tomforde, A. and Brasier, M., 'Bonn and Paris back stand against Iran'

(23.2.89b), Flint, J., 'Rushdie reaction may hit British hostages'

(23.2.89c), Wainwright, M., 'Bradford leaders agree to forum for Rushdie debate'

(23.2.89d), Hirst, D., 'Tehran reacts to sanctions with new death threat'

(24.2.89a), Murtagh, P., 'Muslim group backs Rushdie death edict'

(24.2.89b), Fuentes, C., 'Words apart'

(25.2.89a), Hirst, D., 'Khomeini agrees to meet Shevardnaze'

(25.2.89b), Bose, A. and Hoyland, P., 'Ten die as Bombay police fire on Rushdie protestors'

(25.2.89c), Berger, J., 'Two books and two notions of the sacred'

(27.2.89a), Flint, J., 'Beirut launches holy war against Islam detractors'

(27.2.89b), Martineau, L., 'Japan retreats on Rushdie protest as world fury grows'

(27.2.89c), Martin, P., 'Spurn the book, spare the man'

(27.2.89d), Bowcott, O., 'Bradford Muslims urge Penguin ban'

(27.2.89e), Akhtar, S., 'Whose light, whose darkness?'

(1.3.89a), Elliott, L., 'British trade links become first casualty of the Rushdie affair'

(1.3.89b), Hirst, D., 'Split with UK is "turning point" for Iran'

(3.3.89a), Pallister, D., 'Black voices back Rushdie'

(3.3.89b), Pick, H., 'Howe says Rushdie book is offensive'

(3.3.89c), Phillips, M., 'This book could cause offence'

(3.3.89d), Alrawi, K., 'Letter From Cairo. Rushdie and Mahfouz'

(3.3.89e), O'Higgins, P., 'Relic that has no role'

(4.3.89), Pick, H., 'PM "understands offence" to Islam'

(6.3.89a), Thurgood, L., 'Palestinian guerilla chief "ready to kill Rushdie"'

(6.3.89b), Khomeini, R., 'A challenge to the world-devourers'

(7.3.89), Ezard, J., 'Rushdie urged to withdraw book and "end suffering"'

(8.3.89), Simmons, M., 'Iran breaks off relations with Britain over Rushdie'

(9.3.89), Flint, J. and Simmons, M., 'Embassy urges Britons to get out of Lebanon'

(10.3.89a), Murtagh, P. and Walker, J., 'Rushdie "death squad" denial'

(10.3.89b), Foot, M., 'Historical Rushdie'

(11.3.89a), Targett, J., 'Tight lips for Tehran'

(11.3.89b), 'Rushdie death squad "not in West Germany"'

(13.3.89), Reeve, H., 'Islam's reply to sedition'

(15.3.89), Burman, P., 'Two quit in Nobel row over Rushdie'

(17.3.89), Traynor, I., 'Islamic states refuse to back Rushdie death sentence'

(27.3.89), Smith, M., 'Muslim voters threaten boycott'

(30.3.89a), Wolf, J., 'Imam in Rushdie row shot dead'

(30.3.89b), Wainwright, M., 'Labour MPs unrepentant on Rushdie'

(31.3.89), Webb, W., 'The clocks go back in Cairo'

(3.4.89), Sharrock, D., 'Muslims urged to break law'

(7.4.89), Bern, T., 'An end to blasphemy'

(16.4.89a), Brenton, H., 'A mullah's night in'

(16.4.89b), Knewstubb, N., 'Renton urges more integration in rebuke to Muslim protesters'

(22.4.89), Devlin, A., 'Something indigestible at the writers' lunch'

(4.5.89), Rose, D., 'Rushdie protest may set record'

(5.5.89), Rose, D., 'Muslim march "poses security nightmare"'

(9.5.89), Hebert, H., 'The liberal taboos'

(15.5.89), Schwarz, W., 'Muslim leaders scale down estimates of Rushdie demo'

(26.5.89), Soyinka, W., 'Communication cannot be halted by Bible, Koran or Bhagavad-Gita"

(27.5.89), Pallister, D., 'Muslims plan to march on Downing Street'

(29.5.89), Vulliamy, E., 'March ends in battle at Westminster'

(6.6.89), Rose, D., 'Tehran crush claims 8 lives'

(9.6.89), Thurgood, L., 'Rafsanjani speaks out against Britain'

(20.6.89), 'Bishop seeks end to Satanic demos'

(11.7.89), Wainright, M., 'White gang attack touches raw nerve for Muslims'

(20.7.89), Pallister, D., 'Rushdie call for conciliation'

(22.7.89a), Schwarz, W., 'Satanic Verses demos put on ice'

(22.7.89b), White, M., 'Muslim row "hits 10 Labour seats"'

(25.7.89), Whyte, A., 'Flying in the face of tradition'

(1.8.89), Henry, G., 'BBC goes ahead with play about Rushdie'

(2.8.89), Wainwright, M., 'Church leaders unite to condemn BBC'

(14.8.89), Pallister, D., 'Scholar calls for Rushdie extradition'

(21.8.89), Thompson, J., 'Towards a redefinition of freedom'

(23.8.89), Hirst, D., 'Britain rejects Iran's offer to restore relations'

(25.8.89), Alrawi, K., 'Are you or have you ever been an atheist?'

(26.8.89), Nettleton, P., 'Rushdie living separately from wife for past four weeks'

(15.9.89), Wainwright, M., 'York police hold man after blast'

(16.9.89a), The Bookseller, 'Penguin, the hawks and the ostrich'

(16.9.89b), Ezard, J., 'Books blast suspect sought'

(25.9.89), Bowcott, O., 'Rushdie protest to be stepped up'

(2.10.89), Bowcott, O., 'Rushdie making monkeys of us all, says preacher'

(24.11.89), Young, H., 'Life, death and Mr Rushdie'

(17.1.90), Ahmed, A., 'Salman Rushdie: a new chapter'

(21.4.90), White, M., 'Tebbit's test match swipe goes over the racial boundary for irate Asian community'

(2.5.90), Ahmed, S. and O'Neill, S., 'Protest ends Iran project at school'

(24.7.90), Barker, D., 'Video proprietor with sights set on world fortune'

(18.8.90), Barker, D., 'The man who "killed" Rushdie'

(29.8.90), Wintour, P., 'MP in furore over "Muslims go home"'

(7.9.90), Akhtar, K. and Kennedy, M., 'Screenings of Rushdie film postponed by cinema'

(21.3.93), Ellison, M., 'Midnight's Children earns Rushdie accolade of best Booker winner'

(23.12.94), Branigan, T., 'Stars sign letter in support of playwright in hiding'

(28.9.94), Black, I., 'Britain and Iran in deadlock over Rushdie fatwa'

(23.6.95), Black, I., 'Iran stalls on deal over Rushdie fatwa'

(5.7.07), Milne, S., 'Denial of link with Iraq is delusional and dangerous'

(9.7.07), Bunting, M., 'Hearts and minds of young Muslims will be won or lost in the mosques'

Independent, The

(28.1.89), Helm, S., 'Muslims divided by a faith caught in a period of change'

(16.2.89a), Mills, H., Lister, D. and Morris, H., 'Writers call on Thatcher to denounce murder command'

(16.2.89b), Mills, H., Lister, D. and Morris, H., 'Film writer is "deeply ashamed"'

(16.2.89c), Mills, H., Lister, D. and Morris, H., 'Response left to Shia conscience'

(16.2.89d), Morris, H., 'Khomeini's edict unifies competing factions'

(16.2.89e), Mills, H., Lister, D. and Morris, H., 'Paperback edition "a provocative act"'

(17.2.89a), Lister, D., 'Publishers cancel Rushdie editions'

(17.2.89b), Morris, H., 'Iranian paper criticises $1 bounty for author'

(18.2.89a), Bulloch, J., Morris, H. and Usborne, D., 'Iran's President tells Rushdie to beg forgiveness'

(18.2.89b), Midgley, S. and Ward, S., 'Outraged British Muslims condemn "The Satanic Verses" unseen'

(18.2.89c), Smith, R., 'Holy warriors volunteer to kill'

(18.2.89d), Ward, K., 'The violent gifts of modern Islam'

(21.2.89a), Vahdatkhah, A., 'Review in Tehran journal went unnoticed'

(21.2.89b), Usborne, D., 'Sir Geoffrey swept along by EC enthusiasm'

(21.2.89c), Usborne, D., Morris, H. and Barwick, S., 'Britain puts links with Iran on ice'

(21.2.89d), Barwick, S., 'Runcie calls for broader legislation'

(22.2.89a), Morris, H., 'Tehran loses fragile links to the Little Satan'

(22.2.89b), Brown, C., Bulloch, J., Haeri, S. and Barwick, S, 'Howe demands full retraction'

(22.2.89c), Rice, R., 'Muslim leaders not to be charged'

(22.2.89d), Hoffman, M., 'The pre-eminence of truth in the market-place of ideas'

(22.2.89e), Yapp, M., 'The hubris of the hidden Imam'

(23.2.89), Parekh. B., 'The mutual suspicions which fuelled the Rushdie affair'

(24.2.89a), Ward, S., 'Asian artists join in defence of Rushdie'

(24.2.89b), Bulloch, J., 'Envoys warned of impending furore'

(24.2.89c), Morris, H., 'Rushdie "conspiracy" stokes the fires of Khomeini revolution'

(25.2.89a), 'Hurd tells Muslims not to break law over Rushdie book'

(25.2.89b), Lister, D., ' "Verses" view of women offends Islam'

(27.2.89a), McCarthy, T., 'Indonesia and Malaysia joint Rushdie ban'

(27.2.89b), Nowell, R., 'Blasphemy does not exist for Buddhism'

(27.2.89c), Tweedie, J., 'Xenophobia as a social mechanism'

(28.2.89a), Palling, B., 'Penguin admits it pulped Verses'

(28.2.89b), Brown, C. and Morris, H., 'Muslims' blasphemy law plea fails'

(1.3.89a), Elliott, L., 'British trade links become first casualty of the Rushdie affair'

(1.3.89b) Morris, H., ' "Princess" case led British words of regret'

(1.3.89c), Jenkins, P., 'Is Rushdie just the tool of Allah's will?'

(1.3.89d), Kaufman, G., 'So-called liberals for whom some are more tolerable than others'

(1.3.89e), Bulloch, J. and Brown, J., 'Moscow may mediate on Rushdie Iran row'

(2.3.89a), Lister, D., 'Book world defends Rushdie'

(2.3.89b), Cornwell, R., 'Russia blames press for Rushdie'

(2.3.89c), Jenkins, P., 'The story of free thought and speech'

(3.3.89a), Lister, D., 'Newsreader gets 24-hour guard'

(3.3.89b), Bulloch, J., 'Britain rejects talks with Iran'

(6.3.89a), Reuters, 'Palestinian radical vows to kill Salman Rushdie'

(6.3.89b), Sheridan, M. and Kelsey, T., 'Rushdie denounced as blasphemous by Vatican paper'

(14.3.89a), 'Rushdie refusal'

(14.3.89b), 'Morris, H., 'Saudis deflect Iran's bid for a "Rushdie summit" '

(15.3.89a), Burman, P., 'Two quit in Nobel row over Rushdie'

(15.3.89b), Morris, H., 'Riyadh urges calm over "Verses"'

(15.3.89c), Barker, P., 'Publish and be damned'

(11.4.89), 'Arsonists attack bookshop'

(29.4.89a), United Press Institute, '"Rushdie" threats against diplomats'

(29.4.89b), 'Rushdie affair'

(29.5.89), Reeves, P., 'Muslims may strike for book ban'

(3.5.89), 'Publishers shelve book on Rushdie'

(9.5.89), Maitland, S., 'Unravelling the Rushdie row'

(13.5.89), 'Rushdie "defender" jailed for bomb attack'

(27.5.89), Dalrymple, J., 'Muslims to march over "Satanic Verses"'

(28.5.89), Shrimsley, R. and Dawson, C., 'Riot squad battles Muslims'

(31.5.89), Bulloch, J. and Darwish, A., 'Rushdie protest fights a Muslim power struggle'

(3.6.89), Helm, S., 'Muslim warning on campaign of civil disobedience'

(8.6.89), 'Rushdie offered a truce if "Satanic Verses" is withdrawn'

(13.6.89), 'The Rushdie file'

(17.6.89), Associated Press, 'Britain expels Iranians'

(19.6.89), Dalrymple, J., 'Rushdie attacks newspaper over "false interview"'

(20.6.89), 'Bishop warns of rising fear'

(24.6.89), Dalrymple, J., 'Marches ban imposed over Rushdie protests'

(5.7.89), Helm, S., 'Minister rules out blasphemy law for Islam'

(21.7.89a), Bevins, A., 'Labour Party split over Rushdie'

(21.7.89b) Hattersley, R., 'The racism of asserting that "they" must behave like "us"'

(22.7.89), Bevins, A, 'Labour on the rack over Rushdie'

(24.7.89), Lister, D., 'Rushdie adapts to Le Carré lifestyle in literary captivity'

(31.7.89), Brown, A., 'BBC urged to delay Rushdie programme'

(1.8.89), Ward, S., 'BBC shows Rushdie film despite Archbishop's plea'

(2.8.89), Brown, A., 'Runcie group may seek law change to protect religions'

(3.8.89), Brown, A., 'Disarming the zealot with tea, cakes and conversation'

(5.8.89), Kirby, T., 'Hotel terrorist had two bombs "for Rushdie"'

(28.8.89), 'Muslims call for Rushdie poem ban'

(5.9.89), Dalrymple, J., 'Bomb attack condemned as "lunacy"'

(14.9.89), Wahhab, I., 'Muslims launch political party to contest elections'

(15.9.89), Kirby, T. and Wahhab, I., 'Man held over bookshop bomb'

(25.9.89), O'Sullivan, J., 'Penguin yet to decide on Rushdie paperback'

(29.9.89), 'Rushdie split'

(30.9.89), O'Sullivan, J., 'Rushdie "insulted non-Muslims"'

(10.10.89a), 'Call for blasphemy law change'

(10.10.89b), Akhtar, S., 'The Liberal Inquisition'

(15.10.89), Bailey, M., 'Penguin may print Koranic verses'

(21.10.89), 'King Penguin under threat of extinction'

(27.10.89), Cusick, J., 'Muslim warning stops lecture on Rushdie affair'
(2.11.89), 'CPS to consider threat to Rushdie'
(6.1.90a), 'Young blood takes up fight for rights'
(29.5.90), Reeves, P., 'Muslims may strike for book ban'
(29.12.90), Boggan, S., 'Rushdie reaffirms conversion to Islam'

Independent on Sunday
(4.2.90), Rushdie, S., 'In good faith'

International Herald Tribune
(18–19.2.89), Rushdie, S., 'Please, read "Satanic Verses" before condemning it'

Jewish Chronicle, The
(28.10.88), 'Chief Rabbi backs Moslem protest'
(3.2.89), Bermant, C., 'Bradford burning evokes unhappy memories'
(24.2.89a), Kessel, Y., 'Rushdie row in Israel'
(24.2.89b), 'Rushdie threat outrage'
(10.3.89a), Josephs, B. and Rocker, S., 'Chief in Rushdie row'
(10.3.89b), Kleinman, P., 'Chief Rabbi goes too far'
(10.3.89c), Bermant, C., 'The authentic voice of Jewish intolerance'
(17.3.89), 'Big mail bag for Chief over Rushdie book row'
(12.5.89), Frazer, J., 'Islamic fundamentals'
(26.5.89), 'Blasphemy'
(18.8.89), Rocker, S., 'Rabbi attacks ethnic "bullying"'

Muslim News, The
(9.6.89), 'Hard Labour over Rushdie'
(7.7.89a), 'Bradford call for ten point plan'
(7.7.89b), 'High Court victory against Rushdie'
(22.9.89), Sherif, M. and Mirza, F., 'MPs on the line'

New Life
(9.9.88), 'Vaz to see "harmful" film'
(16.9.88), 'Muslim group calls for Christ film ban'
(16.12.88), 'Satanic Verses protest continues'
(20.1.89), 'Muslim book burning condemned'
(27.1.89), 'Salman defends "right to offend"'
(3.2.89), 'Protests could lead to Muslim boycott'
(17.2.89), Shahin, S., 'British Muslims oppose Khomeini order'
(24.2.89a), Shahin, S., 'Salman affair snowballs into furore'
(24.2.89b), 'CRE calls for tolerance'

(3.3.89a), Shahin, S., 'Hurd stuns British Muslims'
(3.3.89b), Parek, B., 'Liberal versus religious fundamentalism'
(10.3.89a), 'Howe and Thatcher U-turn on Verses'
(10.3.89b), Vaz, K., 'Satanic curses'
(17.3.89), 'Councillor told to quit over Rushdie death call'
(31.3.89), 'Keith will stay vow Asians'
(14.4.89a), 'Koran film scene axed to avoid offence'
(14.4.89b), Agrawal, K., 'Pressing the self-destruct button'
(14.4.89c), Vaz, K., 'Godless Labour'
(14.4.89d), ' "Muslim independent" campaign in Leicester'
(12.5.89a), 'Focus changing from immigration to integration: Renton'
(12.5.89b), Parekh, B., 'Between holy text and moral void'
(23.6.89), 'White youths provoke Bradford Muslims'
(7.7.89), Ahuja, S., 'Women against religious oppression'
(21.7.89a), 'Anti-Rushdie campaign'
(21.7.89b), 'Labour divided over Rushdie affair'
(11.8.89), 'Bradford restaurant owners to sue BBC'
(15.9.89), 'Asian leaders slam Islamic party launch'
(29.9.89), 'Rushdie may sue Penguin'
(3.10.89), 'Rushdie pamphlet ignites race controversy'
(13.10.89), Hussain, A., 'How Rushdie fooled the West'
(1.12.89), 'BBC ordered to hand over Muslim film'

Observer, The
(22.1.89), 'Choice between dark and light'
(9.12.07), 'Opinion'

People, The
(19.2.89), Cliff, P., '20 ways to spot a mad mullah'

Sunday Times, The
(29.1.89), Roy, A. and Wahhab, I., 'How Rushdie lit a world Islamic fire'
(2.7.89), Roy, A., 'Rushdie taunts widen racial gap'
(9.7.89), Davison, J., Elliott, V. and Furbisher, J., 'Muslims on the march'
(3.9.95), Lees, C. and Fowler, R., 'Rushdie's latest upsets Hindus'

Sydney Morning Herald, The
(20.2.89), Glover, R., 'Book feud turns into testing-ground for race relations'

Times, The
(20.2.89), Rushdie, S., 'Statement by Salman Rushdie'

(2.3.89), Vincent, J., 'Outrage we cannot ignore'

(28.12.90), Rushdie, S., 'Why I have embraced Islam'

(12.10.93), 'Rushdie publisher shot'

(1.4.95), Brock, G., 'EU seeks Tehran pledge on safety of Rushdie'

(21.5.95), 'Iran gives hint of Rushdie reprieve'

(22.5.95), Evans, M., 'Tehran hints at lifting of Rushdie death sentence'

(23.6.95), Bremner, C., 'Iran resists EU call to reject fatwa on Rushdie'

(8.9.95), Frost, B., 'Ebulliant Rushdie casts off six years in the shadows to meet his readers'

Online Newspapers and Other Online Resources

BBC.co.uk

(5.10.06) 'Straw's veil comments spark anger' http://news.bbc.co.uk/1/hi/uk_politics/5410472.stm, accessed 7.11.2008

(14.12.07) 'Newsnight response to Policy Exchange Statement' http://www.bbc.co.uk/blogs/newsnight/2007/12/newsnight_response_to_policy_exchange_statement.html, accessed 7.11.2008

(29.5.2008), 'Policy Exchange dispute – update' http://www.bbc.co.uk/blogs/newsnight/2008/05/policy_exchange_dispute_update.html, accessed 7.11.2008

Independent.co.uk

(9.7.2008) Russell, B., 'Former head of MI5 says 42-day detention plan is unworkable' http://www.independent.co.uk/news/uk/home-news/former-head-of-mi5-says-42day-detention-plan-is-unworkable-862947.html, accessed 7.11.2008

Independent Television News

(8.7.2007), 'Tackling terror "will take 15 years"' http://itn.co.uk/news/1bc624f-112b0439417083d4b7ff33116.html, accessed 26.7.2008

Telegraph.co.uk

(31.10.2007), Helm, T., 'Hate literature easily found at UK mosques' http://www.telegraph.co.uk/news/uknews/1567819/Hate-literature-easily-found-at-UK-mosques.html, accessed 26.7.2008

Times Online

(20.2.05), Webster, P., Hoyle, B., Navi, R., 'Ayatollah revives the death fatwa on Salman Rushdie' http://www.timesonline.co.uk/tol/news/uk/article414681.ece, accessed 26.7.2008

(4.2.06), Norfolk, A., 'Bradford takes "insults" calmly as cultures clash over images' http://www.timesonline.co.uk/to/news/world/article726503.ece accessed 7.11.08

Authored and Edited Books and Newspaper, Magazine and Journal Articles

Abbas, T. (2005), 'Recent Developments to British Multicultural Theory, Policy and Practice: The Case of British Muslims'. *Citizenship Studies*, 9, 2, 153–66.

Abbas, T. (2007a), 'Muslim minorities in Britain: integration, multiculturalism and radicalism in the post-7/7 period'. *Journal of Intercultural Studies*, 28, 3, 287–300.

Abbas, T. (ed.) (2007b), *Islamic Political Radicalism: A European Perspective*. Edinburgh: Edinburgh University Press.

Abrams, M., Gerard, D. and Timms, N. (eds.) (1985), *Values and Social Change in Britain*. London: Macmillan.

Afshari, R. (1990), 'The poet and the prophet: the iconoclasm of The Satanic Verses'. *Humanity and Society*, 14, 4, 419–27.

Ahmad, A. (1991), 'Rushdie's *Shame*. Postmodernism, migrancy and the representation of women'. *Economic and Political Weekly*, 15.6.91, 1461–71.

Ahsan, M. (1982), 'The "Satanic Verses" and the Orientalists: a note on the authenticity of the so-called Satanic Verses'. *Hamdard Islamicus*, 5, Spring, 27–36.

Ahsan, M. (1988), 'The Orientalists' "Satanic Verses"'. *Impact International*, 28.10.88–10.11.88, 17–18.

Ahsan, M. (1991), 'The "Satanic Verses" and the Orientalists: (a note on the authenticity of the so-called Satanic Verses)', in M. Ahsan and A. Kidwai (eds.), *Sacrilege Versus Civility: Muslim Perspectives on the Salman Rushdie Affair*, pp. 131–40.

Ahsan, M. and Kidwai, A. (eds.) (1991), *Sacrilege Versus Civility: Muslim Perspectives on the Salman Rushdie Affair*. Leicester: Islamic Foundation.

Aji, A. (1995), 'All names mean something: Salman Rushdie's *Haroun* and the legacy of Islam'. *Contemporary Literature*, 36, 1, 103–29.

Akhtar, S. (1989a), 'Whose light, whose darkness?' *The Guardian*, 27.2.89.

Akhtar, S. (1989b), 'The Liberal Inquisition'. *The Independent*, 10.10.89.

Akhtar, S. (1989c), *Be Careful with Muhammad!: The Salman Rushdie Affair*. London: Bellew Publishing.

Akhtar, S. (1990a), *A Faith for All Seasons: Islam and Western Modernity*. London: Bellew Publishing.

Akhtar, S. (1990b), 'Is freedom holy to liberals?: some remarks on the purpose of law', in Commission for Racial Equality, *Free Speech: Report of a Seminar*. London: Commission for Racial Equality, pp. 18–27.

Akhtar, S. (1990c), 'Art or literary terrorism?', in D. Cohn-Sherbok (ed.) (1990), *The Salman Rushdie Controversy in Interreligious Perspective*, pp. 1–23.

Akhtar, S. (1990d), 'Holy freedom and the "Liberals"'. *Impact International*, 23.2.90–8.3.90, 9–11.

Al-Azmeh, A. (1989), 'The Satanic flame'. *New Statesman and Society*, 20.1.89, 16–17.

Alderman, G. (1983), *The Jewish Community in British Politics*. Oxford: Clarendon Press.

Ali, Y. (1992), 'Muslim women and the politics of ethnicity and culture in northern England', in G. Saghal and N. Yuval-Davis (eds.), *Refusing Holy Orders: Women and Fundamentalism in Britain*. London: Virago, pp. 101–23.

Alibhai-Brown, Y. (1999), *True Colours: Public Attitudes to Multiculturalism and the Role of the Government*. London: Institute for Public Policy Research.

Allen, C. and Nielsen, J. (2002), *Summary Report on Islamophobia in the EU after 11 September 2001*. Vienna: European Monitoring Centre on Racism and Xenophobia.

Allot, A. (1990), 'Religious pluralism and the law in England and Africa: a case study', in I. Hamnett (ed.) (1990), *Religious Pluralism and Unbelief: Studies Critical and Comparative*, London: Routledge, pp. 205–26.

Alrawi, K. (1989a), 'Letter From Cairo. Rushdie and Mahfouz'. *The Guardian*, 3.3.89.

Alrawi, K. (1989b), 'Are you or have you ever been an atheist?'. *The Guardian*, 25.8.89.

Amanuddin, S. (1989), 'The novels of Salman Rushdie: mediated reality as fantasy'. *World Literature Today*, 58, 42–45.

Ammitzboll, P. and Vidino, L. (2007), 'After the Danish Cartoon Controversy'. *Middle East Quarterly*, 14, 1, 3–11.

Anderson, B. (1983), *Imagined Communities: Reflections on the Origin and Spread of Nationalism*. London: Verso.

Andrews, A. (1994a), 'The Inter-Faith movement in the UK: towards religious pluralism'. *The Indo-British Review*, 10, 1, 123–30.

Andrews, A. (1994b), 'The concept of sect and denomination in Islam'. *Religion Today*, 9, 2, 6–10.

Andrews, A. (1996), 'Muslim attitudes towards political activity in the United Kingdom', in W. Shadid and S. van Koningsveld (eds.), *Political Participation and Identities of Muslims in non-Muslim States*, pp. 115–28.

Anees, M. (1989), *The Kiss of Judas: Affairs of a Brown Sahib*. Kuala Lumpur: Quill Publishers.

Anonymous (1989), review of S. Rushdie (1988), *The Satanic Verses*. *Faith and Freedom: A Journal of Progressive Religion*, 42, Summer, 110–12.

Ansari, H. (2002), *Muslims in Britain*. London: Minority Rights Group International.

Appignanesi, L. and Maitland, S. (1989), *The Rushdie File*. London: Fourth Estate.

Applebaum, D. (1991), review of S. Rushdie, (1990), *Haroun and the Sea of Stories*. *Parabola*, 16, May, 126–32.

Aravamudan, S. (1989), ' "Being God's postman is no fun, yaar": Salman Rushdie's *The Satanic Verses*'. *Diacritics*, 19, 3–20.

Armstrong, K. (1988), *Holy War: The Crusades and Their Impact on Today's World*. London: Macmillan.

Asad, T. (1990), 'Multiculturalism and British identity in the wake of the Rushdie affair'. *Politics and Society*, 18, December, 455–80.

Ashcroft, B., Griffiths, G. and Tiffin, H. (1989), *The Empire Writes Back: Theory and Practice of Post-Colonial Literatures*. London: Routledge.

Ashford, S. and Timms, N. (1992), *What Europe Thinks: A Study of Western European Values*. Aldershot: Dartmouth.

Azm, S. (1991), 'The importance of being earnest about Salman Rushdie'. *Welt des Islams*, ns 31, 1, 1–49.

Bacal, A. (1991), *Ethnicity in the Social Sciences: A View and Review of the Literature on Ethnicity* (Reprint Paper on Ethnic Relations, No. 3). Coventry: Centre for Research in Ethnic Relations, University of Warwick.

Bader, R. (1992), '*The Satanic Verses*: an intercultural experiment by Salman Rushdie'. *International Fiction Review*, 19, 2, 65–75.

Badham, P. (ed.) (1989), *Religion, State and Society in Modern Britain*, Lewiston: NY; Lampeter: Mellen.

Baena, R. (2001), 'Telling a bath-time story: Haroun and the Sea of Stories as a modern literary fairy tale'. *Journal of Commonwealth Literature*, 36, 2, 73–84.

Baker, S. (2000), ' "You must remember this": Salman Rushdie's The Moor's Last Sigh'. *Journal of Commonwealth Literature*, 35, 1, 43–54.

Bakhtin, M. (1981), *The Dialogic Imagination: Four Essays*. Austin: University of Texas Press.

Balibar, E. and Wallerstein, I. (1992), *Race, Nation, Class: Ambiguous Identities*. London: Verso.

Barker, D., Halman, L. and Vloet, A. (n.d.), *The European Values Study 1981–1990*. Aberdeen. The Gordon Cook Foundation.

Barker, E., Beckford, J. and Dobbelaere, K. (eds.) (1993), *Secularization, Rationalism and Sectarianism*. Oxford: Oxford University Press.

Barton, S. (1986), *The Bengali Muslims of Bradford*. Leeds: Commmunity Religions Project, University of Leeds.

Batty, N. (1987), 'The art of suspense: Rushdie's 1001 (Mid-)Nights'. *Ariel: Review of International English Literature*, 18, 3, 49–65.

Baumann, G. (1999), *The Multicultural Riddle: Rethinking National, Ethnic, and Religious Identities*. London: Routledge.

Baumann, G. (2001), 'Cross-faith conflict and interfaith community in Britain: from the "Rushdie Affair" to the present'. *Bulletin of the Royal Institute for Inter-Faith Studies*, 3, 1, 127–47.

Bennett, C. (1990), 'The Rushdie affair: some underlying issues'. *Discernment: A Christian Journal for Inter-Religious Encounter*, 4, 2, 3–11.

Benn, T. (1989), 'An end to blasphemy'. *The Guardian*, 7.4.89.

Bennett, C. (1994), 'The Salman Rushdie affair in Anglo-Indian perspective'. *Indo-British Review*, 20, 1, 237–43.

Berger, J. (1989), 'Two books and two notions of the sacred'. *The Guardian*, 25.2.89.

Berger, P. (1967), *The Social Reality of Religion: Elements of a Sociological Theory of Religion*. London: Faber and Faber.

Berman, H. (1974), *The Interaction of Law and Religion*. London: SCM.

Beyer, P. (1990), 'Privatisation and the public influence of religion in a global society'. *Theory, Culture and Society*. 7, 2–3, 373–95.

Bhabha, H. (1994), review of S. Rushdie, *East, West. The Guardian*, 4.10.94.

Blackwood, C. (1644), *The Storming of the Antichrist, in His Two Last and Strongest Garrisons: Of Compulsion of Conscience and Infant Baptism*. London.

Blair, T. (2006), 'Speech to the Los Angeles World Affairs Council, 1 August 2006'. London: Tony Blair Archive 2006 Speeches, at: http://www.number10.gov.uk/output/Page9948.asp, accessed on 1.8.08.

Blishen, E. (1990), review of S. Rushdie, (1990), *Haroun and the Sea of Stories. New Statesman and Society*, 28.9.90, 33.

Blom-Cooper, L. (1981), *Blasphemy: An Ancient Wrong or a Modern Right?* London: Unitarian Information.

Blom-Cooper, L. and Drewry, C. (1976), *Law and Morality*. London: Duckworth.

Bongartz, C. and Richey, E. (2001), ' "Kahani Means Story and City": Wittgenstein, Chomsky, and the Linguistics of Narrative in Haroun and the Sea of Stories'. *Southern Journal of Linguistics*, 25, 1–2, 87–106.

Bowen, D. (1992a), 'Bradford and *The Satanic Verses*', in D. Bowen (ed.), *The Satanic Verses: Bradford Responds*, pp. 5–21.

Bowen, D. (ed.) (1992b), *The Satanic Verses: Bradford Responds*. Bradford: Bradford and Ilkley Community College.

Boyd, S. (1997), 'Blasphemy: verbal offense against the sacred, from Moses to Salman Rushdie'. *Church History*, 66, 1, 177–9.

Boyle, K. (1990), 'Freedom of religion, freedom of expression – Salman Rushdie case'. *Conscience and Liberty*, 2, Spring, 82–5.

Bradbury, M. (1995), review of S. Rushdie, (1995), *The Moor's Last Sigh. The Times*, 31.8.95.

Bradford Council of Mosques (1989), *Bradford's 10 Point Plan of Action*. Bradford: Bradford Council of Mosques, 17.6.89.

Bradney, A. (1993), *Religions, Rights and Laws*. Leicester: Leicester University Press.

Breiner, B. (1995a), '*Sharī'ah* and religious pluralism', in T. Mitri (ed.), *Religion, Law and Society*, pp. 51–62.

Breiner, B. (1995b), 'Secularism and religion: alternative bases for the quest for a genuine pluralism', in T. Mitri (ed.) (1995), *Religion, Law and Society*, pp. 92–99.

Brennan, T. (1990), *Salman Rushdie and the Third World: Myths of the Nation*. London: Macmillan.

British Council of Churches (1978), *The New Black Presence in Britain: A Christian Scrutiny*. London: British Council of Churches.

British Council of Churches (1989), *BCC 'Grave Concern' At Impact of*

Rushdie Controversy (press release). London: British Council of Churches, 15.2.89.

Brouillette, S. (2005), 'Authorship as crisis in Salman Rushdie's Fury'. *Journal of Commonwealth Literature*, 40, 1, 137–56.

Brown, M. (2006), 'Comparative analysis of mainstream discourses, media narratives and representations of Islam in Britain and France prior to 9/11.' *Journal of Muslim Minority Affairs*, 26, 3, 297–312.

Bruce, S. (1992), *Religion and Modernization: Sociologists and Historians Debate the Secularization Thesis*. Oxford: Oxford University Press.

Bunting, M. (2007), 'Hearts and minds of young Muslims will be won or lost in the mosques'. *The Guardian*, 9.7.2007.

Burgess, A. (1989), 'The burning truth'. *The Daily Mail*, 31.1.89.

Burningham, B. (2003), 'Salman Rushdie, author of the Captive's Tale'. *Journal of Commonwealth Literature*, 38, 1 2003, 113–33 (*Moor's Last Sigh*).

Cable, V. (1994), *The World's New Fissures: Identities in Crisis*. London: Demos.

Cantle, T. and the Community Cohesion Team (2001), *Community Cohesion: A Report of the Independent Review Chaired by Ted Cantle*. London: Home Office.

Centre for the Study of Islam and Christian-Muslim Relations (1989), *The 'Rushdie Affair': A Documentation*. Research Papers on Muslims in Europe No. 42, June.

Chryssides, G. (1990), 'Fact and fiction in the Salman Rushdie affair'. *Discernment: A Christian Journal of Inter-Religious Encounter*, 4, 2, 19–25.

Cohen, C. (1922), *Blasphemy: a Plea for Religious Equality*. London: Pioneer Press.

Cohn-Sherbok, D. (ed.) (1990), *The Salman Rushdie Affair in Interreligious Perspective*. Lampeter: Edwin Mellen Press.

Commission for Racial Equality (1989), *Satanic Verses Controversy – CRE calls for Tolerance* (press release). London: Commission for Racial Equality, 20.4.89.

Commission for Racial Equality (1990a), *Britain: A Plural Society. Report of a Seminar*. London: Commission for Racial Equality.

Commission for Racial Equality (1990b), *Free Speech: Report of a Seminar*. London: Commission for Racial Equality.

Commission for Racial Equality (1990c), *Law, Blasphemy and the Multi-Faith Society: Report of a Seminar*. London: Commission for Racial Equality.

Commission on British Muslims and Islamophobia (1997), *Islamophobia: A Challenge for Us All*. London: Runnymede Trust.

Commission on Integration and Cohesion (2007), *Our Shared Future*. London: Commission on Integration and Cohesion.

Commission on the Future of Multi-Ethnic Britain (2000), *The Future of Multi-Ethnic Britain: The Parekh Report*. London: Profile Books.

Concerned Individuals of Asian Origin (1989), 'Statement' (advertisement). *The Guardian*, 25.2.89.

Connolly, C. (1991), 'Washing our linen: one year of women against fundamentalism'. *Feminist Review*, 37, 68–77.

Cooper, H. and Morrison, P. (1991), *A Sense of Belonging: Dilemmas of British Jewish identity*. London: Weidenfeld and Nicholson/Channel 4.

Coppola, C. (1991), 'Salman Rushdie's *Haroun and the Sea of Stories*: Fighting the good fight or knuckling under'. *The Journal of South Asian Literature*, 26, 1–2, 229–37.

Cottle, S. (1991), 'Reporting the Rushdie affair: a case study in the orchestration of public opinion'. *Race and Class*, 32, April–June, 45–64.

Cottrell, R. (1984), 'Interview: Richard Cottrell, MEP'. *Update: A Quarterly Journal on New Religious Movements*, 8, 3–4, 30–34.

Cumper, T. (2007), 'Inciting religious hatred: balancing free speech and religious sensibilities in a multi-faith society', in N. Ghanea, A. Stephens and R. Walden (eds.), *Does God Believe in Human Rights?* pp. 233–58.

Cundy, C. (1992), 'Rehearsing voices: Salman Rushdie's *Grimus*'. *The Journal of Commonwealth Literature*, 27, 1, 128–38.

Daniels, N. (1960), *Islam and the West: The Making of an Image, 1000–1300AD, Volume I*. Edinburgh: Edinburgh University Press.

Daniels, N. (1967), *Islam and the West: Islam, Europe and Empire, Volume II*. Edinburgh: Edinburgh University Press.

Davie, G. (1994), *Religion in Britain Since 1945: Believing Without Belonging*. Oxford: Blackwell.

Davies, C. (1989), 'Religion, politics and "permissive" legislation', in P. Badham (ed.), *Religion, State and Society in Modern Britain*, pp. 321–42.

Day, M. (1990), 'The Salman Rushdie affair: implications for the CRE and race relations', in Commission for Racial Equality, *Free Speech: Report of a Seminar*, pp. 104–10.

Dayal, S. (1992), 'Talking dirty – Salman Rushdie and "Midnight's Children"'. *College English*, 54, 4, 431–45.

D'Costa, G. (1990), 'Secular discourse and the clash of faiths: "The Satanic Verses" in British society'. *New Blackfriars*, October, 418–32.

Deedat, A., (n.d.), *How Rushdie Fooled the West: 'The Satanic Verses', Unexpurgated*. Birmingham: Islamic Propagation Centre.

Denham, J. and the Ministerial Group on Public Order and Community Cohesion (2001), *Building Cohesive Communities: A Report of the Ministerial Group on Public Order and Community Cohesion*. London: The Home Office.

Denning, A. (1949), *Freedom Under the Law*. London: Stevens and Sons.

Deszcz, J. (2004), 'Research article: Salman Rushdie's attempt at a feminist fairytale reconfiguration in Shame'. *Folklore*, 115, 1, 27–44.

Dhawan, R. (1985), *Three Contemporary Novelists: Khushwant Singh, Chaman Nahal, Salman Rushdie*. New Delhi: Classical Publishing Company.

Dhawan, R. and Taneja, G. (1992), *The Novels of Salman Rushdie*. New Delhi: Indian Society for Commonwealth Studies.

Dhondy, F. (1991), review of S. Rushdie (1991), *Imaginary Homelands: Essays and Criticisms, 1981–1991*. *The Times Educational Supplement*, 29.3.94.

Dickstein, M. (1993), 'After the Cold War: culture as politics, politics as culture'. *Social Research*. 60, 3, 531–44.

Didur, J. (2004), 'Secularism beyond the East/West divide: literary reading, ethics, and The Moor's Last Sigh'. *Textual Practice*. 18, 4, 541–62.

Discernment: A Christian Journal for Inter-Religious Encounter (1990), *Focus on the Salman Rushdie Affair* (special issue), 4, 2.

Dobbelaere, K. (1981), 'Secularisation: a multi-dimensional concept'. *Current Sociology*, 39, 2.

Dobbelaere, K. (1984), 'Secularisation theories and sociological paradigms: convergences and divergences'. *Social Compass*, 31, 199–219.

Dobbelaere, K. (1988a), 'Secularisation, pillarisation, religious involvement and religious change in the Low Countries', in T. Gannon (ed.), *World Catholicism in Transition*, pp. 80–115.

Dobbelaere, K. (1988b), 'Secularisation theories and sociological paradigms: a reformulation of the private–public dichotomy and the problem of societal integration'. *Sociological Analysis*. 46, 377–87.

Donoghue, D. (1990), review of S. Rushdie, (1990), *Haroun and the Sea of Stories*. *New Republic*, 10.12.90, 37–38.

Dossa, S. (1989), 'Satanic Verses: imagination and its political context'. *Crosscurrents*, 39, Summer, 204–12.

Durant, A. (1990), 'From the Rushdie controversy to social pluralism'. *New Formations*, 12, Winter, 143–50.

Durix, J-P. (1985), 'Magic realism in Midnight's Children'. *Commonwealth Essays and Studies*, 8, 1, 57–63.

Durix, J-P. (1993), ' "The gardener of stories": Salman Rushdie's *Haroun and the Sea of Stories'. The Journal of Commonwealth Literature*, 29, August, 114–22.

Dyson, A. (1990), 'Looking below the surface', in D. Cohn-Sherbok (ed.), *The Salman Rushdie Controversy in Interreligious Perspective*, pp. 59–69.

Easterman, D. (1992), *New Jerusalems: Reflections on Islam, Fundamentalism and the Rushdie Affair*. London: Grafton.

Enright, D. (1989), review of S. Rushdie (1988), *The Satanic Verses. New York Review of Books*, 36, March 2, 25–26.

Evans, B. (1855), *Modern Popery: A Series of Letters on Some of its More Important Aspects*. London: Houlston and Stoneman.

Featherstone, M. (ed.) (1990), *Global Culture, Nationalism, Globalisation, Modernity*. London: Sage.

Feinberg, M., Samuels, S. and Weitzman, M. (eds.) (2007), *Antisemitism: The Generic Hatred: Essays in Memory of Simon Wiesenthal*. London: Vallentine Mitchell.

Fekete, L. (2004), 'Anti-Muslim racism and the European security state'. *Race and Class*, 46, July–September, 3–29.

Fenwick, M. (2004), 'Crossing the figurative gap: metaphor and metonymy in Midnight's Children'. *Journal of Commonwealth Literature*, 39, 3, 45–68.

Ferdinand, K. and Mozaffari, M. (eds.) (1988), *Islam: State and Society*. London: Curzon Press.

Fischer, M. and Abedi, M. (1990), 'Bombay talkies, the word and the world: Salman Rushdie's Satanic Verses'. *Cultural Anthropology*, 5, 2, 107–59.

Flower, D. (1991), review of S. Rushdie (1990), *Haroun and the Sea of Stories*. *The Hudson Review*, 44, 317–25.

Fong, D. (2004), 'Satanic v. Angelic. The world welterweight fight: Rushdie takes on hegemony!' *Commonwealth*. 26, 2. 91–106.

Foot, M. (1989), 'Historical Rushdie'. *The Guardian*, 10.3.89.

Fowler, B. (2000), 'A sociological analysis of The Satanic Verses'. *Theory, Culture and Society*, 17, 1, 39–61.

Frazer, J. (1989), 'Islamic fundamentals'. *The Jewish Chronicle*, 12.5.89.

Friends of the Western Buddhist Order (1990), *Statement*, in Commission for Racial Equality, *Law, Blasphemy and the Multi-Faith Society*, pp. 88–9.

Fuentes, C. (1989), 'Words apart'. *The Guardian*. 24.2.89.

Furedi, F. (2007), *Invitation to Terror: The Expanding Empire of the Unknown*. London: Continuum.

Gane, G. (2006), 'Postcolonial Literature and the Magic Radio: The Language of Rushdie's "Midnight's Children"'. *Poetics Today*, 27, 3, 569–96.

Gannon, T. (1988) (ed.), *World Catholicism in Transition*. New York: Macmillan.

Gardels, N. *et al.* (1989), 'Salman Rushdie: a collage of comment'. *New Perspectives Quarterly*, 6, Spring, 48–55.

Garvey, J. (1989), 'Offensive defenders: Rushdie's rights and wrongs'. *Commonweal*, 116, 24.3.89, 166–8.

General Assembly of the Unitarian and Free Christian Churches (1989), *Unitarians Speak Out on 'Satanic Verses'*. London: General Assembly of the Unitarian and Free Christian Churches, 7.3.89.

General Synod of the Church of England (1981), *Offences Against Religion and Public Worship*, G.S. Misc. 149. London: General Synod of the Church of England.

General Synod of the Church of England (1988), *Offences Against Religion and Public Worship*, G.S. Misc. 286. London: General Synod of the Church of England.

George, T. (1984), 'Between pacifism and coercion: the English Baptist doctrine of religious toleration'. *Mennonite Quartely Review*, 58, 1, 30–49.

Ghanea, N., Stephens, A. and Walden, R. (eds.) (2007), *Does God Believe in Human Rights?: Essays on Religion and Human Rights*. Leiden: Martinus Nijhoff Publishers.

Goddard, H. (1991), 'Stranger than fiction: the affair of The Satanic Verses'. *Scottish Journal of Religious Studies*, 12, 2, 88–106.

Green, S. (1990), 'Beyond The Satanic Verses: conservative religion and the liberal society'. *Encounter*, June, 12–20.

Griffith, L. (2002), *The War on Terrorism and the Terror of God*. Grand Rapids: Eerdmans.

Groves, R. (ed.) (1998), *Thomas Helwys: A Short Declaration of the Mystery of Iniquity*. Macon, GA: Mercer University Press.

Guelke, A. (2006), *Terrorism and Global Disorder: Political Violence in the Contemporary World*. London: I.B Tauris.

Guillaume, A. (1987), *The Life of Muhammad: A Translation of Ishaq's Sirat Rasul Allah*. Oxford: Oxford University Press.

Gülen, F. (2004), *Towards a Global Civilization of Love and Tolerance*. New York: The Light.

Gutman, A. (1994), *Multiculturalism: Examining the Politics of Recognition*. Princeton: Princeton University Press.

Habermas, J. (1994), 'Struggles for recognition in the democratic constitutional state', in A. Gutman (ed.), *Multiculturalism*, pp. 107–48.

Halsell, G. (1999), *Forcing God's Hand: Why Millions pray for a Quick Rapture – and Destruction of Planet Earth*. Washington DC: Crossroads International Publishing.

Hamnett, I. (ed.) (1990), *Religious Pluralism and Unbelief: Studies Critical and Comparative*. London: Routledge.

Hanna, J. (1992), 'Satanic Verses in academic publishing: truth, politics and consequences. Commentary'. *Knowledge – Creation, Diffusion, Utilisation*, 13, 471–78.

Hardy, P. (1972), *The Muslims of British India*. Cambridge: Cambridge University Press.

Harket, H. (1993), 'Outrage in Oslo: the murder of William Nygard, a Norwegian publisher of Salman Rushdie's *The Satanic Verses*'. *Index on Censorship*, 22, 10, 40–41.

Harrison, J. (1992), *Salman Rushdie*. New York: Maxwell Macmillan International.

Hartley, A. (1989), 'Saving Mr. Rushdie?' *Encounter*, 73, 1, 73–7.

Hattersley, R. (1989), 'The racism of asserting that "they" must behave like "us"'. *The Independent*, 21.7.89.

Hawes, C. (1993), 'Leading history by the nose – the turn to the 18th century in *Midnight's Children*'. *Modern Fiction Studies*, 39, 1, 147–68.

Haynes, G. (1998), *Religion in Global Politics*. London: Longman.

Hebert, D. (1993), 'God and free speech: a Quaker perspective on the Satanic Verses Controversy'. *Islam and Christian–Muslim Relations*, 4, 2, 257–67.

Hebert, H. (1989), 'The liberal taboos'. *The Guardian*, 9.5.89.

Helwys, T. (1612), *A Short Declaration of the Mystery of Iniquity*, in R. Groves (ed.) (1998), *Thomas Helwys: A Short Declatration of the Mystery of Iniquity*.

Henighan, S. (1998), 'Coming to Benengeli: the genesis of Salman Rushdie's rewriting of Juan Rulfo in The Moor's Last Sigh'. *Journal of Commonwealth Literature*, 33, 2, 55–74.

Hepple, B. and Szyszczak, E. (eds.) (1992), *Discrimination and the Limits of the Law?* London: Mansell.

Hewson, K. (1989), 'Opening up the universe a little more: Salman Rushdie and the migrant as story-teller'. *Span: Journal of the South Pacific Association for Commonwealth Literature and Language,* 29, October, 88.

Hick, J. (ed.) (1974), *Truth and Dialogue: The Relationship Between World Religions.* London: Sheldon Press.

Hoffman, B. (2006), *Inside Terrorism* (revised and expanded edition). New York: Colombia University Press.

Hoffman, M. (1989), 'The pre-eminence of truth in the market-place of ideas'. *The Independent,* 22.2.89.

Horton, J. (ed.) (1993), *Liberalism, Multiculturalism and Toleration.* London: Macmillan.

Hulmes, E. (1992), '*The Satanic Verses*: A Test-Case for Pluralism', in D. Bowen (ed.), *The Satanic Verses: Bradford Responds,* pp. 45–50.

Huntington, S. (1993), 'The clash of civilizations?' *Foreign Affairs,* 72, 3, 22–49.

Huntington, S. (1996), *The Clash of Civilizations and the Remaking of World Order.* New York: Simon and Schuster.

Hurd, D. (1989), *Race Relations and the Rule of Law.* London: The Home Office, 24.2.89.

Husain, E. (2007), *The Islamist: Why I Joined Radical Islam in Britain, What I Saw Inside and Why I Left.* London: Penguin.

Hussain, Amir (2002), 'Misunderstandings and hurt: how Canadians joined worldwide Muslim reactions to Salman Rushdie's The Satanic Verses'. *Journal of the American Academy of Religion,* 70, 1, 1–32.

Hussain, Asaf (1992), *Beyond Islamic Fundamentalism.* Leicester: Volcano Press.

Hussain, F. (1990), *The Anti-Islamic Tradition in the West.* Leicester: Muslim Community Studies Institute.

Iganski, P. (ed.) (2002), *The Hate Debate: Should Hate Be Punished as a Crime?* London: Profile Books.

Impact International (1988a), 'Anti-Islam's new find "Simon Rushton" aka Salman Rushdie'. *Impact International,* 28.10.88–10.11.88, 15.

Impact International (1988b), 'Quote, unquote Satanic Verses'. *Impact International,* 28.10.88–10.11.88, 13.

Impact International (1990), *Impact International* (special issue), 23.3.90–28.3.90.

India Today, '"My theme is fanaticism." Madhu Jain interviews Salman Rushdie', in *India Today,* 15.9.88.

Institute of Race Relations, 'Racism, liberty and the war on terror: extracts from a conference held by the Institute of Race Relations in September 2006'. *Race and Class,* 48, 4, 45–92.

Inter Faith Network for the United Kingdom (1989), *Statement,* in Centre for the

Study of Islam and Christian Muslim Relations (1989), *The Rushdie Affair: A Documentation*. Research Papers on Muslims in Europe No. 42, June, 18–19.

Inter Faith Network for the United Kingdom (1991), *Law, Respect for Religious Identity and the Multi-Faith Society*. London: Commission for Racial Equality.

International Committee for the Defence of Salman Rushdie and his Publishers (1989a), *The Crime of Blasphemy – Why it Should be Abolished*. London: International Committee for the Defence of Salman Rushdie and his Publishers.

International Committee for the Defence of Salman Rushdie and his Publishers (1989b), 'Statement'. *The Guardian*, 2.3.89.

Inayatullah, S. (1990), 'Understanding the postmodern world: why Khomeini wants Rushdie dead'. *Third Text*. 11, summer, 91–8.

Islam, S. (1999), 'Writing the postcolonial event: Salman Rushdie's August Fifteenth, 1947'. *Textual Practice*, 13, 1, 119–35.

Islamic Defence Council (1989), 'Memorandum of Request From the Muslim Community in Great Britain to the Owners of Penguin Books Ltd, 28.1.89,', in A-R Sambhli (ed.) (1990), *Our Campaign Against 'The Satanic Verses' and the Death Edict*, pp. 37–9.

Islamic Foundation (1989), *Focus on Christian–Muslim Relations (The Rushdie Affair – Responses and Reactions)*, 3, March.

Ivory, J. (2004), 'Salman Rushdie's postcolonial metaphors: migration, translation, hybridity, blasphemy, and globalization.' *Journal of Third World Studies*, 21, 1, 343–44.

Iyer, N. (1999), 'Fictions to live in: narration as an argument for fiction in Salman Rushdie's novels'. *Contemporary South Asia*, 8, 2, 246.

Jackson, M. and Rogan, J. (eds.) (1962), *Thomas Arnold's Principles of Church Reform*. London: SPCK.

Jain, M. (1988) ' "My theme is fanaticism". Madhn Jain interviews Salman Rushdie. *India Today*, 15.9.88.

Jameson, F. (1991), *Postmodernism: or, The Cultural Logic of Late Capitalism*. London: Verso.

Jenkins, P. (1989a) 'Is Rushdie just the tool of Allah's will?' *The Independent*, 1.3.89.

Jenkins, P. (1989b), 'The story of free thought and speech'. *The Independent*, 2.3.89.

Jenkins, R. (1967), *Essays and Speeches*. Collins: London.

Jenkins, R. (1989), 'On race relations and the Rushdie affair'. *The Independent Magazine*, 14.3.89.

Jewett, R. and Lawrence, J. (2003), *Captain America and the Crusade Against Evil: The Dilemma of Zealous Nationalism*. Grand Rapids: Eerdmans.

Johanssen, I. (1985), 'The flight from the enchanter: reflections on Salman Rushdie's *Grimus*'. *Kunapipi*, 7, 1, 20–30.

Jones, P. (1990a), 'Rushdie, race and religion'. *Political Studies*, 38, 4, 687–94.

Jones, P. (1990b), 'Respecting beliefs and rebuking Rushdie'. *British Journal of Political Science*, 20, October, 415–37.

Kabbani, R. (1989), *Letter to Christendom*. London: Virago.

Kane, J. (2006), 'Embodied panic: revisiting modernist "religion" in the controversies over Ulysses and The Satanic Verses'. *Textual Practice*, 20, 3, 419–40.

Kanga, F. (1991), review of S. Rushdie, (1991), *Imaginary Homelands: Essays and Criticism, 1981–1991. The Times Literary Supplement*, 29.3.91.

Karamcheti, I. (1986), 'Salman Rushdie's *Midnight's Children*: an alternate Genesis'. *Pacific Coast Philology*, 21, 1–2, 81–4.

Kaufman, G. (1989), 'So-called liberals for whom some are more tolerable than others'. *The Independent*, 1.3.89.

Kayhan Farangi (1989), 'Rushdie has fallen into total moral degradation'. *The Independent*, 21.2.89.

Kazantzakis, N. (1985), *The Last Temptation of Christ*. London: Faber and Faber.

Kemp, P. (1995), review of S. Rushdie (1995), *The Moor's Last Sigh. The Times*, 3.9.95.

Kerr, D. (1989a), 'What *The Satanic Verses* mean in Brick Lane'. *Reform*, April, 3–4.

Kerr, D. (1989b), 'The Satanic Verses and beyond'. *Christian Century*, 106, 11, 354–8.

Khomeini, R. (1981), *Islam and Revolution: Writings and Declarations of Imam Khomeini*. Berkeley: Mizan.

Khomeini, R. (1989), 'A challenge to the world-devourers'. *The Guardian*, 6.3.89.

Khuri, F. (1990), *Imams and Emirs: State, Religion and Sects in Islam*. London: Saqi Books.

Klassen, W. (1981), 'The Anabaptist critique of Constantinian Christendom'. *The Mennonite Quarterly Review*, 55, July, 218–30.

Knönagel, A. (1991), 'The "Satanic Verses": narrative structure and Islamic doctrine'. *International Fiction Review*, 18, 2, 69–75.

Kundnani, A. (2007), 'Integrationism: the politics of anti-Muslim racism'. *Race and Class*, 48, 4, 24–44.

Kuortti, J. (1997), 'Dreams, intercultural identification and The Satanic Verses'. *Contemporary South Asia*, 6, 2, 191–200.

Kuortti, J. (1998), 'Unending metamorphoses: myth, satire and religion in Salman Rushdie's novels/after Empire: Scott, Naipaul, Rushdie'. *Contemporary South Asia*, 7, 3, 371–3.

Kuortti, J. (1999), ' "Nomsense": Salman Rushdie's The Satanic Verses'. *Textual Practice*, 13, 1, 137–46.

Lægard, S. (2007), 'The cartoon controversy: offence, identity, oppression?'. *Political Studies*, 55, 3, 481–98.

LaHaye, T. and Jenkins, J. (1995), *Left Behind*. Wheaton, IL: Tyndale House.

Lahr, J. (1992), review of S. Rushdie, (1992), *The Wizard of Oz. New Statesman and Society*, 29.5.92, 39–41.

Lamb, C. (1985), *Belief in a Mixed Society*. Tring: Lion.

Langeland, A. (1996), 'Rushdie's Language'. *English Today*, 12, 1, 16–22.

Larsen, T. (1999), *Friends of Religious Equality: Nonconformist Politics in Mid-Victorian England*. Woodbridge: The Boydell Press.

Law Commission, The (1981), *Offences Against Religion and Public Worship: Working Paper No. 79*. London: Her Majesty's Stationery Office.

Law Commission, The (1985), *Offences Against Religion and Public Worship: Law Commission Report No. 145*. London: Her Majesty's Stationery Office.

Lee, S. (1990), 'Religion in the UK: legal ways forward', in The Inter Faith Network and The Commission for Racial Equality, *Law, Respect for Religious Identity and the Multi Faith Society*, pp. 6–15.

Lee, S. (1993), 'Protecting both Gods and books: abolish blasphemy law and make incitement to religious hatred a crime', in UK Action Committee on Islamic Affairs, *Muslims and the Law in Multi-Faith Britain*, pp. 56–7.

Lewis, B. (1991), 'Behind the Rushdie affair'. *American Scholar*, 60, Spring, 185–96.

Lewis, P. (1989), 'The Salman Rushdie affair: a view from Bradford'. *InPrint: Church Missionary Society Information Service*, March.

Lewis, P. (1990), 'From book-burning to vigil: Bradford Muslims a year on'. *Discernment: A Christian Journal for Inter-Religious Encounter*, 4, 2, 26–34.

Lewis, P. (1994a), *Islamic Britain: Religion, Politics and Identity Among British Muslims. Bradford in the 1990s*. London: I.B. Tauris.

Lewis, P. (1994b), 'Being Muslim and being British: the dynamics of Islamic reconstruction in Bradford', in R. Ballard (ed.), *Desh Pardesh: Britain*, pp. 58–87.

Liechty, J. and Clegg, C. (2001), *Moving Beyond Sectarianism: Religion, Conflict and Reconciliation in Northern Ireland*. Dublin: The Colomba Press.

Lindsey, H. (1971), *The Late Great Planet Earth*. Grand Rapids: Zondervan Press.

Lindsey, H. (1980), *The 1980s: Countdown to Armageddon*. New York: Bantam Books.

Ling, T. (1974), 'Communalism and the social structure of religion', in J. Hick (ed.), *Truth and Dialogue*, pp. 59–76.

Lijphart, A. (1968), *The Politics of Accommodation: Pluralism and Democracy in the Netherlands*. Berkeley: University of California Press.

Local Government Association, Inner Cities Religious Council, Active Community Unit, the Home Office and the Inter Faith Network for the UK (2002a), *Faith and Community: A Good Practice Guide For Local Authorities*. London: Local Government Association Publications.

Local Government Association, Office of the Deputy Prime Minister, Home Office, Commission for Racial Equality, and the Inter Faith Network for the United Kingdom (2002b), *Guidance on Community Cohesion*. London: Local Government Association Publications.

Lomas, A. (1989), 'Muslim unity proves greater than third rate novel'. *New Life*, 2.6.89.

MacCabe, C., Ali, M., Carlin, P., Gilroy, P., Hext, K., Kureishi, H., Rushdie, S., Serret, N.

and Young, S. (2006), 'Multiculturalism after 7/7: a CQ seminar'. *Critical Quarterly*, 48, 2, 1–44.

MacDonogh, S. (ed.) (1993), *Rushdie Letters: Freedom to Speak, Freedom to Write*. County Kerry: Brandon.

MacEoin, D. (ed.) (2007), *The Hijacking of British Islam: How Extremist Literature is Subverting Mosques in the UK*. London: Policy Exchange.

McGrath, P. (1967), *Papists and Puritans Under Elizabeth I*. Poole: Blandford Press.

McLoughlin, S. (1996), 'In the name of the *Umma*: globalisation, "race" relations and Muslim identity politics in Bradford', in W. Shadid and S. van Koningsveld (eds.), *Political Participation and Identities of Muslims in non-Muslim States*, pp. 207–28.

McRoy, A. (2006), *From Rushdie to 7/7: the radicalisation of Islam in Britain*. London: Social Affairs Unit.

Mahfouz, N. (1981), *Children of Gebelawi*. London: Heinemann.

Maitland, S. (1989), 'Unravelling the Rushdie row'. *The Independent*, 9.5.89.

Maitland, S. (1990), 'Blasphemy and creativity', in D. Cohn-Sherbok (ed.), *The Salman Rushdie Affair in Interreligious Perspective*, pp. 115–30.

Malak, A. (1989), 'Reading the crisis: the polemics of Salman Rushdie's "The Satanic Verses"'. *Ariel: A Review of International English Literature*, 20, October, 176–86.

Malik, J. (ed.) (2004), *Muslim Minority Societies in Europe: from the Margin to the Centre*. Münster, LIT Verlag.

Marotti, A. (2005), *Religious Ideology and Cultural Fantasy: Catholic and Anti-Catholic Discourses in Early Modern England*. Notre Dame, IN: University of Notre Dame Press.

Martin, D. (1978), *A General Theory of Secularisation*. Oxford: Blackwell.

Mazrui, A. (1989), *The Satanic Verses or a Satanic Novel? The Moral Dilemmas of the Rushdie Affair*. New York: The Committee of Muslim Scholars and Leaders of North America.

Mazrui, A. (1990a), 'The Satanic Verses or a satanic novel? the moral dilemmas of the Rushdie affair', in Commission for Racial Equality, *Free Speech: Report of a Seminar*, pp. 79–103.

Mazrui, A. (1990b), 'Witness for the prosecution: a cross-examination on *The Satanic Verses*'. *Third Text*, Summer, 31–40.

Mehdi, M. (1989), *Islam and Intolerance: Reply to Salman Rushdie*. New York: New World Press.

Mendus, S. (1989), *Toleration and the Limits of Liberalism*. London: Macmillan.

Mezey, J. (2006), 'Neocolonial narcissism and postcolonial paranoia: Midnight's Children and the "Psychoanalysis" of the state interventions, 8, 2, 178–92.

Mijares, L. (2003), '"You are an Anglo-Indian?": Eurasians and hybridity and cosmopolitanism in Salman Rushdie's Midnight's Children'. *Journal of Commonwealth Literature*, 38, 2, 125–45.

Mills, J. (1989), review of S. Rushdie (1988), *The Satanic Verses. New Blackfriars*, 70, March, 106–8.

Millward, C. (1994), 'Games with names in Midnight's Children'. *Names*, 42, 2, 91–9.

Milne, S. (2007), 'Denial of the link with Iraq is delusional and dangerous'. *The Guardian*, 5.7.07.

Mitchell, B. (1967), *Law, Morality and Religion in a Secular Society*. Oxford: Oxford University Press.

Mitri, T. (ed.) (1995), *Religion, Law and Society*. Geneva: World Council of Churches.

Modood, T. (1989), 'Religious anger and minority rights'. *Political Quarterly*, 60, July–September, 280–5.

Modood, T. (1990a), 'The Rushdie affair: texts and contexts'. *The Independent*, 5.2.90.

Modood, T. (1990b), *Muslims, Race and Equality in Britain: Some Post-Rushdie Affair Reflections*. Papers No. 1, June. Birmingham: Centre for the Study of Islam and Christian–Muslim Relations.

Modood, T. (1990c), 'Muslims, race and equality in Britain: some post-Rushdie Affair Reflections'. *Third Text*, Summer, 127–34.

Modood, T. (1990d), 'Catching up with Jesse Jackson: being somebody and being oppressed'. *New Community*, 17, 1, 85–96.

Modood, T. (1990e), 'British Asian Muslims and the Salman Rushdie affair'. *The Political Quarterly*, 61, April–June, 143–60.

Modood, T. (1992), 'Minorities, faith and citizenship'. *Discernment: A Christian Journal for Inter-Religious Encounter*, 6, 2, 58–60.

Modood, T. (1993a), 'Muslims, incitement to hatred and the law', in UK Action Committee on Islamic Affairs, *Muslims and the Law in Multi-Faith Britain*, pp. 69–81.

Moin, B. (1994), 'Khomeini's search for perfection: theory and reality', in A. Rahnema (ed.), *Pioneers of Islamic Revival*, pp. 64–94.

Moore, K. (1997), 'Legal pluralism in Britain: the rights of Muslims after the Rushdie affair'. *Legal Studies Forum*, 21, 4, 443–68.

Mosley, B. (2007), 'Naguib Mahfouz's window on the world of Islam'. *New Politics*, 11, 2, 131–4.

Mozaffari, M. (1990), 'The Rushdie affair: blasphemy as a new form of international conflict and crisis'. *Terrorism and Political Violence*, 2, 3, 415–41.

Mullen, P. (1990), 'Satanic asides', in D. Cohn-Sherbok (ed.), *The Salman Rushdie Controversy in Interreligious Perspective*, pp. 25–35.

Muslim Institute, The (1990), *The Muslim Manifesto: A Strategy For Survival*. London: The Muslim Institute.

Mustapha, M. (1989), *An Islamic Overview of The Satanic Verses by Western Writers*. Trinidad and Tobago: T.K. Industries.

Naidu, M. (1989), 'Religionism, rationalism and violence: a study in religious terrorism'. *Peace Research*, 21, 2, 1–12.

Naik, M. (1985), 'A life of fragments: the fate of identity in *Midnight's Children*'. *The Indian Literary Review: A Tri-Quarterly of Indian Literature*, 3, 3, 63–8.

Nair, R. and Battacharya, R. (1990), 'Salman Rushdie: the migrant in the metropolis'. *Third Text*, Summer, 17–30.

Nasr, S. (1994), 'Mawdudi and the Jam'at-i Islami: the origins, theory and practice of Islamic revivalism, in A. Rahnema (ed.), *Pioneers of Islamic Revival*, pp. 98–124.

Needham, A. (1988–89), 'The politics of post-colonial identity in Salman Rushdie'. *The Massachusetts Review*, 29, 602–4.

Newbigin, L. (1990), 'Blasphemy and the free society'. *Discernment: A Christian Journal for Inter-Religious Encounter*, 4, 2, 12–18.

Newell, S. (1992), 'The other God – Salman Rushdie's new aesthetic'. *Literature and History* (3rd series), 1, 2, 67–87.

Newton, K. (1992), 'Literary theory and the Rushdie affair'. *English*, 41, Autumn, 235–47.

Nokes, G. (1928), *A History of the Crime of Blasphemy*. London: Sweet and Maxwell.

O'Higgins, P. (1989), 'Relic that has no role'. *The Guardian*, 3.3.89.

Omer, M. (1989), *The Holy Prophet and the Satanic Slander*. Madras: The Women's Islamic Social and Educational Trust.

O'Neill, D. (1999), 'Multicultural liberals and the Rushdie affair: a critique of Kymlicka, Taylor, and Walzer'. *Review of Politics*, 61, 2, 219.

Organisation of the Islamic Conference (1989), *Statement*, 5.11.89, in A-R. Sambhli (ed.) (1990), *Our Campaign Against 'The Satanic Verses' and The Death Edict*, pp. 42–5.

Parameswaran, U. (1989), review of S. Rushdie (1988), *The Satanic Verses*. Littcrit, 14, 77–83.

Parashkevova, V. (2007), ' "Turn your watch upside down in Bombay and you see the time in London": Catoptric urban configurations in Salman Rushdie's The Satanic Verses'. *Journal of Commonwealth Literature*, 42, 3, 5–24.

Parekh, B. (1989a), 'Between holy text and moral void', in *New Statesman and Society*, 23.3.89, 29–33.

Parekh, B. (1989b), 'The mutual suspicions which fuelled the Rushdie affair'. *The Independent*, 23.2.89.

Parekh, B. (1989c), 'Liberal versus religious fundamentalism'. *New Life*, 3.3.89.

Parekh, B. (1989d), 'Between holy text and moral void'. *New Life*, 12.5.89.

Parekh, B. (1990a), 'The Rushdie affair and the British press', in D. Cohn-Sherbok (ed.), *The Salman Rushdie Controversy in Interreligious Perspective*, pp. 71–95.

Parekh, B. (1990b), 'The Rushdie affair and the British press: some salutary lessons', in Commission for Racial Equality, *Free Speech*, pp. 59–78.

Parekh, B. (1990c), 'The Rushdie affair: the research agenda for political philosophy'. *Political Studies*, 28, December, 695–709.

Parekh, B. (1992), *The Concept of Fundamentalism*. Leeds: Peepal Tree.

Parsons, G. (ed.) (1994a), *The Growth of Religious Diversity: Britain From 1945. Volume II: Issues*. London: Routledge.

Parsons, G. (1994b), 'From consensus to confrontation: religion and politics in Britain since 1945', in G. Parsons (ed.), *The Growth of Religious Diversity: Britain From 1945. Volume II: Issues*, pp. 123–59.

Parsons, G. (1994c), 'Introduction: deciding how far you can go', in G. Parsons (ed.), *The Growth of Religious Diversity. Volume II: Issues*, pp. 5–21.

Patten, J. (1989a), *Muslims in Britain Today*. London: The Home Office, 4.7.89.

Patten, J. (1989b), *On Being British*. London: The Home Office, 18.7.89.

Phillips, M. (1989), 'This book could cause offence'. *The Guardian*, 3.3.89.

Phillips, T. (2005), 'After 7/7: sleepwalking to segregation'. *Commission for Racial Equality*, 22, September.

Pidcock, D. (ed.) (1992), *Satanic Voices Ancient and Modern*. Milton Keynes: Mustaaqim Islamic Art and Literature.

Pipes, D. (1990), *The Rushdie Affair: the Novel, the Ayatollah, and the West*. New York: Birch Lane Press.

Pipes, D. (1998), 'Salman Rushdie's delusions, and ours'. *Commentary*, 106, 6, 51–3.

Piscatori, J. (1990), 'The Rushdie affair and the politics of ambiguity'. *International Affairs*, 66, 767–89.

Poulter, S. (1986), *English Law and Ethnic Minority Customs*. London: Butterworths.

Poulter, S. (1990a), *Asian Traditions and English Law*. London: Runnymede Trust.

Poulter, S. (1990b), 'Cultural pluralism and its limits: a legal perspective', in Commission for Racial Equality, *Britain: A Plural Society*, pp. 3–28.

Poulter, S. (1993), 'Towards legislative reform of the blasphemy and racial hatred laws', in UK Action Committee on Islamic Affairs, *Muslims and the Law in Multi-Faith Britain*, pp. 58–68.

Price, D. (1994), 'Salman Rushdie's "use and abuse of history" in *Midnight's Children*'. *Ariel: A Review of International English Literature*, 25, 2, 91–107.

Publishers Weekly (1989), 'A Rushdie paperback?' *Publishers Weekly*, 13.10.89.

Purdam, K. (1996), 'Settler political participation: Muslim local councillors', in W. Shadid and S. van Koningsveld (eds.), *Political Participation and Identities of Muslims in non-Muslim States*, pp. 129–43.

Qureshi, S. and Khan, J. (1989), *The Politics of The Satanic Verses: Unmasking Western Attitudes*. Leicester: Muslim Community Surveys, Occasional Paper 3.

Race, A. and Shafer, I. (eds.) (2002), *Religions in Dialogue: From Theory to Democracy*. Aldershot, Ashgate.

Rahman, T. (1991), 'Politics in the novels of Salman Rushdie'. *Commonwealth Novel in English*, 4, 1, pp. 24–37.

Rahnema, A. (ed.) (1994), *Pioneers of Islamic Revival*. London: Zed Books.

Ramachandaran, H. (2005), 'Salman Rushdie's The Satanic Verses: hearing the post-colonial cinematic novel'. *Journal of Commonwealth Literature*, 40, 3, 102–17.

Ramadan, T. (2004), *Western Muslims and the Future of Islam*. Oxford: Oxford University Press.

Ramsey-Kurz, H. (2001), 'Does Saleem really miss the spittoon?: script and scriptlessness in Midnight's Children'. *Journal of Commonwealth Literature*, 36, 1, 127–45.

Rashadath, A. (1990), *The Satanic Conspiracy*. Calcutta: Peacock Publications.

Raza, M. (1992), *Islam in Britain: Past, Present and Future* (2nd edition). Leicester: Volcano Press.

Reeve, H. (1989), 'Islam's reply to sedition'. *The Guardian*, 13.3.89.

Rex, J. (1985), 'The Concept of a Multi-Cultural Society'. Occasional Papers in Ethnic Relations, No. 3, Centre for Research in Ethnic Relations, University of Warwick, Coventry.

Rex, J. (1990), 'Research on Muslims and the Rushdie Affair', unpublished paper at the New Issues in Black Politics conference, Centre for Research in Ethnic Relations, University of Warwick, Coventry, 14.5.90–16.5.90.

Rex, J. (1991), 'The political sociology of a multi-cultural society'. *European Journal for Intercultural Studies*, 2, 1, 7–19.

Riordan, J. (1990), review of S. Rushdie (1990), *Haroun and the Sea of Stories*, *The Times Educational Supplement*, 5.10.90.

Robilliard, St. John A. (1984), *Religion and The Law: Religious Liberty in Modern English Law*. Manchester: Manchester University Press.

Robinson, F. (1988), *Varieties of South Asian Islam*. Research Paper No. 8, Centre for Research in Ethnic Relations, University of Warwick, Coventry.

Robinson, N. (1992), 'Reflections on the Rushdie Affair – 18th April 1989', in D. Bowen (ed.), *The Satanic Verses: Bradford Responds*, pp. 33–44.

Roy, O. (2003), 'EuroIslam: the jihad within?' *National Interest*, 71, Spring, 63–73.

Runcie, R. (1989), *The Archbishop of Canterbury Speaking on Offence Caused by Publication of Satanic Verses*. London: Lambeth Palace, 20.2.89.

Rushdie, S. (1972), *The Book of the Pir* (unpublished manuscript).

Rushdie, S. (1975), *Grimus*. London: Paladin.

Rushdie, S. (1981), *Midnight's Children*. London: Picador.

Rushdie, S. (1982), 'The new Empire within Britain', in S. Rushdie (ed.) (1991a), *Imaginary Homelands*, pp. 129–38.

Rushdie, S. (1983), *Shame*. London: Jonathan Cape.

Rushdie, S. (1987), *The Jaguar Smile: A Nicaraguan Journey*. Harmondsworth: Penguin.

Rushdie, S. (1988), *The Satanic Verses*. London: Viking Penguin.

Rushdie, S. (1989a), 'Choice between dark and light'. *The Observer*, 22.1.89.

Rushdie, S. (1989b), 'Bonfire of the certainties'. *The Guardian*, 15.2.89.

Rushdie, S. (1989c), *Statement of Apology*, in L. Appignanesi and S. Maitland (eds.), *The Rushdie File*, p. 120.

Rushdie, S. (1989d), 'Please, read "Satanic Verses" before condemning it'. *The International Herald Tribune*, 18–19.2.89.

Rushdie, S. (1989e), 'Statement by Salman Rushdie'. *The Times*, 20.2.89.

Rushdie, S. (1989f), 'Open Letter to Rajiv Gandhi', in L. Appignanesi and S. Maitland (eds.), *The Rushdie File*, pp. 42–5.

Rushdie, S. (1989g) '6 March 1989'. *Granta*. 1.9.89.

Rushdie, S. (1990a), *Haroun and the Sea of Stories*. London: Granta.

Rushdie, S. (1990b), *Is Nothing Sacred?* Cambridge: Granta.

Rushdie, S. (1990c), 'Is nothing sacred?', in S. Rushdie (1991a), *Imaginary Homelands: Essays and Criticism, 1981–1992*, pp. 415–29.

Rushdie, S. (1990d), 'In good faith'. *The Independent on Sunday*, 4.2.90.

Rushdie, S. (1990e), 'Why I have embraced Islam'. *The Times*, 28.12.90.

Rushdie, S. (1991a), *Imaginary Homelands: Essays and Criticism, 1981–1992*. London: Granta.

Rushdie, S. (1991b), 'One thousand days in a balloon', in S. Rushdie (1991a), *Imaginary Homelands*, pp. 430–9.

Rushdie, S. (1992), *The Wizard of Oz: An Appreciation*. London: British Film Institute.

Rushdie, S. (1994), *East, West: Stories*. London: Jonathan Cape.

Rushdie, S. (1995), *The Moor's Last Sigh*. London: Jonathan Cape.

Rushdie, S. (1996), 'Interview'. *Critical Quarterly*, 38, 2, 51–70.

Rushdie, S. (1999), *The Ground Beneath Her Feet*. London: Jonathan Cape.

Rushdie, S. (2001a), *Fury*. London: Jonathan Cape.

Rushdie, S. (2001b), *Step Across This Line: Collected Non-Fiction, 1992–2002*. London: Jonathan Cape.

Rushdie, S. (2005), *Shalimar the Clown*. London: Jonathan Cape.

Rushdie, S. (2008), *The Enchantress of Florence*. London: Jonathan Cape.

Rushdie, S., Ali, Ayaan H., Nasree, T., Levy, B-H., Chafiq, C., Fourest, C., Manji, I., Mozaffari, M., Namazie, M., Sfeir, A., Warraq, I. and Val, P. (2006), 'Confronting Islamist totalitarianism'. *Mediation Quarterly*, 13, 3, 82–3.

Ruthven, M. (1991), *A Satanic Affair: Salman Rushdie and the Wrath of Islam*. (revised and updated edition). London: The Hogarth Press.

Sacks, J. (1991), *The Persistence of Faith: Religion, Morality and Society in a Secular Age*. London: Weidenfeld and Nicolson.

Sacranie, I. (1989), 'Muslim response to Mr. Patten'. *Impact International*, 28.7.89–11.8.89.

Sadri, A. (1991), 'What Rushdie wrote and wrought'. *International Journal of Politics, Culture and Society*, 4, 3, 371–85.

Saeed, A. and Saeed, H. (2004), *Freedom of Religion, Apostasy and Islam*. Aldershot: Ashgate.

Saghal, G. and Yuval-Davis, N. (eds.) (1992a), *Refusing Holy Orders: Women and Fundamentalism in Britain*. London: Virago.

Saghal, G. and Yuval-Davis, N. (1992b), 'Introduction: fundamentalism, multiculturalism and women in Britain', in G. Saghal and N. Yuval-Davis (eds.), *Refusing Holy Orders*, pp. 1–25.

Saghal, G. and Yuval-Davis, N. (1992c), 'Secular spaces: the experience of Asian women organising', in G. Saghal and N. Yuval-Davis (eds.), *Refusing Holy Orders*, pp. 163–97.

Said, E. (1978), *Orientalism: Western Conceptions of the Orient*. Harmondsworth: Penguin.

Said, E. (1981), *Covering Islam: How the Media and the Experts Determine How we See the Rest of the World*. London: Routledge and Kegan Paul.

Samad, Y. (1992), 'Book burning and race relations: political mobilisation of Bradford Muslims'. *New Community*, 18, July, 507–19.

Samartha, S. (1991), *One Christ – Many Religions: Towards a Revised Christology*. New York: Orbis.

Sambhli, A-R. (ed.) (1990), *Our Campaign Against 'The Satanic Verses' and the Death Edict*. London: Islamic Defence Council.

Sangharakshita, Venerable (1978), *Buddhism and Blasphemy: Buddhist Reflections on the 1977 Blasphemy Trial*. London: Windhorse Publications.

Sardar, Z. and Wyn Davies, M. (1990), *Distorted Imagination: Lessons from the Rushdie Affair*. London: Grey Seal Books.

Schmid, A. (1984), *Political Terrorism: A Research Guide*. New Brunswick, NJ: Transaction Publishers.

Scorsese, M. (1988), *The Last Temptation of Christ* (film). Los Angeles: MCA/Universal.

Searchlight (1998), 'Blood on the streets'. *Searchlight*, September, 3.

Semminck, H. (1993), *A Novel Visible But Unseen: A Thematic Analysis of Salman Rushdie's The Satanic Verses*. Ghent: Studia Germanica Gandensia.

Senghaas, D. (1998), *The Clash Within Civilizations: Coming to Terms with Cultural Conflicts*. Routledge: London.

Shadid, W. and van Koningsveld, S. (eds.) (1996a), *Muslims in the Margin: Political Responses to the Presence of Islam in Western Europe*. Kampen: Kok Pharos.

Shadid, W. and van Koningsveld, S. (1996b), *Political Participation and Identities of Muslims in non-Muslim States*. Kampen: Kok Pharos.

Shadid, W. and van Koningsveld, S. (1996c), 'Politics and Islam in Western Europe', in W. Shadid and S. van Koningsveld (eds.), *Muslims in the Margin*, pp. 1–14.

Shadid, W. and van Koningsveld, S. (1996d), 'Dutch political views on the multi-cultural society', in W. Shadid and S. van Koningsveld (eds.), *Muslims in the Margin*, pp. 93–113.

Shadid, W. and van Koningsveld, S. (1996e), 'Political participation: the Muslim perspective', in W. Shadid and S. van Koningsveld (eds.), *Political Participation and Identities of Muslims in non-Muslim States*, pp. 2–13.

Shadid, W. and van Koningsveld, S. (1996f), 'Loyalty to a non-Muslim government: an analysis of Islamic normative discussions and of the views of some contemporary Islamicists', in W. Shadid and S. van Koningsveld (eds.), *Political Participation and Identities of Muslims in non-Muslim States*, pp. 84–114.

Shahabuddin, S. (1988), 'We shall not permit literary colonialism, nor religious pornography'. *Impact International*, 11.11.88–24.11.89, 17–18.

Shepard, W. (1992), 'Satanic Verses and the death of God – Salman Rushdie and Najib Mahfuz'. *Muslim World*, 82, 1–2, 91–111.

Shepherd, R. (1985), 'Midnight's Children: the parody of an Indian novel'. *Span: Journal of the South Pacific Association for Commonwealth Literature*, 21, October, 55–67.

Siddiqui, H. (1989), 'A woman's banner for doubt and dissent', in Southall Black Sisters, *Against the Grain: A Celebration of Survival and Struggle*. London: Southall Black Sisters, p. 2.

Simawe, S. (1990), 'Rushdie's *The Satanic Verses* and heretical literature in Islam'. *Iowa Review*. 81, 185–98.

Simpson, R. (1993), *Blasphemy and the Law in a Plural Society*, Grove Ethical Studies No. 90. Bramcote: Grove.

Singh, S. (1985), 'Salman Rushdie's Midnight's Children: rethinking the life and times of modern India'. *Panjab University Research Bulletin (Arts)*, 16, 1, 55–67.

Slaughter, M. (1993), 'The Salman Rushdie affair: apostasy, honour, freedom of speech'. *Virginia Law Review*, 129, 1, 153–204.

Smith, W. C. (1946), *Modern Islam in India*. London: Victor Gollancz.

Smith, W. C. (1957), *Islam in Modern History*. Princeton, NJ : Princeton University Press.

Smith, W. C. (1978), *The Meaning and End of Religion*. London: SPCK.

Smith, W. C. (1981), *Towards a World Theology*. London: Macmillan.

Somervell, D. C. (1960), Abridgement of A. Toynbee, *A Study of History: Abridgement of Volumes 1–X*. Oxford: Oxford University Press.

Southall Black Sisters (1989), *Against the Grain: A Celebration of Survival and Struggle*. London: Southall Black Sisters.

Southern, R. (1962), *Western Views of Islam in the Middle Ages*. Cambridge: Harvard University Press.

Soyinka, W. (1989), 'Communication cannot be halted by Bible, Koran or Bhagavad-Gita'. *The Guardian*, 26.5.89.

Speelman, G., (1995), 'Muslim Minorities and *Sharīah* in Europe', in T. Mitri (ed.), *Religion, Law and Society*, pp. 70–9.

Spivak, G. (1990), 'Reading The Satanic Verses'. *Third Text*, 11, Summer, 41–60.

Sprigge, T. (1990), 'The Satanic novel: a philosophical dialogue on blasphemy and censorship'. *Inquiry*, 33, December, 277–300.

Srivastava, A. (1989), ' "The Empire writes back": language and history in "Shame" and "Midnight's Children" '. *Ariel: A Review of International English Literature*, 20, 4, 62–78.

Stern, J. (1989), 'By any other name'. *The Guardian*, 17.2.89.

Swann, J. (1986), 'East is East and West is West? Salman Rushdie's *Midnight's Children* as an Indian novel'. *World Literature Written in English*, 26, 2, 353–62.

Syed, M. (1994), 'Warped mythologies: Salman Rushdie's Grimus'. *Ariel: A Review of International English Literature*, 25, 4, 135–51.

Taylor, C. (1994), 'The politics of recognition', in A. Gutman (ed.), *Multiculturalism*, pp. 25–73.

Teverson, A. (2004), 'Salman Rushdie and Aijaz Ahmad: satire, ideology and Shame'. *Journal of Commonwealth Literature*, 39, 2, 45–60.

Third Text (1990), *Beyond the Rushdie Affair* (special issue), Summer.

Thompson, J. (1989), 'Towards a redefinition of freedom'. *The Guardian*, 21.8.89.

Toynbee, A. (1946), *A Study of History: Abridgement of Volumes 1–VI*, abridged by D. C. Somervell. Oxford: Oxford University Press.

Toynbee, A. (1960), *A Study of History: Abridgement of Volumes 1–X*, abridged by D. C. Somervell. Oxford: Oxford University Press.

Toynbee, A. (1956), *An Historian's Approach to Religion*. Oxford: Oxford University Press.

Toynbee, A. (1958), *Christianity Among the Religions of the World*. Oxford: Oxford University Press.

Trevor-Roper, H. (1989), 'Home Thoughts'. *The Independent Magazine*, 10.6.89.

Tripp, C. (1994), 'Sayyid Qutb: the political vision', in A. Rahnema (ed.), *Pioneers of Islamic Revival*, pp. 154–83.

Trousdale, R. (2004), ' "City of mongrel joy": Bombay and the Shiv Sena in Midnight's Children and The Moor's Last Sigh". *Journal of Commonwealth Literature*, 39, 2, 95–110.

Tweedie, J. (1989), 'Xenophobia as a social mechanism'. *The Independent*, 27.2.89.

UK Action Committee on Islamic Affairs (1992), 'Response of the UK Action Committee on Islamic Affairs to the Commission for Racial Equality's Second Review of the Race Relations Act, 1976', in UK Action Committee on Islamic Affairs (1993), *Muslims and the Law in Multi-Faith Britain*, pp. 38–40.

UK Action Committee on Islamic Affairs (1993), *Muslims and the Law in Multi-Faith Britain: The Need for Reform*. London: UK Action Committee on Islamic Affairs.

Ünal, A. and Williams, A. (eds.) (2000), *Advocate of Dialogue*. Fairfax, VA: The Fountain.

Unterman, A. (1990), 'A Jewish perspective on "the Rushdie affair"', in D. Cohn-Sherbok (ed.), *The Salman Rushdie Controversy in Interreligious Perspective*, pp. 97–114.

Vaz, K. (1989a), 'Satanic curses'. *New Life*, 10.3.89.

Vaz, K. (1989b), 'Godless Labour'. *New Life*, 14.4.89.

Vincent, J. (1989), 'Outrage we cannot ignore'. *The Times*. 2.3.89.

Walter, N. (1990), *Blasphemy: Ancient and Modern*. London: Rationalist Press Association.

Walters, G. (1995), review of S. Rushdie (1995), *The Moor's Last Sigh*. *The Times*, 5.10.95.

Ward, K. (1989), 'The violent gifts of modern Islam', *The Independent*, 18.2.89.

Warraq, I. (2003), *Why I am Not a Muslim*. New York: Prometheus Books.

Watson-Williams, H. (1984), 'An antique land: Salman Rushdie's *Shame*'. *Westerly: A Quarterly Review*, 29, 4, 38.

Weasel, The (1989), 'Up and Down the City Road'. *The Independent Magazine*, 25.2.89.

Weatherby, W. (1990), *Salman Rushdie: Sentenced to Death*. New York: Caroll and Graff.

Webb, W. (1989a), 'The Imam and the scribe'. *The Guardian*, 17.2.89

Webb, W. (1989b), 'The clocks go back in Cairo'. *The Guardian*, 31.3.89.

Webster, R. (1990), *A Brief History of Blasphemy: Liberalism, Censorship and the Satanic Verses*. Southwell: Orwell Press.

Weiser, S. (1993), 'Varieties of censorship and response in the Satanic Verses'. *Journal of Information Ethics*, 2, 1, 42–7.

Weldon, F. (1989), *Sacred Cows: A Portrait of Britain, Post-Rushdie, Pre-Utopia*. London: Chatto and Windus.

Weller, P. (1990a), 'The Rushdie controversy and inter-faith relations', in D. Cohn-Sherbok (ed.), *The Salman Rushdie Controversy in Inter-Religious Perspective*, pp. 37–57.

Weller, P. (1990b) 'Literature update on the Rushdie affair'. *Discernment: A Christian Journal for Inter-Religious Encounter*, 4, 2, 35–41.

Weller, P. (1990c), 'The Rushdie affair, plurality of values and the ideal of a multi-cultural society'. *National Association for the Values of Education and Training Working Papers*, 2, October, 1–9.

Weller, P. (1996), 'The Salman Rushdie Controversy, Religious Plurality and Established Religion in England' (unpublished doctoral thesis). Leeds: Department of Theology and Religious Studies, University of Leeds.

Weller, P. (2002a), 'Insiders or outsiders?: religions(s), state(s) and societies: propositions for Europe. Part I'. *The Baptist Quarterly*, 39, 5, 211–22.

Weller, P. (2002b), 'Insiders or outsiders?: religions(s), state(s) and societies: propositions for Europe. Part II'. *The Baptist Quarterly*, 39, 6, 276–86.

Weller, P. (2002c), 'Insiders or outsiders?: propositions for European religions, states and societies', in A. Race and I. Shafer (eds.), *Religions in Dialogue*, pp. 193–208.

Weller, P. (2005a), *Time for a Change: Reconfiguring Religion, State and Society*. London: T & T Clark.

Weller, P. (2005b), 'Religions and social capital: theses on religion(s), state(s) and societ(ies): with particular reference to the United Kingdom and the European Union'. *Journal of International Migration and Integration*, 6, 2, 271–89.

Weller, P. (2006a), '"Human rights", "religion" and the "secular": variant configurations of religion(s), state(s) and society(ies)'. *Religion and Human Rights: An International Journal*, 1, 1, 17–39.

Weller, P. (2006b), 'Addressing religious discrimination and Islamophobia: Muslims and liberal democracies. The case of the United Kingdom'. *The Journal of Islamic Studies*, 17, 3, 295–325.

Weller, P. (2007a), 'Conspiracy theories and the incitement of hatred: the dynamics of deception, plausibility and defamation,' in M. Feinberg, S. Samuels and M. Weitzman (eds.), *Antisemitism: The Generic Hatred*, pp. 182–97.

Weller, P. (2007b), 'Robustness and civility: themes from Fethullah Gülen as resource and challenge for Government, Muslims and civil society in the United Kingdom', in I. Yilmaz (ed.), *The Muslim World in Transition*, pp. 268–84.

Weller, P. (2007c), 'Dialogical and transformative resources: perspectives from Fethullah Gülen on religion and public life', in I. Yilmaz (ed.), *Peaceful Co-Existence*, pp. 242–65.

Weller, P. (2008), *Religious Diversity in the UK: Contours and Issues*. London: Continuum.

Weller, P., Feldman, A. and Purdam, K. *et al* (2001), *Religious Discrimination in England and Wales*. Home Office Research Study 220. London: The Home Office Research, Development Statistics Directorate.

Weller, P., Feldman, A. and Purdam, K. (2004), 'Muslims and Religious Discrimination in England and Wales', in J. Malik (ed.), *Muslim Minority Societies in Europe*, pp. 115–44.

Werbner, P. (1996), 'Allegories of sacred imperfection: magic, hermeneutics, and passion in *The Satanic Verses*'. *Current Anthropology*, 37, Supplement, February, S55–69.

Werbner, P. (2000), 'Divided loyalties, empowered citizenship? Muslims in Britain'. *Citizenship Studies*, 4, 3, 307–24.

Werbner, P. (2004), 'The predicament of diaspora and millennial Islam: reflections on September 11, 2001'. *Ethnicities*, 4, 4, 451–76.

Wiemann, D. (2007), 'From forked tongue to forked tongue: Rushdie and Milton in the Postcolonial Conversation' *Journal of Commonwealth Literature*, 42, 2, 47–63.

Wiens, E. (1989), review of S. Rushdie (1988), *The Satanic Verses. The Conrad Grebel Review*, 7, Spring, 198–203.

Wilson, A. (1978), *Finding a Voice: Asian Women in Britain*. London: Virago.

Wilson, B. (1966), *Religion in a Secular Society*. Harmondsworth: Pelican.

Wilson, B. (1989), *Old Laws and New Religions*, Pamphlet Library No. 20 of the Centre for the Study of Religion and Society, Canterbury: University of Kent.

Wilson, K. (1984), '*Midnight's Children* and reader responsibility'. *Critical Quarterly*, 26, 3, 23–37.

Wolffe, J. (1994), ' "And there's another country . . .": religion, the state and British identities', in G. Parsons (ed.), *The Growth of Religious Diversity, Volume II. Issues*, pp. 85–159.

Wood, J. (1995), review of S. Rushdie (1995), *The Moor's Last Sigh. The Guardian*, 8.11.95.

Wright, L. (2006), *The Looming Tower: Al-Qaeda's Road to 9/11*. London: Penguin Books.

Wright, T., Jr. (1990), 'The Rushdie controversy: the spread of communalism from South Asia to the west'. *Plural Societies*, 20, 3, 31–40.

Yapp, M. (1989), 'The hubris of the hidden Imam'. *The Independent*, 22.2.89.

Yilmaz, I. (ed.) (2007a), *The Muslim World in Transition: Contributions of the Gülen Movement* (Conference Proceedings of an International Conference of the same name, held at the House of Lords, the School of Oriental and African Studies and the London School of Economics, London, 25–27 October 2007). London: Leeds Metropolitan University Press.

Yilmaz, I. (ed.) (2007b), *Peaceful Co-Existence: Fethullah Gülen's Initiatives in the Contemporary World* (Conference Proceedings of an International Conference of the same name, held at Erasmus University, Rotterdam, 22–23 November 2007). London: Leeds Metropolitan University Press.

Young, H. (1989), 'Life, death and Mr Rushdie', *The Guardian*, 24.11.89.

Zamora, L. and Faris, W. (1996), *Magical Realism: Theory, History, Community*. North Carolina: Duke University Press.

Zucker, D. (2008), 'Roth, Rushdie and rage: religious reactions to Portnoy and The Verses'. *Journal of Ecumenical Studies*. 43, 1, 31–44.

Index

The index is organized into several parts, as follows:

Chapter Section Index
Sections highlighted in bold are main sections of chapters, while others are chapter subsections

Topic Index
The following entries reflect key topics referred to in the text of the book

Index of Acts of Parliament, Parliamentary Orders, Parliamentary Bills, International Conventions, Agreements, Reports of Commissions and Other Official Documents
As mentioned in the text of the book

Authors and Editors Index
Where the book quotes from their published work

Named Individuals Index
Where identified in the text of the book by name or title, other than when quoted or referred to as authors or editors. This includes when they are quoted in newspaper articles or in other publications of which they are not the named author or editor.

Organization Index
As referred to by name in the text of the book

Place Index
Of places referred to within the text of the book.

Chapter Section Index

Sections highlighted in bold are main sections of chapters, while others are chapter sub-sections

Topic Index

The following entries reflect key topics referred to in the text of the book

Index of Acts of Parliament, Parliamentary Orders, Parliamentary Bills, International Conventions, Agreements, Reports of Commissions and Other Official Documents

As mentioned in the text of the book

Authors and Editors Index

Named Individuals Index

Where identified in the text of the book by name or title, other than when quoted or referred to as authors. This includes when quoted in newspaper articles or in other publications of which they are not the named author or editor.

Organization Index

Place Index

Of places referred to within the text of the book.